THE ACQUISITION OF COMEDIC SKILLS AS A
COMPONENT OF GROWTH AND INDIVIDUATION:
POST-JUNGIAN AND PSYCHOANALYTIC PERSPECTIVES.


DR. MARIA KEMPINSKA MBE

Copyright © Maria Kempinska 2019
Published: August 2019 by
FCM Publishing

ISBN: 978-1-9160643-7-9
Hardback Edition

All rights reserved.

The right of Maria Kempinska to be identified as author of this work has been asserted by her in accordance with sections 77 and 78 of the Copyright, Designs and Patents Act 1988.

No part of this publication may be reproduced, stored in a retrieval system, copied in any form or by any means, electronic, mechanical, photocopying, recording or otherwise transmitted without written permission from the publisher. You must not circulate this book in any format.

Typeset in 12pt Times New Roman

Cover Design by FCM Publishing

# Summary

This dissertation proposes that the comedic performance triggers and utilises Jung's symbolic and archetypal theories. Stand-up comedy reflects the social and psychological change in our society towards class, gender equality, re-distribution of wealth and re-structuring of social systems. Jungian theories are particularly pertinent to this study because they capture the psychological implications of transformation in both the inter- and intra- psyche of the individual and of society . Freudian and post-Freudian theories prove to be more appropriate for examining the details of the agencies activated within inter- and intra-psychic dynamic affecting the delivery of the comedians' material during the performance.

Jungian and post-Jungian theory examines the impact of social and mythological aspect of stand-up comedy on the comedian himself and society in general focusing on the Trickster archetype and Amfortas Wound. Stand-up comedy and in particular women as stand-up comedians become a litmus test for society's problems and issues and the rebalancing thereof. Archetypally the comedy club becomes a Vas, a symbolic sacred transformational space where stand-up comedy has the potential to become a transformative process for both the comedian and the .audience.

The stand up comedian's internal struggle is recreated into a personal comedic story, of the individual within the collective; Thanatos and Eros, personal versus social, responsibility versus irresponsibility, power, race, gender and hierarchy can be assessed. The audience reflects upon these comedic stories and by doing so whether the comedian is successful or unsuccessful the comedian also reflects upon it hence transformation occurs.

Within this alchemical process it is arguable the joke on occasion becomes the Trickster, which cuts through consciousness and is transformative of which the most powerful becomes the Supra-joke. Plus the comedian is transmuted into a Supra-comedian who not only transforms himself but also is the vehicle of social transformation. The personal revelations of the comedian in the comedy club setting creates a self-initiating, morphing and mutating imagery induced by the desire to create humour. Through this creative alchemical stand-up ritual individuation becomes viable.

This transformative processes are explored using a range of Jungian theories; namely Individuation, Enantiodromia, Alchemy, Temenos, Amfortas Wound and the Self.

The comedian's issues are exposed to the audience, and the changes to his psyche are being encouraged by the verbal transaction of the comedic practise comparable to the therapist and his client. The comedians' psychic development is being watched by a great number of people, and although the audience is not personally selected, they affect his development, and they monitor his or her progress by loving the comedian and thereby attaching themselves or, conversely, disowning and rejecting him. It is my assertion that the audience is the symbolic mother and her response nurtures the attachment process as recognised by Bowlby and if successful the comedian's secure base is established.

The stand-up comedian's art consists of creating jokes. The joke then becomes the tool of personal and social transformation. In the arena of stand-up my proposal is that the Trickster, as the joke, is one perfectly united moment between the stand up himself and his material, whose delivery and impact is swift, unexpected and transformative. The comedian is in constant search to create the perfect joke in order to capture the audience. The joke breaks into our psyche and announces a profoundly altering viewpoint. It is in that moment that opposing (or at least unexpected) views, ideas and opinions collide, and laughter occurs. The Supra-comedians' personal issues are often bound within the problems of their society; hence the audience is influenced, at times enraged and often enlightened by this comedic exchange. Chris Rock acknowledges this moment where he aims to 'incorporate more quiet moments into the show. To me, that's the best part of the show, to bring them down and then pow, hit them with an explosive line' (Rock quoted in Ajaye, 2002:183)

Stand-up as therapy is an emotional and intellectual exchange in which neither the comedian nor the audience are omniscient or entirely in control of the situation. Humour can be regarded as a process of reparation, resolution and re-integration of personal and social conflicts whilst the stand –up comedians' conscious focus is to make the audience laugh. Their ability to reveal themselves and to reframe their inner turmoil affects the audience. The impact of their material due to modern technology is far reaching.

Not all comedians directly affect society, but those that do can make profound changes and on occasion can be prophetic foreseeing the changes that will occur in society or expose activities or people whose activities at that time are hidden. They intuitively perceive the problems of society and mirror issues with humour and often they are not successful comedians and may not be recognised in their lifetime as in the case of Bill Hicks.

It is clear that stand-up comedy is a unique phenomenon of a time of global social transformation how it affects the individual is dependent upon the individual. It is a process without boundaries and can be the most powerful artistic medium for change.

# Table of Contents

| | | |
|---|---|---|
| **SUMMARY** | | i |

**CHAPTER 1**

| | | | |
|---|---|---|---|
| **INTRODUCTION** | | | **1** |
| 1. | Definitions | | 2 |
| 1.1. | The Roots of Stand-Up Comedy | | 2 |
| 1.1.1. | Stand-up Comedy as a Genre | | 5 |
| 1.1.2. | Definitions of a Stand-up Comedian | | 7 |
| 1.2. | Basic Premise of the Dissertation | | 8 |
| 1.2.1. | Chapter Outline | | 8 |
| 1.2.2. | Stand Up Comedy as a Form of Therapy | | 11 |

**CHAPTER 2**

| | | |
|---|---|---|
| **CRITICAL LITERATURE REVIEW** | | **14** |
| 2.1. | General Psychological Literature on Humour | 15 |
| 2.2. | Jungian and Post-Jungian Theories | 17 |
| 2.2.1. | The Concept of Individuation | 17 |
| 2.2.2. | The Wound Metaphor | 18 |
| 2.2.3. | The Trickster Archetype | 20 |
| 2.3. | Psychoanalysis and the Post-Freudians | 20 |
| 2.3.1. | Humour as a Defence Mechanism | 20 |
| 2.3.2. | The Oedipus Complex | 23 |
| 2.3.3. | Freud's Concept of Libido | 25 |
| 2.3.4. | Lacan and the Symbolic Order | 26 |
| 2.3.5. | Melanie Klein and the Pre-Oedipal Issues | 27 |
| 2.3.6. | Attachment Theories | 30 |
| 2.4. | Conclusion | 32 |

## CHAPTER 3
## JUNGIAN AND POST-JUNGIAN IDEAS IN RELATION TO THE COMEDIAN     34
- 3.1. Individuation     35
- 3.2. The Amfortas Wound     36
- 3.3. The Ego and the Self     39
- 3.4. The Persona     40
- 3.5. Enantiodromia     43
- 3.6. Temenos     44
- 3.7. The Trickster     45
- 3.8. Conclusion     50

## CHAPTER 4
## STAND-UP COMEDY AND THE FREUDIAN LEGACY     51
- 4.1. Freud     52
- 4.1.1. The Oedipus Complex     52
- 4.1.2. Freud's Concept of libido     54
- 4.2. Lacan – Signified and Signifier     55
- 4.2.1. The Phallus     55
- 4.2.2. Phallus as the Signifier and the Symbolic Order.     57
- 4.3. Melanie Klein and the Object Relations Theory     58
- 4.3.1. Audience Responsiveness: The Good Breast and the Bad Breast     59
- 4.3.2. Trauma and Phantasy     63
- 4.4. John Bowlby and Heinz Kohut – Attachment and the Formation of the Self     64
- 4.4.1. Bowlby     64
- 4.4.2. Heinz Kohut     67
- 4.5. Mirroring, Attunement and Shame     71
- 4.5.1. Mirroring and Control     71
- 4.5.2. Transitional Objects in Comedic Performance     73
- 4.6. Conclusion:     78

**CHAPTER 5**

## A JUNGIAN THEORY OF COMEDY    **79**
    5.1.    The Supra Joke    81
    5.2.    The Supra Comedian    89
    5.3.    Supra Jokes, Alchemy and the Transcendent Function    93
    5.4.    Comedy as Alchemical Composition    95
    5.5.    The Comedian as a Trickster and the Alchemical Transformation    102
    5.6.    Conclusion    103

**CHAPTER 6**

## CREATIVITY AND THE COMEDIAN    **104**
    6.1.    Comedic Creativity from a Freudian View    104
    6.2.    A Positive View of Creativity in Comedy: Carl Jung, James Hillman, Otto Rank and D.W. Winnicott    114
    6.3.    Conclusion:    126

**CHAPTER 7**

## GOING ON STAGE: INTER-AND-INTRAPSYCHIC MATRIX OF STAND-UP COMEDY    **127**
    7.1.    Before    127
    7.2.    During    131
    7.2.1.    The Comedian's Individuation Process on Stage    132
    7.2.2.    Attachment and Seduction    135
    7.3.    After    140
    7.3.1.    Reflection    142
    7.3.2.    Repair    143
    7.4.    Stand Up Comedy as a Maturation Process    147
    7.5.    Conclusion    148

## CHAPTER 8
### THE COMEDIAN AND DEPRESSION — 149
    8.1. The Insecure Comedian — 149
    8.2. The Audience as Psychological Filler: the Hunger for Love — 153
    8.3. Audience as an Abusive or Neglectful Parent — 159
    8.4. Early Childhood Experiences and Depression — 167
    8.5. Conclusion — 171

## CHAPTER 9
### GENDER, CULTURE AND COMEDY — 172
    9.1. Baubo – the Greek Goddess – the First Female Comedian — 174
    9.2. The Issue of Male Envy — 186
    9.3. Gay Women on the Circuit — 188
    9.4. The Comedic Animus — 192
    9.5. My Own Experience as a Comedian — 199

## CHAPTER 10
### CONCLUSION — 202
    10.1. Developing Stand up Comedy Therapy: — 204

### BIBLIOGRAPHY — 205

# CHAPTER 1

## INTRODUCTION

How does the joke affect society? How does it affect the stand-up comedian? The premise of this thesis is that the comedian goes through transformational change on stage, as does his audience. Humour is the medium, which enables this personal change, this Analytical Psychology termed as the Individuation process. The performer uses creativity as a way of examining himself and social issues. The audience participates in the comedian's jokes because both share or recognise the same issues. As Andrew Samuels reminds us that the individual's problems and social issues are closely related (Samuels, 2001: 5). I propose that the stand-up genre can be seen as a form of psychotherapy both for the comedian and society. In fact the two happen simultaneously, as the people in the audience reflect on the issues mentioned by the comedian in his performance. Individuation is intrinsically linked to society, and this link can be explored through the medium of comedy. The people in the audience, alongside the man on stage, go through the four stages of the therapeutic process as defined by Jung: confession, elucidation, education and transformation (Jung CW16: para. 55).

The psychological and psychotherapeutic aspects of the stand-up performance are of paramount importance. Each stand-up comedian has his own perspective on the world, which must have the capacity to resonate with the audience. In their performances, comedians demonstrate their ability to interpret the world through the uniqueness of their own experience. Their personal lives become the foil for their analysis and criticism of society. They use storytelling methods and are raconteurs who manage to draw the audience into their creative aura. The intensity of this complex interaction, which involves a web of projections and introjections between the performer as the stand-up comedian and the audience means that there are various therapeutic processes being activated.

This dissertation is an attempt to deconstruct and define the psychological exchanges between the three participants of this interaction: the Stand-up, the Third Space and the audience. Although our primary interest is the comedian's own personal transformation, the audience's reaction to comedy and the far-reaching social reaction to the role of the Stand-up and humorous material are vital as they are all interdependent. Particularly important is the recent upsurge of interest in comedy because it is a genre, which reflects the individual's struggle with the collective. Comedy debates the issue of individual identity in our times of globalisation, mass production, corporate structures and the patriarchal hierarchical deconstruction and the shift towards the integration of matriarchal values.

# 1. Definitions

## 1.1. The Roots of Stand-Up Comedy

Comedic performance presented before an audience is a very ancient phenomenon. *Plato in Philebus* considered humour as based on malevolence and envy, which was an act of hostility. This theory was highlighted by Ludovici who remarked 'in laughing we bare our fangs' (Krichtafovich, 2006: 16).

Aristotle in his *Poetics* (430 BC) gave a basic analysis of the psychology and purpose of professional comedy. Aristotle defines comedy by comparing it to another genre, tragedy. From his view, all arts are based on the process of imitation (II). However, while tragedy aims at presenting men as better in actual life, comedy presents them as worse (I). In fact, comedy exaggerates the worst components of human character to make them more noticeable. Aristotle writes that comedy is 'an imitation of characters of a lower type not, however, in the full sense of the word bad, the ludicrous being merely a subdivision of the ugly. To take an obvious example, the comic mask is ugly and distorted, but does not imply pain' (V). While tragedy aims at arousing fear and pity in the spectator, comedy merely highlights the imperfect in human beings (XIV). Fundamentally he believed that humour also separates humans from animals.

The *Oxford Dictionary* defines comedy as:

> **1** A narrative poem with a happy ending. obs. exc. in The Divine Comedy [tr. La Divina Commedia] of Dante. b A drama (on stage, film, or radio) with a happy ending, chiefly representing everyday life and of a light, amusing, and often satirical character; any literary composition with similar characteristics.
> **2** A genre of drama etc. characterized by its depiction of amusing characters or incidents and an informal style. b Humour; humorous behaviour.
> **3** A humorous or farcical incident in life; such incidents collectively.

In his book *The Death of Comedy* (2001), Erich Segal delves into the etymology of the word 'comedy' to provide its definitions. He reminds us that for the Greeks comedy consists of two words: *koma* (sleep) and *oide* (song). Segal then writes that 'comedy is a night song. It was born at night'. (Segal, 2001: 1). His analysis of comedy is close to my own vision of comedy as being triggered by the unconscious, as both as a therapeutic process of an avenue through which a cluster of complexes and defences are conveyed. Comedy is rooted in the unconscious. Segal argues:

> What then would a Nightsong be? Perchance a dream. On several occasions Freud equalled the psychodynamics of the comic and the oneiric, once alluding to his essays on jokes and dreams as 'twin brothers'. These mental actions have many important features in common, among which are punning word-play, the relaxation of inhibition, and the liberation of 'primary process thinking'. Nightsong thus represents a temporary return to childhood, which Wordsworth called 'the glory and the freshness of a dream'.
>
> In both dream and comedy, the impossible wish comes true. In each case the aim is pleasure, and the joy comes with no loss of energy or pang of conscience – the normal experience of spirit borne free. […]
>
> (Segal, 2001: 1)

Moreover, he argues, '*koma* is a rare word with rare connotations, whenever it appears instead of the more common *hypnos*. It can have an erotic sense of letting go, not merely nodding off. In *The Iliad,* for example, Hypnos, the god of sleep, declares that he has covered Zeus with an especially soft slumber (*melakon koma*) – just after Zeus and Hera have made love. The sense of indulgence and release adds a metalinguistic validity to the alleged etymology of comedy' (2001: 4).

I agree with this view because comedic performance is a heightened exchange, at night mostly, between human beings; between the performer and the audience. It is the highest form of human exchange without the physical contact. It involves elation and revelry both on the part of the performer and on the part of the audience. Quintilian hypothesised that humour contains a certain amount of truth and lies, whereas Immanuel Kant in his critique of pure reason states that in humour and jokes there is nothing of value, it is an empty intellectual jostling for meaning or depth; 'laughter is an emotion which is born from the sudden change of an anxious expectation into nothing'. His view can be challenged in the light of the socially provocative content of the Supra-comedian and Supra-joke.

John Morreall separates all theories of comedy and laughter into three groups: Incongruity theory, Superiority theory and Relief theory. Incongruity theory includes, for instance, the views of Immanuel Kant and Arthur Schopenhauer. They theorised that the comic is born out of the tension between the external, so-called 'normal' reality and the possible alternative perceptions of it. For instance, in his work *Critique of Judgement,* Kant wrote: 'in everything that is to excite a lively convulsive laugh there must be something absurd (in which the understanding, therefore, can find no satisfaction). Laughter is an affection arising from sudden transformation of a strained expectation into nothing' (Morreall, 1987: 47). Schopenhauer's view of the psycho-philosophical origins of laughter is similar to that of Kant. According to him, humour has its roots in human ability to perceive the absurd and the incongruous in seemingly 'normal' things. In his essay *'On the Theory of the Ludicrous'* he argues that:

> … the source of the ludicrous is always the paradoxical, and therefore unexpected, subsumption of an object under a conception which in other respects is different from it, and accordingly the phenomenon of laughter always signifies the sudden apprehension of an incongruity between such a conception and the real object thought under it, thus between the abstract and the concrete object of perception.
> 
> (Morreall, 1987: 54)

In his analysis of comedy, the existentialist philosopher Soren Kierkegaard also determined contradiction and incongruity as being the principal ingredients of the comedic experience. In the essay *'Concluding Unscientific Postscript'* he wrote that

> The tragic and the comic are the same, in so far as both are based on contradiction; but the tragic is the suffering contradiction, the comical, the painless contradiction. […] the comic apprehension evokes the contradiction or makes it manifest by having in mind the way out, which is why the contradiction is painless. The tragic apprehension sees the contradiction and despairs of a way out.
> 
> (Morreall, 1987: 83)

The Superiority theory, which encompasses, for instance, the views of Thomas Hobbes, states that human beings laugh at all things that they perceive as 'lowly' and 'ugly'. In Leviathan he writes that the human race is an instant power struggle. And that it should not be surprising that victory goes to one who laughs. He also suggested that 'laughter is an expression of sudden triumph, caused by a no less sudden feeling of superiority over others or over one's past'.

Mikhail Bakhtin explains folk humour and forms of laughter in various spheres of human creation. Folk culture invented carnival; it is characterised by serious overtones, as it was their only method of expressing truth and other important things. Laughter contains the history of society and a conception of the world. During the

Renaissance laughter always conquered fear. Victory over fear was believed to come through laughter.

Igor Krichtafovich highlights the aggressive roots of humour during public executions; jesters and fools entertained the crowd whilst people distributed food and drink and were generally festive. He also suggests that when Jesus was dying people were laughing and joking around him.

> *'When Jesus was dying on the cross many among the crowd found this amusing, and exchanged jokes.* They found it funny'
> (Krichtafovich, 2006:28.)

This indicates that sheer joy in the macabre is potentially inherent. There have been many theories about the use of humour about its purpose and affect. This dissertation aims to establish that the emergence of the Stand-up and contemporary humour is more than a series of verbal constructs and affectations dependent on a number of variables, including the inter and intra-psychic structure and agencies activated in the moment of performance, for both the comedian and the audience. Essentially this phenomenon is a contemporary depiction, which echoes and illustrates its effect individually, socially and in the collective, as Jung termed the 'anima mundi', within the 'unus mundus' connecting the spirit of the world change within the essence of the one world fusion.

### *1.1.1. Stand-up Comedy as a Genre*

Stand-up performance, however, is a distinct genre with clear characteristics. In his study of stand-up comedy as a genre, Robert Stebbins writes:

> Stand-up comedy is the art, initially developed in the United States, of humorous dialogue presented before an audience. The talk itself is memorised, and, today, usually expressed in a spontaneous conversational manner, as if the performer were speaking to friends. Although it tends to be one-sided, there may be interaction between performer and audience, which the former does not always want. […] The typical narrative consists of anecdotes, narrative jokes, one-liners, and short descriptive monologues, which may or may not be related.
> (Stebbins, 2003: 3)

The chief characteristics of stand-up comedy are the domination of verbal content over any other component of performance (2003: 3-4). In stand-up comedy, the verbal supersedes any other physical manifestation of humour. Stebbins argues: 'Verbal content is the essence of stand-up comedy. Other stock-in-trade aspects of legitimate theatre – notably costumes, scenery, and make-up – are either avoided or considered minor (Mintz, 1985: 71). Although stand-up comedy was originally presented only to live audiences, later it became available over radio and still later on television and long-playing records' (2003: 4). Stebbins also goes back to the genre roots of stand-up comedy. He writes that in its pure form it is 'a type of *variety comedy*, which is, in turn, one area of the variety arts. There are variety arts that are entertaining but not humorous, such as dance routines and feats of skills, and although it has clowns, the circus, a series of variety acts is not a particularly humorous form of entertainment' (2003: 4).

However, there are similarities and differences between stand-up comedy and variety performances. Unlike the variety genre, stand-up comedy does not necessarily require props (although some comedians choose to use them). As genre, stand-up is entirely dependent and focused on the personality of the individual comedian. His personality is paramount and different comedians can perform the same script in totally different ways. The reaction of the audience also depends on the delivery of the joke. The flexibility of the comedian is also essential, as they have to adapt their material to the audience. In other words, comedic performance staged in this kind of setting is never entirely predictable; the outcome depends on the combination of the particular audience and the comedian's persona. There are other ingredients in the stand-up performance, which cannot be predictable or planned with precision. For instance, the flow between the comedian and the audience depends on a number of things, including the amount of alcohol consumed by the audience.

In this dissertation I am connecting my personal history with my thirty-three years' experience of working in the UK comedy scene and owning the *Jongleurs* chain. My parents were post Second World War political refugees; they were prisoners of war in Siberia under the Russians and having joined the Polish Free Army alongside the British 8th army fought against Nazi Germany. They settled in England where I was brought up speaking both Polish and English experiencing the joys and hardship of impoverished refugees along with the paradoxical emotional states of elation and depression of the survivor, including guilt and the affect of PTSD. My mother, a mathematician in Poland, made Christmas Crackers and my father a barrister in Poland, worked in a various factories. The extreme dichotomy of their traumatic painful being pain and shame of existing, plus the humour from various jokes from the Christmas cracker and TV made my early upbringing the basis of my drive and understanding. Creating *Jongleurs* was pivotal to my personal development along with the expansion of stand-up comedy in the UK. A number of famous comedians have performed for *Jongleurs* since its creation in 1983, including Stephen Fry, Eddie Izzard, Michael McIntyre, Rory Bremner, Al Murray, Stephen Coogan, Mike Myers, Jack Dee, Frank Skinner, Arthur Smith, Ben Alton, Harry Enfield, Lee Mack, Russell Brand, Rita Rudner, Sam Kinison, Emo Philips and Mitch Hedberg..

The English-speaking comedy scene has been expanding since the nineteen eighties. The genre of Stand-up Comedy started in the USA in the nineteen-sixties with Lenny Bruce, Richard Pryor and in England Alexi Sayle and Billy Connolly. The most popular and important comedy club chains include *'The Comedy Store'*, *Jongleurs* and *'The Glee Club'*. There are also small independent comedy clubs offering different types of stand-up comedy. Although *Jongleurs* has been instrumental in development and promotion of the comedy talent, I am not going to look exclusively at this particular chain but analyse the stand-up comedy phenomenon in the English-speaking world. It is important to do so because stand-up as a genre reflects the spirit, problems and anxieties of our fast-changing post-industrial society where the shift is from the man manning the machine in industry to becoming a cog in the corporate sector wheel. This unprecedented expansion of comedy has occurred because it answers a psychological need in our society today. Mankind is exposed to greater opportunities yet greater pressure to perform individually is expected and rewarded. Man's need to stand out and be noticed in a capitalist, competitive environment encompasses a number of postmodern issues, including the engulfment of individual identity by the mass character of late managerial cult which although seems easier than the industrial period is psychologically dangerous. The threat to the individual, represented by the competitive capitalist institutions such as banking, mass media and mass culture to the individual, is of oblivion and mediocrity. Comedians have the unique ability to express their individual anxieties publicly. They represent rebellion in the face of these engulfing mass structures. It could be said that we are engaging in a time where 'the comic spirit,' (Lemma, 2000:10) recognises the 'inescapable difficulty of being'.

## *1.1.2. Definitions of a Stand-up Comedian*

A stand-up comedian is an entertainer who has the ability to reframe a situation through the use of humour with the aim of arousing laughter in the audience. From the psychological point of view, the comedian can be seen as activating the unconscious material (both personal and belonging to the audience – i.e., collective) for purposes of humour. This enables him to look at his internal world with the detachment he needs to assimilate the content. He also learns how to formulate and debate his unconscious material interactively and recollect it spontaneously into a socially acceptable format, namely a comedy routine. Traditionally, the term 'comedian' will refer to the stand-up comedian and is used to define both female and male performers. In this dissertation the term will be used in relation to both sexes, but will be used in masculine gender.

It is important to differentiate the stand-up comedian as a profession from other forms of comedic entertainment involving humorous encounters. The Comedian works with his own material. This material is personal; he edits the intimate information internally and turns it into performance pieces. By contrast, the Comic is a person who primarily works with pre-structured material, which is repeated in a manner similar to that of an actor. The joke can give pleasure in its own right; it has an entity in itself and can be taken away from the comedian.

Another type of performer, the Joker, differs from the Comedian in that he operates purely in the social sphere and uses humour for verbal sparring in order to seduce his social circle. His purposes are purely social although his motives can be personal. The Comedian as a profession should also be differentiated from that of the Clown/Fool, which lies in their manner of arousing laughter in viewers. The Fool uses the absurd to highlight the truth by showing the absurd aspect of the social order. According to Ulanov, 'the Fool, the Clown 'alternates between destruction and restitution, between wreckage and reparation. He personifies our worst and hidden fears of inferiority' (Ulanov: 4). Historically the Court Jester in England had an accepted role in the Royal Court of mocking the royal rulings one day per year. Jesters would have visibly comedic apparel and had permission to make fun of the royal legislation in order to show up potential absurdity, foolish decision making and also to deliver bad news. The purpose of his role was also to keep the Royal ruler level headed and for him to avoid the potential destructive decision making of the affect of hubris. The clown costume whose intention is to cause laughter, mostly through mime, wore the overt absurd and exaggerated. The jester or clown was a familiar character cross-culturally as Beatrice K Otto reveals 'he seems to have arisen spontaneously and independently within societies without their necessarily being aware of his existence elsewhere, suggesting that he fulfils a deep and widespread cultural need.' (Otto, 2007 xvvi).
The closest resemblance to the comedian is the Court Jester. The comedian's role is to comment on the problems in life and living of everyman hence he wears everyday clothing.

## 1.2. *Basic Premise of the Dissertation*

### 1.2.1. *Chapter Outline*

The emergence of stand-up comedy as a widely enjoyable form of entertainment has an individual, psychosocial and archetypal resonance. However, there is relatively little psychotherapeutic literature observing the complex psychic agencies that are activated in the comedian during the concentrated and creative moment of performance. My earlier work as a *Pilot Study of Psychological Types in Stand-up Comedy (2004)* encouraged my further interest in the psychological dynamics of the comedian and his relationship with society. In my dissertation, I will attempt to explain the psychosocial and psychotherapeutic bases of stand-up performance and outline the psychological processes that drive the comedian in his quest for the perfect connection with the audience. My proposition is that the comedian is seeking a perfect connection shown through affectionate attention and laughter with the audience in order to heal his own psychological wound and by the same interaction potentially that of various members of the audience. By exploring the contents of the wound and by transforming the repressed unconscious material into jokes, the comedian advances in his personal development and potentially into what Jung termed Individuation which is also linked to the comedian's personal transformation and to his environment and society.

To construct my argument, I will be drawing on a combination of ideas and theories: Analytical Psychology (Carl Gustav Jung, Marie Louise von Franz, Erich Neumann, James Hillman, Jolande Jacobi), psychoanalysis (Sigmund Freud, Melanie Klein), cultural anthropology (Arnold van Gennep, Victor Turner, Hynes and Doty) and theories of humour (Martin A. Rod, Fisher and Fisher). I will employ an integrative approach, which involves using a constellation of concepts by different theorists. Jungian theories in particular the individuation process, alchemy, the transcendent function, archetypes, enantiodromia, the wound.' form the core of this thesis; Freudian ideas are used in relation to the act of stand-up.

These concepts will be united by the principal idea of the comedian's interaction with the audience and the psychological change triggered by this interaction. Jung's concept of individuation will serve as a theoretical canvas for my research. The decision to use an integrative approach is influenced by the fact that all comedians differ in their relationships with the audience. Each of them employs unique content paired with a distinctive emotional tone during their interaction. Jung's ideas of society and its links with individual psyche will also be used. I argue that with the right comedian, the stand-up performance is a form of collective therapy, dependent upon the comedian's own psychological awareness, his social knowledge and ability to relate to his audience at that time. Fundamentally, the social acceptance of the stand-up creating laughter as a means of acceptance of the premise of the joke enables a collective form of therapy.

Freud and the post-Freudians, especially Melanie Klein, define childhood complexes, early experiences, the construction and deconstruction of developmental stages and the aggressive aspects of human nature (greed and envy, attachment and seduction, and sexual libido) .In his essay, 'Jokes and Their Relation to the Unconscious' (1905), Freud links human propensity to generate humour to aggressive and sexual impulses; as a form of release for the energy otherwise not acceptable in a civilised society.

At the same time, this thesis insists that the Freudian approach to humour does not take into consideration the transformational aspects of comedy. The social and personal transformation will be explored in this thesis. There have been numerous studies of humour based on, or referring to Freud's theory of humour. This thesis is the first of its kind as it develops a Jungian theory of humour, and even attempts to go beyond it and into the realm of the social effect. A key argument of this theory is that the joke is one of the primary media of social and personal transformation. It combines the social and the therapeutic, and can even be compared to a psychotherapeutic session. As Christopher Hauke argues in his book *Jung and the Postmodern: The Interpretation of Realities* (2000),

> … Freudian psychoanalytic theorising of society comes under some strain, which certain approaches from the Jungian perspective are able to avoid. This is partly due to the Freudians' less critical attitude to prevailing consciousness and an overvaluing of the ego-function, but, connected with this, it is also due to a further major difference between the Freudian and Jungian perspective. Whereas in the former there is an emphasis on past causes – the reductive point of view – the Jungian position emphasises the understanding of phenomena – including social conditions – by asking 'Where is this heading? What are these conditions – or 'symptoms' – leading us *towards*?
>
> (Hauke, 2000: 57)

In Chapter 3, 'Stand-up Comedy and the Freudian Legacy,' will explore the central concept of Freud's psychology and how the Oedipus complex is played out in the comedy club setting. The chapter will argue that the relationship between the comedian and the audience is that of the child and the symbolic mother and the issues that arise during the process of performance concern the comedian's conflict with the mother and father figure in various manifestations.

Chapter 4, 'The Jungian Theory of Comedy,' explores the transformative aspects of comedy and humour. It introduces the concepts of the Supra Joke and the Supra Comedian. It also argues that, during a live comedic performance an alchemical individuation takes place, which is a two-way process during which both the comedian and the audience alter each other psychologically and change each other's personal, political and social views.

In Chapter 5, 'Creativity and Stand-Up Comedy,' the comedian's creative process is discussed, and linked to the audience's psychological transformation. It is arguable that creativity forms a big part of the performer's individuation process; as well as assisting the audience in its self-analysis and self-reflection. The creative process is, essentially an alchemical process as it makes something out of dark matter via transmutation. Ultimately, comedy is a giving profession as it entails making other people better by making them laugh, by sharing one's creativity with them.

Chapter 6 'Going On Stage: the Inter and Intra-Psychic Matrix of the Stand-Up Comedian' demonstrates how the inter and intra-psychic mechanisms are activated within the comedian during the process of the performance. This includes the preparation for the performance in terms of his material and his persona, plus reflections upon his past performance/s. Throughout the performance various separate and interdependent psychological agencies are activated oscillating between the comedian and the audience. This study includes psychoanalytic theoretical approaches: by referring to Melanie Klein and John Bowlby. I revisit the Oedipus complex in order to explore the comedian's relationship with the symbolic mother. I use Klein's object relations' theory, her concept of phantasy and John Bowlby's ideas on attachment to explore the immediate and intense dynamic between the comedian and the audience during the performance. This chapter also deals the performer's relationships with other comedians as he competes with them for the attention of the symbolic mother (the audience).

Chapter 7, 'The Comedian and Depression' uncovers the dark aspects of stand-up comedy: depression, mental health problems and suicide. It explores the observable link between mental health issues and stand-up comedy as well as gives accounts of famous comedians' encounters with mental health problems. It also investigates why the adulation of the audience is often not enough to cure the comedian's depression.

Chapter 8, 'Gender, Culture and Comedy' explains the core political issues in relation to stand up comedy as a genre. These issues include the female voice, sexist and patronising treatment by the male representatives of the industry, male envy, the compatibility of comedy and femininity, of the material of female jokes, gender identity on stage and dealing with aggressive audiences. Stand-up comedy is a male-dominated industry. It is still difficult for a female comedian to break through because she is immediately seen as breaking gender expectation.

### *1.2.2. Stand Up Comedy as a Form of Therapy*

One of the central concerns of this thesis is the therapeutic role of stand-up comedy as a genre. I will argue that comedy is a form of therapy for both the comedian and society. This function of comedy can be regarded from both the Jungian and Freudian perspectives. Importantly, the central theory is; only when a person is prepared to self-reflect and self-analyse via his self-created joke, does he become able to individuate. Individuation means that our complexes are no longer in the Shadow, and the true (individuating) comedian illuminates his unconscious transforming his inspiration into joke form which in turn has the potential to reveal the problems of their society. The true comedian is comparable to the role of a therapist where self-analysis is paramount. Moreover, it also implies the willingness of the performer to self-deprecate in the joke in order to engage with the audience.

This phenomenon can be called the 'self-participating joke'. Comedians should be able to mock themselves. In Chapter three, this idea will be explored further, and the concept of Supra Comedian will be introduced. It will be argued that the Supra Comedian has a more powerful urge to use themselves and their jokes to confront their own issues and the issues of their society. The Supra Comedian is immensely aware of his impact on society and of the fact that they are tangibly influencing society through self-awareness and self-analysis. This differs from the narcissistic use of comedic realm of 'celebrity' where fame is narcissistic tool used to gain attention for personal advancement and notoriety with no real social interest.

By trying to understand themselves, comedians reassess their position within their society. They try to define their place in the fast-changing Western culture. They try to work out what their feelings are in relation to these changing issues. They try to find new ways of identifying themselves. It can be said that they appeal to the audience for validation and reflection in that they try to establish whether other people in the audience also experience their problems.

I suggest there is a Jungian style of humour, which is bound within this constant conflict of self-evaluation between the personal and the collective, and produces personal humour, which is a route to individuation. The process of understanding oneself is both serious and dangerous because it inevitably involves dealing with the collective: 'are we going to let ourselves be robbed of our individual freedom, and what can we do to stop it?' (Jung CW10: para. 718). Individuation is;

> … a process informed by the archetypal ideal of wholeness, which in turn depends on a vital relationship between ego and unconscious. The aim is not to overcome one's personal psychology, to become perfect, but to become familiar with it. Thus individuation involves an increasing awareness of one's unique psychological reality, including personal strengths and limitations, and at the same time a deeper appreciation of humanity in general. As the individual is not just a single, separate being, but by his very existence presupposes a collective relationship, it follows that the process of individuation must lead to more intense and broader collective relationships and not to isolation.
> (Jung CW 6, par. 758/para: Smith et al., 2012: 141).

The 'self-participating joke' is a form of self-sacrifice, which gives them the ability to be subversive without alienating the audience. The laughter creates a cushion and power for the vulnerable psychic component, which has divested itself of strength and compensates for the potential instinct of anger. The ability to self-deprecate in joke form supports the individuals' quest to distinguish himself from the mass. It is imperative that the comedian, by nature and by profession, finds his 'distinctiveness' amongst the social and personal collective. He does this by creating his unique humour bound within his personal complex where the archetypes emerging from his collective unconscious are being woven into a socially accepted humorous anecdotal framework juxtaposed against social norms and expectations. The Supra-Comedian is the master who is aware of his elevated status along with its power and weaves his self-created humorous material to make a social comment, thus making a multi-layered impact. For the Supra-Comedian making an impact through the social commentary is more important than the narcissistic reward of an adoring audience.

I will argue in this thesis that the multi-layered effect of the comedian has profound significance upon the personal and social, psychological and archetypal aspect of mankind. Stand-up comedy is a unique phenomenon arising from fear, uncertainty and the need to adjust to the forces of global integration sweeping across all strata and structures of society. The comedian can alleviate the uncertainty and by engaging the process he can individuate. By individuating, he can heal himself and his society, which become inseparable, and both are of paramount importance for the psychological health of society.

# CHAPTER 2

## CRITICAL LITERATURE REVIEW

The emergence of stand-up comedy as a widely enjoyable form of entertainment has individual, psychosocial and archetypal resonance. However, there is relatively little psychotherapeutic literature observing the complex psychic agencies activated in the comedian during the concentrated and creative moment of performance. In my dissertation, I will attempt to explain the psychosocial and psychotherapeutic bases of stand-up performance and outline the psychological processes that drive the comedian in his fantasy of perfect connection with the audience. My proposition is that the comedian is seeking a perfect connection with the audience in order to integrate a psychological wound. By 'exploring' the contents of the wound and by transforming the repressed material and that which is unconscious, into jokes, the comedian advances in his/her individuation I will also link his personal transformation to his environment and society.

To construct my argument, I will be drawing on a number of theories from several branches of the social sciences: psychoanalysis (Sigmund Freud, Melanie Klein), analytical psychology (Carl Gustav Jung, Marie Louise von Franz, Erich Neumann, James Hillman, Jolande Jacobi), cultural anthropology (Arnold van Gennep, Victor Turner, Hynes and Doty) and theories of humour (Martin A. Rod, Fisher and Fisher). The reason why I employ a patchwork of concepts, instead of using one theory for my analysis of stand-up comedy, is that the psychological and psychotherapeutic literature on the subject of humour is inconsistent. Firstly, the psychotherapy does not have unified concepts of either the psychological origins or therapeutic effects of humour. Secondly, every branch of the humanities that has ever attempted to define humour – mainstream psychology, Freudian and post-Freudian psychoanalysis, Analytical Psychology, cultural anthropology, mythology and folklore – has its own, predictably narrow, angle on the issue. My task, as I see it, is constructing a psychotherapeutic model of the inter-and-intrapsychic processes within the comedian.

Therefore, in my dissertation I will employ an integrative approach, which involves using a constellation of concepts by different theorists. These concepts will be united in the principal concept of the comedian's interaction with the audience and the psychological change triggered by this interaction within the performer. The decision to use an integrative approach is also influenced by the fact that all comedians differ in their relationships with the audience. Each of them employs a unique emotional tone during their creative process.

In my analysis of stand-up performance, I will mostly concentrate on the figure of the comedian and his side of psychological exchange with the audience. However, one of the chapters of my thesis will be devoted to the social role and political resonance of humour in general, and stand up comedy in particular.

## 2.
### *2.1. General Psychological Literature on Humour*

Humour is defined by the Encyclopaedia Britannica as 'a type of stimulation that tends to elicit the laughter reflex.' (Humour,2010:http://www.britannica.com). However, the exact functioning of the mechanisms and processes that trigger laughter in humans remain unclear. A number of branches of psychology have approached the phenomenon of humour scientifically, and attempted to explore and explain these mechanisms.

General psychological literature about humour can be divided into several categories. One of these categories deals with the social importance of humour and jokes. A number of recent studies (Martin 2007; Martin and Kuiper 1999; Provine and Fischer 1989; Ruch 1992; 2007) have concentrated on the role of humour as an inherent element of social interaction. As the psychologist Rod A. Martin writes,

> We laugh and joke much more frequently when we are with other people than when we are by ourselves […]. People do occasionally laugh when they are alone, such as while watching a comedy show on television, reading a humorous book or remembering a funny personal experience. However, these instances of laughter can usually be seen as 'pseudo-social' in nature because one is still responding to the characters in the television program or the author of the book, or reliving in memory an even that involved other people.
> 
> (Martin, 2007: 5).

From the point of view of social psychology, humour operates as a facilitator of interaction between members of a community and eases internal and interpersonal tensions. Several researchers (Martin, 2007; Morreall, 1991) have noted the importance of laughter as a form of social play assisting human beings in social communication and influence which also acts as a coping mechanism and an effective tension relief system. A number of empirical studies have measured (however impossible it may sound) the degree of creativity necessary for humour appreciation and humour production (Babad, 1974; Brodzinsky and Rubien, 1976; Clabby, 1980). Doris and Fierman, 1956 even found a correlation between humour appreciation and anxiety. The famous German-British experimental psychologist Hans Eysenck (1942; 1943) devised a series of experiments measuring individual differences in the perception of jokes (Ruch, 2007: 35). Other attempts to develop an objective and empirically based theory of sense of humour have been made by Cattell and Luborsky (1947), Levine and Abelson (1959) and Willibald Ruch (1992).

Theories of humour investigating the social aspect are important for our argument because stand-up at its core, is an intense social interaction. The fact that it is planned, framed and controlled in a certain way raises the questions of why spectators seek this particular type of stimulation, and why the performer seeks contact with the audience by provoking in them the sense of exhilaration (Ruch, 2007: 205) or 'the emotion of mirth' (Martin, 2007: 9). It is obvious that the audience and the comedian are moved by different psychological needs when they engage in this kind of interaction. It is our aim to investigate these needs and to determine the psychotherapeutic mechanisms of the emotional exchange happening between the audience and the comedian.

Where experimental psychologists concentrate on the social side of the comedic interaction, psycholinguists attempt to define the exact linguistic processes behind the production of jokes. Thus, they are more concerned with the 'joker' and the techniques he or she employs to achieve the desired result (to elicit the emotion of mirth, to use Rod A. Martin's expression) rather than the audience's reaction to these techniques. For instance, Alan Partington (2006) uses methodologies and software derived from Corpus Linguistics (the study of language as expressed in samples) and integrates quantitative and qualitative approaches in his study of 'laughter-talk'. His aim is to pinpoint the exact linguistic triggers (for instance, wordplay, sarcasm or facework) of bouts of lauger. Other psycholinguistic approaches include, for instance, General Theory of Verbal Humour (GTVH) (Attardo, 2001; Attardo and Ruskin, 1985). Whereas the linguistic theories of humour and laughter are interesting and important, semantics of humour is not included in the scope of this thesis.

Of all empirical investigations of humour, thematically closest to this thesis is the qualitative study by Seymour Fisher and Rhoda Lee Fisher (1981), in which they conducted an investigation into the psychology of the comedian. They interviewed a group of performers collectively referred to as 'comics', and drew a number of conclusions about the personal conflicts of the performer drawn to this profession. Their findings led them to ascertain that the conflicts in early life either directly or indirectly led to their profession. In their own words,

> One of the points that particularly impressed us about these people, who are so dedicated to being funny, is that they forever feel called upon to shield people from the threats and forebodings typifying modal life on this planet. As a result of early transactions with their parents they feel obliged to soothe others and to interpose themselves against the bad things 'out there'. They are weighted down by a poignant sense of duty to help those who come asking for the antidote provided by humour against the human misfortune.
>
> (Fisher and Fisher, 1981: 1)

Fisher and Fisher's empirical findings and philosophical conclusions are useful for our own investigation of the 'wounded' comedian and his or her eternal quest for the lost wholeness, for the completion, which they see and seek in the audience. However, not all the comedians came from dysfunctional or neglected backgrounds as is implied. There are a number who through their personalities are in need of adoration or attention and found that the art of humour gave them the limelight they required. Their drives link to both Jungian ideas primarily individuation and the theme of the 'wounded child.' The wounded child according to both Jung and Freud has an inherent guilt, which is carried through the generations exemplified for Freud by the myth of the Oedipus and for Jung as Parsifal. The theoretical apparatus borrowed from cultural anthropology (the trickster, rites of passage). By eliciting a response from the audience, the comedian attempts to heal himself, to close the wound (caused by those 'early transactions with the parents'), while at the same time potentially healing and educating the audience as in the case of Chris Rock and George Carling.

## 2.2. *Jungian and Post-Jungian Theories*

### 2.2.1. *The Concept of Individuation*

To further investigate the theme of psychological woundedness and the metaphor of 'lost wholeness', we will employ a number of Jungian and post-Jungian theories. Central to the thesis is Carl Gustav Jung's concept of *Individuation* – which, in its core, means becoming oneself while also dealing with society's pressures and demands. According to Jolande Jacobi, individuation is a 'spontaneous, natural process within the psyche' which is 'potentially present in every man, although most men are unaware of it' (Jacobi, 1973: 107). However, this process does not merely mean *finding oneself* – its ultimate aim is to create an independent thinking, unique individual who would at the same be 'a member of collectivity'. The aim of the individuation process is not the individual's supposed individuality as opposed to his collective obligations but 'the fulfilment of his own nature as it is related to the whole' (1973: 107). Thus, individuation does not mean some kind of narcissistic loneliness, but always presupposes involvement with one's fellow human beings (CW7: para. 267).

As Christopher Hauke (2000) notes, for Jung, individuation is

> ...nothing more or less than being fully oneself. This means including parts of oneself that have been lost or neglected not only due to circumstances or personal history – parents, upbringing and so on – but have also been lost or neglected due to the collective conditions of the era and culture [...] However, the personal and the collective, as well as the past and the present, are difficult to differentiate and separate in any final way.
> 
> (Hauke, 2000: 109).

This aspect of individuation is relevant to our idea of the comedian who feels incomplete and therefore chooses an unusual, creative and very public way of exposing his Shadow aspect. Thus, the process of solving intimate problems is turned into a social act. The comedian's individuation, observable in his stand-up performances, Thus, the 'wound' is opened and examined publicly as a painful and a public form of self-therapy, during and after the performance. As a result, an internal conflict is activated which triggers the process which Jung called individuation.

## 2.2.2. *The Wound Metaphor*

Closely related to the idea of individuation in stand-up comedy is the metaphor of the wounded Fisher King (the Amfortas wound). Amfortas is the king from the Grail Legend who 'suffers from a wound which cannot be healed; he cannot recover and hand over the authority to Parzifal' (Von Franz, 1998: 274). In his essay on the Child archetype, Jung reminds us that in many myths and fairy tales the child is often abandoned. He explains that the motif of abandonment is linked to the child's creativity (CW 9/I: para. 285). He writes that the child archetype symbolises the future personality. The motif of abandonment represents separation from the mother; loss of security, and a break-up of primal relationship'. However, this kind of pain is necessary for the child's future progression and maturation. Pain is part of individuation:

> 'Child' means something evolving towards independence. This it cannot do without detaching itself from its origins: abandonment therefore is a necessary condition, not just a concomitant symptom. The conflict is not to be overcome by the conscious mind remaining

caught between the opposites, and for this very reason it needs a symbol to point out the necessity of detaching itself from its origins.

(CW 9/I: para. 287)

The idea of pain and abandonment in relation to the child archetype has been developed by a number of Jung's disciples. For instance, Marie-Louise von Franz argues that 'the true process of individuation – the *conscious* relationship with the great inner man or one's own psychic centre – usually begins with an injury or some suffering, represents a kind of vocation which is not often recognised as such' (Von Frantz, 1994: 300). In his book *The Child: Structure and Dynamics of the Nascent Personality* (1973) Jung's disciple Erich Neumann writes about the primal relationship (which, for him, is the initial relationship between the mother and the child) and links the emergence of creativity in individuals to various disturbances in this relationship. According to Neumann, the 'abandoned' ('injured', 'wounded') child feels unwanted and grows up gasping for love and acceptance. However, narcissism is also borne out of the neglected child who retaliates by demanding attention along with creativity he can become a comedian. Neumann writes: 'the guilt feeling of the matriarchal phase, deriving from a disturbed primal relationship follows the formula: "To be good is to be loved by one's mother; you are bad because your mother does not love you"' (Neumann, 2002: 87). Following this argument, creativity is born out of a negative primal relationship, out of the necessity to re-live or recreate the relationship with the mother (we will discuss the post-Freudian take on this phenomenon in section 2.3).

James Hillman (1987) establishes a link between the motif of the wounded hero in mythology and the hero's problem with his parents. He also links the hero's wound to his drive and creativity. Interestingly enough (and appropriate for our analysis of the male stand-up comedian), Hillman's *puer* is male rather than female. Instead of fleeing castration, Hillman's *puer* is initiated by his wound (1987: 114). Thus, the individuation/wound cluster of Jungian and post-Jungian ideas are vital for our vision of the stand-up comedian as a wounded hero, bravely displaying his problems to his audience in the hope to heal them.

It would be neglectful to term the comedian per se, a Puer Aeternus, some clearly symbolise the quest for youth and irresponsibility others transform during the process, yet some use the process as a creative medium. Metaphorically speaking, 'healing the wound' can be seen as part of the process of healing the father image in a patriarchal society. I believe this change will transform the 'Amfotas wound ' which Jung called the 'eternal split in the male psyche' (CW6: para. 150. This process can be a significant transition to heal the dominating social wounds in contemporary Western society.

## 2.2.3. The Trickster Archetype

Another aspect of Jungian psychology important for our argument is the trickster archetype. We will use the trickster in our analysis of the interaction between the comedian and the audience. It can be used (in conjunction with other theories) to describe comedy's subversive and revolutionary character.

In his essay on the trickster archetype (*CW9*), Jung gives it a number of definitions. According to one of them, the trickster is 'a faithful reflection of an absolutely undifferentiated human consciousness, corresponding to a psyche that has hardly left the animal level' (CW9/I: para. 465). According to another, this archetype is the remainder of an earlier stage of human development; its task is to remind highly conscious and civilized human beings of their animal roots. Jung also notes the trickster's link with the divine. It represents 'God, man and animal at once'. It is both 'subhuman and superhuman, a bestial and divine being, whose chief and most alarming characteristic is his unconsciousness' (CW 9/I: para. 472). The trickster figure metaphorically represents the psychological principle that makes human beings question cultural imperatives thus allowing them to individuate and start thinking independently (Bassil-Morozow, 2011). As it stands for the flexibility of thinking and the fluidity of perception, the trickster resists rigid definitions. Writing about the trickster in myth, William Hynes notes that 'to define (de-finis) is to draw borders around phenomena, and tricksters seem amazingly resistant to such capture, they are notorious border breakers' (Hynes and Doty, 1993: 33).
Jungian-orientated scholars of film and media have broadened Jung's definition of the trickster figure in myth, fairy tales and non-mythological narratives. These findings, since they deal with the trickster's manifestations in contemporary culture, are important for our project. For instance, Ricki Stephanie Tannen (2007) writes about the representations of the female trickster in media and film; Terrie Waddell' (2009) is interested in the role of liminality in various television series, while Helena Bassil-Morozow (2011) analyses manifestations of the trickster in contemporary film.

## 2.3. Psychoanalysis and the Post-Freudians

## 2.3.1. Humour as a Defence Mechanism

We will use Jung's idea of individuation as the base for our body of ideas. However, our analysis of the agencies and mechanisms of stand-up performance will come from the Freudian and post-Freudian schools of thought. While Jung's theorising of humour is limited to his analysis of the trickster archetype, Freud actually produced his own theory of humour.

The stand-up is significantly different from the clown. The clown, the word clown is an English composition was created to define a character in a costume; makeup and distinctive footwear in order to be seen at a distance and to highlight his humour through the use of exaggerate actions in order to create laughter.

1. a comic entertainer, especially one in a circus, wearing a traditional costume and exaggerated make-up.

    "a circus clown"

He can amplify various characteristics of either playfulness or viciousness, depending on the other performers included in the piece, in the form of mime, extravagant actions and facial expressions for the purpose of laughter. Originated from the rustic fool of Roman and Greek theatre, the fool e.g. Lee Evans early work is a modern version of this style. In various tribes the fool was both the bringer of truth and the shaman. He is considered to be the one who can make fun of the observer from the king, to the priest or the commoner.

In his book *Jokes and Their Relation to the Unconscious* (1905), he outlined his theory of humour as a defence mechanism as a form of sublimation of instincts. Basing himself on the current philosophical theories of humour (Jean Paul Richter, Theodor Vischer, Kuno Fischer and Theodore Lipps), Freud examined the psychosocial role of the joke. He came to the conclusion that the role of the joke in society is to protect the social order from the surge of the instinctual. He writes that 'brutal hostility, forbidden by law, has been replaced by verbal invective' (1975: 102) and 'though as children we are still endowed with a powerful inherited disposition to hostility, we are later taught by a higher personal civilization that it is an unworthy thing to use an abusive language; and even where fighting has itself remained permissible, the number of things which may not be employed as methods of fighting has extraordinarily increased' (1975: 102). Put simply, jokes help us to deal with our own aggression.

In 1927 Freud further expanded his analysis of the psychotherapeutic aspects of the comic in his book *Humour*. In it he continues to develop his early concept of humour as a defence mechanism helping the ego to cope with the unpleasant and difficult external and internal realities. For instance, he writes that 'the grandeur [in humour] clearly lies in the triumph of narcissism, the victorious assertion of the ego's invulnerability. The ego refuses to be distressed by the provocations of reality, to let itself be compelled to suffer. It insists that it cannot be affected by the traumas of the external world' (Freud, 1961: 162). Freud's vision of humour as a way of dealing with personal problems taps into our idea that, by using humour, the comedian is defending his narcissistic wound. Humour also becomes a kind of harbour for the comedian's narcissistic needs.

The role of humour as a defence and coping mechanism can be successfully employed in psychotherapy and has been discussed by other authors including Barron (1999), Kulhman (1994), Lemma (2000), Bergmann (1999), Strean (1993; 1994) and Bollas (1995). These authors tend to discuss humour in terms of its direct psychotherapeutic outcome for the client. Lemma (2000) examines humour in terms of a 'space,' which adds a component of 'distancing' as an attitude whereas Kohut (1991) sees it both as 'defensive' and 'offensive'. Discussing the humour as an important element of psychotherapy, Kulhman (1994) concludes that humour provides detachment necessary for distancing oneself from pain and suffering associated with the wound. He postulates that 'detachment strategies seek to move the client *away* from a problem, to decrease the client's investment in or preoccupation with it' (Kulhman, 1994: 59).

The purpose of shares humour, Lemma points out also has the pleasure of interpersonal relationships, and they 're-arrange 'implicit relational knowing' (p149 Lemma) *"such that a person operates from within a different mental landscape, resulting in new behaviours and experiences in the present and future." (Stern et al: International Journal of Psychoanalysis (79 (5)1998)*

Strean (1994) ascertains the sexual relevance of the joke:
*'For many individuals, including myself, the act of telling and listening to jokes has many similarities to making love, and the laughter that can erupt can be likened to an orgasm. Further, mutual laughter between two-confreres as they exchange jokes can be similar to a mutual orgasm.' (Humour and Psyche –J.W. Barron Analytic Press 1999)*

The joke give the comedian an opportunity to recontextualise a series of thoughts and events and also it announces our social commentary in an abridged view testing the response of our audience. It also offers a glimpse into our personal psyche with a defensive caveat of relinquishing ownership should the audience not laugh and hence not agree with the central premise of the joke.

Moreover, for the joke to be activated it needs an audience. The pleasure of a joke comes from the response of the audience. It is they who validate the joke-tellers existence and creates enjoyment within the proceedings. However, it is also very controversial in that creating jokes consistently can be avoidance of personal self-reflection and avoids true connection with an understanding of oneself within a social or familial setting.

Strean points out that *"jokes and the emergence of a sense of humour, which represents ego strength, paralleled psychosexual development and the development of mature object relations."* (Barron 73:1999)

As has been mentioned previously in this chapter, stand-up can be regarded as a form of self-therapy. Detachment allows the comedian to distance himself from the wound and the pain that comes with it. He does it by creating a 'humorous construct' (the joke), which the audience can then criticise as an entity that is separate from the comedian. In fact, joke serves as a psychological barrier between himself and the audience. The joke becomes the means of detachment.

Christie (1994) mentions that sometimes the 'defence' aspect of humour can be drawn into the service of manic defence, or into providing slightly modified avenues for destructive impulses such as obscenity and sarcasm (1994: 479). Comedians often pick on (or even start verbal fights with) members on the audience, which can be interpreted both as a way of making a connection and as a way of announcing their superior position. The comedian has to put himself above the audience – this is one of the key defence mechanisms displayed during performance. Of course, they are physically 'elevated' by the stage, but they often feel the need to remain in the superior position even when they step off their podium and become members of the audience.

To sum up, the whole performance is the process when the comedian is trying to paradoxically, reveal and defend his own wound on stage. He detaches himself from his wound and almost forgets that humour comes from his own unconscious.

*'Humorous expressions often serve to cloak overly intense emotions, as when a very personal confession is being made or a lament uttered, especially one concerning their health or some great sorrow. (p.163 Humour and Psyche –J.W. Barron Analytic Press 1999)*

He splits himself off from his humour as if the humour does not really belong to him. It can be said that, in dealing with his problems, the comedian employs a number of defence mechanisms, including splitting, detachment and sublimation. However, whilst he announces and confesses the shadow and darker aspect of his psyche he is still accepted which may deflect from the process of self-analysis and therefore individuation.

## 2.3.2. *The Oedipus Complex*

The idea of humour being used as a means to challenge the social order and the so-called 'civilised behaviour' is closely linked with Freud's Oedipus complex (first mentioned in *Five Lectures on Psychoanalysis,* 1910). By using humour, the (predominantly male) comedian attempts to displace the Father figure in its many incarnations. He challenges several Father figures at once: the internal father, other male comedians (by challenging them to a competition) and, ultimately, the social order.

Although Freud did not write directly about the Oedipal colouring of jokes and humour, his analysis of jokes as a defence mechanism is steeped in the Oedipus complex. Freud theorised that the Oedipus complex (first formulated in 1905) comprises the third stage of child development, preceded by the oral and the anal stages. As Laplanche explains

> oral stage is the first stage of libidinal development: sexual pleasure at this period is bound predominantly to that excitation of the oral cavity and lips, which accompanies feeding. The activity of nutrition is the source of the particular meanings through which the object relationship is expressed and organised: the love relationship to the mother, for example, is marked by the meanings of eating and being eaten.
>
> (Laplanche, 1973: 292)

The oral phase of libidinal development will be discussed in more detail in section 2.3.6. Freud's second stage of libidinal development occurs approximately between the ages of two and four. Laplanche writes that, 'the stage is characterised by an organisation of the libido under the primacy of the anal erotogenic zone. The object relation at this time is invested with meanings having to do with tension of defecation (expulsion/retention) and with a symbolic value of faeces. The anal-sadistic stage sees the strengthening of sado-masochism in correlation with the development of mascular control' (Laplanche, 1973: 345).

Strean (1993) links all three stages in humans' relationship to humour when he writes about the pleasure both the teller of the joke and the listener derive from participating in the humorous exchange. He theorises that joke telling is psychologically similar to engaging in sexual activities: 'A fulfilling sexual encounter is usually initiated by words and kisses (oral), accumulations of tension (anal), and consummation in penetration (genital). When the teller and listener are together in the sensually loving, the mutual laughter that evolves from a joke can be similar to mutual orgasm. In telling and listening to a joke (oral) lead to tensions (anal), which result in laughter (genital)' (Strean, 1993: xiii).

The Oedipus complex is basically the desire for death of the rival (the parent of the same sex) and sexual desire for the parent of the opposite sex. The child's identification with the same-sex parent leads to the successful resolution of the Oedipus complex. However, according to Freud, the complex is subsequently revived at puberty (Laplanche and Pontalis, 1973: 283). Lemma (2000) expounds on the role of humour in the resolution of the Oedipus complex. From her view, humour acts as a mechanism that manages the internal Oedipus complex.

Lemma writes that

> Healthy humour … rests on the capacity to tolerate antithetical ideas, to manage opposites. This capacity is won at a cost. We can have to tread the arduous route and endure dis-identification from our parents. This rests on a relinquishment of an exclusive relationship with both parents along with the acknowledgement that they have an exclusive relationship with each other. If the child negotiates the Oedipal stage in a relatively healthy way he acquires an internal model of an intercourse (between the parents) which is, on the whole, a creative activity.
>
> (Lemma, 2000: 57)

We can theorise that at puberty the Oedipus complex reaches a new stage. The idea of the 'father' shifts from the physical parent and onto the social order as a system. As such, comedy may be said to be all about provocation of the 'masculine' binary opposition in society. Following this train of thought, making comedy is all about 'Oedipal revival'. His desire to make comedy and to create jokes may be interpreted as the Oedipal desire to challenge and overpower 'the father' represented within the joke. Thus, it can be assumed that there are two principal libidinal drives at work during the stand-up performance: the drive to question the order by joking about it (kill the father) and the drive to attract the mother (receive love and attention from the audience). Following Lemma's idea, the comical process can also be regarded as an attempt to lessen the tension, which comes with an unresolved Oedipus complex (an attempt at resolution which, in fact, is the attempt to close 'the wound').

## 2.3.3. *Freud's Concept of Libido*

Freud's concept of libido is also crucial to our argument. As Freud defined it in *Group Psychology and the Analysis of the Ego* (1921), libido is 'the energy regarded as a quantitative magnitude of those instincts which maybe comprised under the word "love"' It is also 'the dynamic manifestation of [the sexual instinct] in mental life.'

Freud stated:
> *Libido is an expression taken from the theory of the emotions. We call by that name the energy………. have to do with all that may be comprised under the word 'love'. The nucleus of what we mean by love naturally consists (and this is what is commonly called love, and what the poets sing of) in sexual love with sexual union as its aim………………. though always preserving enough of their original nature to keep their identity recognisable (as in such features as the longing for proximity, and self-sacrifice).*

Thus, it can be theorised the comedian sublimates his sexual energy and aggression in his performance, and transforms them into jokes. The comedian uses the framework of stand-up performance to express his creative aggression and individuality in a relatively safe environment.

By making fun of prohibitions and serious issues, the joker challenges the superego imposed on him or her by parents as representatives of society and civilization. A number of authors from different branches of the humanities have expanded on the relation of the Oedipus complex to humour. For instance, Mahon, following Arieti (1967) argues that 'humour is a result of the secondary revision that may be needed in order to displace the meaning a little further from the Oedipal core' (Mahon, 1992, quoted in Barron, 1999: 74). Simon Critchley points out that 'in humour the childlike super-ego that experiences parental prohibition and Oedipal guilt is replaced with a more grown up super-ego, let is call it super-ego II' (Critchley, 2007: 102-103). Drawing on Freud's ideas, Lemma (2000) writes that it is during the Oedipal phase that the infant's appreciations of humour develops. Most of these researchers, however, did not analyse the Oedipal element of humour in detail but only mentioned that the Oedipus complex can be used as means of explaining the human desire to create and perform jokes. One of the aims of this thesis is to explore the Oedipal (father-challenging) dimension of humour.

## *2.3.4. Lacan and the Symbolic Order*

Jacque Lacan's ideas concerning the Symbolic Order are also important in our analysis of the psychological dimension of humour. In 'The Function and Field of Speech and Language in Psychoanalysis' (1956) Lacan discusses the Symbolic Order as having many manifestations, including the law and the language. In *The Seminar. Book I. Freud's Papers on Technique* (1953) he refers to Symbolic Father as the Name-of The-Father. Reworking the Oedipus complex, Lacan states that the Symbolic Father is also the dead father, the father of the primal horde who has been murdered by his sons (Evans, 2001: 62).

From Lacan's perspective (1938), the figure of the father is an oxymoron as it incorporates two conflicting functions: the protective function and the prohibitive functions. Also, the Oedipus complex is nothing less than the passage from the imaginary (pre-Oedipal) order to the symbolic order, the conquest of the symbolic relation as such (Evans, 2001: 127). Thus, it may be said that the comedian's personal issues extend (via Oedipus complex) onto the symbolic order. By re-working his conflict with the father, the performer also identifies and attempts to resolve the current issues of society. By breaking the taboos imposed on him by the personal father, the comedian breaks the taboos currently prevalent in his or her culture. This theory has equivalents in cultural anthropology. Anthropologists (including Victor Turner (1968); Hynes and Doty (1993))) regard the trickster's desire to thwart the social order ('kill or de-throne the father') and replace it with a new version ('possess the mother') as an indispensable part of society's development which ensures its progress and renewal. Thus, the comedian may be regarded as attacking the symbolic father (or a constellation of fathers) and defending himself from castration at the same time. This also links with the idea of Amfortas Wound and its mytho-sexual implications. Jung ascribed the mythic narrative to Wagner's opera Parsifal. The priest King Amfortas languished wounded for many years from a wound to 'thigh' – it was argued that his 'thigh' was a polite reference to his penis. (The Amfortas Myth is discussed further in Chapter 3)

Interestingly enough, the comedian uses language (Lacan's *langage*) – the Father's weapon of choice – to attack the Symbolic Order from within. In appropriating language, the comedian alters the order and opens up a new perspective on the world. It is not only the social order (symbolic order, the law) that is being challenged by the 'wounded child', but also the language pattern itself. The comedian re-works the patriarchal structure by attacking it from within.

### 2.3.5. *Melanie Klein and the Pre-Oedipal Issues*

If Freud's Oedipus complex can be useful for analysing the comedian's Oedipal dilemma and his dialogue (or fight) with the 'order' in its many incarnations, Melanie Klein's ideas can throw light on the influence of Oedipal issues on the comedian's creativity. Particularly, the Oral and Anal stages defined in depth by Klein as the Paranoid Schizophrenic and Depressive Positions. Before the arrival of the 'order' (in whatever form) there was the unity with the mother (real or symbolic). If the comedian's desire to challenge the symbolic father (other men, social order, the internal patriarch) has its roots in the Oedipus complex, the origin of his wild desire for love from the audience is largely related to 'oral' ('feeding') issues. The performer's hunger for love and attention becomes sublimated in his or her attempt to 'seduce' the audience.

One of the most prominent features of the comedian's relationship with the audience is his emotional connectivity. From my view, the mystery of this intensity can be explained by the ideas borrowed from Klein's object relations theory. During his stand-up performance, the audience represents the symbolic mother with whom the comedian seeks to establish a relationship. The connection with this kind of mother figure can turn out to be either good or bad.

In order to describe the infant's relationship with its primary caregiver, Klein used the metaphors of the 'good breast' and the 'bad breast'. 'Breasts' are part of the object world of the child' which play an important part in the formation of the ego and symbolise, respectively, the caregiver who keeps the child well fed (literally, physically, emotionally, attention-wise), or the one who neglects the child. (Klein,

1988: 141, 50) Thus, the 'breast' is an 'object' which is internalised by the baby along with a constellation of anxieties and defences are processed. These primal instincts and emotional responses can re-occur and replay consistently throughout life. The infant's survival depends on the attention the caregiver is willing to give it, the relationship between the 'breast' and the child is very intense. 'In this early connection, predominantly oral in character, originates the child's subsequent ability to adapt to and interact with the external world (Klein, 1988: 59).

Kleins' theory runs parallel to the more optimistic model of mother-infant relationship proposed by Neumann (1973), presents audience interaction as a reflection (or a repetition, a return) of the primal relationship.
*'The primary attachment of the Self to the thou as mother, she, as embodiment of that which confers security, is the child's firs model for the experience of its own Self" (p60 E. Neumann The Child Hodder & Staunton 1973)*

Speaking metaphorically, the comedian ('the child') seeks the attention of the audience ('the mother' who can give him 'milk'). The condition of a child seeking his mother's approval is consistent with Klein's view of the repetition of the Paranoid Schizoid position characterised by splitting, projection, identification, idealisation, omnipotence, denial and paranoid anxiety i.e. persecution in the consistent search for reverie. As Klein points out, ' they are potentially present at any time in the here and now, "a 'position' is an always available state, not something one passes through' ( Klein, M. (1935) A Contribution to the Psychogenesis of Manic Depressive States, in The Selected Melanie Klein, ed. Mitchell, J. Penguin Books, London. 1986 p.11)'

Bion's concept of reverie is consistently sought by the comedian 'Mother's mind needs to be in state of calm receptiveness to take in the infants own feelings and give them meaning." (P420 Hinchelwood) It is through the introjection of a receptive, understanding mother he in fact can begin to develop his own capacity for reflection in his own states of mind.

Jung differentiated between the wounded and redeeming characteristics of a child who is, 'the "child" is all that is abandoned and exposed and at the same time divinely powerful; the insignificant, dubious beginning, and the triumphal end.' And the 'eternal child' lost in his youth, which is irreconcilable psychic forces, hindering his existence.

The "eternal child" in man is an indescribable experience, an incongruity, a handicap, and a divine prerogative; an imponderable that determines the ultimate worth or worthlessness of a personality. ["The Psychology of the Child Archetype," CW 9i, par. 300.]

The comedian on stage can either become the child who re-emerses himself within the paranoid-schizoid conflicting, threatening and overwhelming psychic forces and by dramatising these forces he projects and introjects his anxieties and destructive instincts thereby potentially healing himself organically over a period of time. Or alternatively he is the Puer Aeternus who chooses to linger in the adolescent phase of irresponsibility, exploration and conflict projected into the world through anecodes and relationships without empathy, assimilation or self-reflection.

Like the notorious ambivalent Kleinian breast, the audience is not always reliable. Sometimes it provides the comedian with love and attention he or she craves, and sometimes it goes cold and unresponsive (withdraws the 'breast'). According to Klein (1935), the infant possesses a number of psychic defence mechanisms, which help it cope with 'bad' part-objects such as 'unreliable' breasts. The infant regards bad objects as 'internal persecutors' (1988: 116-17). The infant's ways of dealing with them include introjection, projection, expulsion and denial of external reality (1988: 117). We can certainly apply Klein's ideas regarding defence mechanisms to the comedian's behaviour on stage, as they tend to split off their unsuccessful performances and regard them as something separate from their own persona. The internal link between their persona and their very personal material is split the good stays with their persona and the bad with their material or the audience.

They also tend to project the sense failure onto the audience ('they are a bad audience'). Stand-up comedians often react aggressively to any verbal challenge from members of the audience in order to avoid real or imaginary failure. These instances bring to mind Klein's theory of the depressive position (1935) – a defensive state in which the child dreads persecutors ('bad objects') and tries to ward them off by attacking them (1988: 117).

Interestingly enough, Klein linked her 'milk' metaphor to the development of creativity in an infant. She wrote that the feeding breast is regarded by the baby as a source of creativity (Klein, 1997a: 331). Seen in this light, the comedian wants to attract the audience's attention in order to keep his creativity alive; it is as if the audience 'feeds' him or her with their laughter. Klein theorises: 'For the talent to develop … in fixation to the primal scene (or phantasies), the degree of activity which is so important for the sublimation itself, undoubtedly also determines whether the subject develops a talent for creation or reproduction' (Klein, 1997a: 103). In *Envy and Gratitude,* she argues: 'we find in the analysis of our patients that the breast in its good aspect is the prototype of maternal goodness, inexhaustible patience and generosity, as well as of creativeness. It is these phantasies and instinctual needs that so enrich the primal object that it remains the foundation for hope, trust and belief in goodness' (Klein, 1997a: 180). Moreover, as many comedians (whose interviews are provided in the forthcoming chapters) admit, humour is born out of the sense of loss, and exists for the purpose of helping human beings deal with this lamentable state. This certainly taps into Klein's idea concerning the depressive and the comedian's attempt to reconnect with lost and broken objects. This also runs parallel to our main image of the 'wound' and the stand-up performance as a radical way of dealing with it.

Psychologists and psychotherapists researching humour have also adopted the 'breast' element of the object relations theory. For instance, Chris Bollas (1995) writes that the mother-baby relationship is one of farce – not only because the mother's behaviour towards the infant is full of mimicry, vocalizations and all sorts of comical exaggerations – but also because the mother is full of good milk and good humour (quoted in Barron, 1999: 39-40). According to Bollas (1995), the mother can be regarded as the first clown. Lemma also observes that 'the shared laughter rekindles the pre-verbal memory of similar exchanges in infancy, when the mother's smile and face lit up and conveyed that there was nothing to fear, that we were understood and loved' (Lemma, 2000: 57).

Closely linked with the 'audience as a mother' metaphor is Klein's idea of *phantasy*, which can be defined as a form of therapeutic play. Phantasy is both 'activity and its products' (Klein, 1988: 23). Klein's own treatment of her little patients consisted of triggering their phantasies (with the help of toys), and then observing and examining them. This is very similar to triggering a psychotherapeutic creative process and analysing its contents. Lemma notes that Klein's method was 'a prototypical example of the sublimated activity which represented the symbolic expression of anxieties and wishes' (Lemma, 2000: 47-48).

Seen in this light, the comedian's union with the audience can be represented as a kind of *phantasy* of the ideal primal relationship. The performer phantasies' about 'the ideal' audience and 'the ideal' (and plentiful) love they give him or her. It is as if they 'replay' this relationship during the performance. The comedian plays out their own anxieties and phantasies in the hope to heal or modify them. To recap, several of Klein's ideas, including phantasy, the depressive position and the concept of the good/bad objects can be used to analyse the comedian's intensive, tense and sometimes even aggressive and controversial relationship with the audience.

## 2.3.6. *Attachment Theories*

Attachment theories also tap well into the metaphor of the 'wounded comedian'. During the performance, the comedian establishes a relationship with the audience, which is short-lived but very intense. In a way, the performer does not see the audience as a conglomeration of individuals but regards it as a kind of volatile mother figure, an object of courtship. This is where attachment theories come into play. The comedian 'attaches' himself to the audience, expecting it to be accepting and empathic. In this respect, theorists like Bowlby can assist in the construction of the argument. Attachment is defined by Bowlby as 'a form of instinctive behaviour that develops in humans, as in other mammals, during infancy, and has as its aim or goal proximity to a mother-figure' (Bowlby, 2010: 106). In his essay 'Separation and Loss Within the Family' (1970) Bowlby writes that, while attachment behaviour is directed towards the child's actual parents, 'it none the less continues to be active during adult life when it is usually directed towards some active and dominant figure, often a relative but sometimes an employer or some elder of the community' (2010: 106).

Seen in this light, the audience becomes a psychological extension of the mother figure. The comedian needs to ensure that the audience become a positive attachment figure in order to gain a reinforcing reaction. In the essay 'Childhood Mourning and Its Implications for Psychiatry' (1961), Bowlby theorises that, 'in infants and young children the experience of separation habitually initiates defensive processes which lead to yearning for the lost person and reproach for desertion both become unconscious' (2010: 69). It is arguable that the desire to become a stand-up comedian can be regarded as originating in the disruption of an emotional bond or bonds, while the desire to win over and retain the audience can be seen as an urge to recover the lost person. 'If all goes well – Bowlby writes – there is joy and a sense of security. If it is threatened, there is jealousy, anxiety, and anger' (2005: 4). This can be used as a metaphor for the stand-up performance because, while on stage and seeking a secure connection with the audience, the comedian feels emotionally fragile and vulnerable. The perfect connection brings with it the feelings of being loved and even 'omnipotence'. However, when things go wrong, the comedian feels deflated and depressed. Comedians tend to blame the audience for the failure. They use 'stock' phrases such as 'I have died' or 'they are not a good audience' when describing their failure to please the listeners.

The 'lost' person is not a concrete person or a real 'lost carer' in the comedian's life but rather a symbol of the lost mother, a symbol of the primal unity, something that stands for the individual's ideal paradisiacal relationship with the world. This, again, brings us back to Neumann's theorising (1973) on the disruption of the primal relationship, its psychological implications for the individual, and its influence on the individual's creativity.

Bowlby's ideas on aggression (1958) and secure base (1988) are also pertinent to our argument. He postulates (1961) that the biological function of aggression is to achieve reunion with the lost person. In 'Effects on Behaviour of Disruption of an Affectional Bond' (1978) he writes that 'behaviour of an aggressive sort plays a key role in maintaining affectional bonds' (2010: 85). Bowlby writes in 'Psychoanalysis and Childcare' (1958) writes that 'an aggressive child is acting on the basis that attack is the best means of defence' (2010: 13). This directly relates to our analysis of the performer-audience relationship. A comedy club is a space where verbal

aggression is permitted. However, the comedian has to establish what Bowlby terms (1973) a 'secure base' – an attachment figure who can provide the individual (child) with a safe emotional environment. Before displaying any aggression in jokes (aimed against the symbolic father), the comedian has to establish a secure emotional connection with the audience (the symbolic mother). Once this connection is established, the comedian is safe to express aggression in his jokes and in his physical performance as long as this aggression is not directed against individual members of the audience. The attack has to be 'detached' from the audience and aimed at the 'father': the social structure, the law, the symbolic order. However, the comedian may become offensive towards the audience when he or she feels that the audience is apathetic, unresponsive and generally hostile. The idea of 'attack on the father' also links with Turner's concept of ritual (1968) as a way of renewing and challenging the established order of things.
Turner states:

> *'Men use their authority vested in their office to misuse and abuse the incumbents of lower positions and confuse position with its incumbent. Rituals of status reversal, either placed at strategic points in the annual circle or generated by disasters conceived of as being the result of grave social sins, are thought of as bringing social structure and communitas into right relation once again"*
> (p 178 V. Turner. Library of Congress.1969)

## *2.4. Conclusion*

The choice of the integrative approach is informed by the fact that the comedian fulfils a number of psychosocial and anthropological functions during his performance. On the very basic level, the comedian (predominantly male) attempts to resolve his own personal problems (both Oedipal and pre-Oedipal) by acting out his personal and psychological dramas on stage. In the case of a successful stand-up process, the comedian both receives the love of the audience and challenges the real and symbolic patriarch.

At a higher level (and in the long term), stand-up comedy and creative processes associated with it allow the comedian to individuate by exploring his 'Amfortas wound' on stage. In order to activate his creativity, the comedian delves into his unconscious and extracts any material that has the potential for creating tension, laughter and release – both in the audience and the comedian. Thus, the comedian's urge to challenge 'the father' outgrows its personal dimensions and acquires political and social aspects.

In my view, it is crucial to discuss stand-up comedy on all levels as they complement each other. In stand-up comedy, the personal is virtually inseparable from the social, and the comedian's intimate issues also happen to be the problems of his or her society. The comedian articulates these problems thus enlightening (and shocking) the audience while simultaneously healing himself.

# CHAPTER 3

## JUNGIAN AND POST-JUNGIAN IDEAS IN RELATION TO THE COMEDIAN

I believe that stand-up comedy reflects social and psychological change in our society. Jungian theories are particularly pertinent to this study because they capture the psychological implications of social transformations. In this thesis I will argue that the comedic performance triggers and utilises Jung's symbolic and archetypal processes. In fact, stand-up comedy can be regarded as a metaphorical litmus test for society's problems and issues.

The comedy club can become the alchemical term 'vas' a transformational space wherein the audience are prepared to engage and accept the role of the stand-up comedian. In order for the stand-up comedian to engage he has to identify with the audience and the modern audience is prepared for social discourse and personal emotional dilemmas which are bound in the main of societies conflicts and social change. The audience wants to identify with the comedian with the issues he reflects in his personal experiences and the experiences the audience also encounter with an observable detachment and humorous slant. If the transformational space is not established or the comedian does not engage with the audience there will be no 'participation mystique.'

The further we go back into history, the more we see personality disappearing beneath the wrappings of collectivity. And if we go right back to primitive psychology, we find absolutely no trace of the concept of an individual. Instead of individuality we find only collective relationship or what Lévy-Bruhl calls *participation mystique* (Jung, [1921] 1971: par. 12).

Without the unconscious connection humour and transformation becomes negligible.

Whereas Freud interpreted the joke as independent from the individual, which has to standalone and could be passed on like a gift-wrapped in eloquent comedic construct and intonation. The resonance of which is cerebral not ontological.

Therefore for the comedian to be identified with the whole audience or individual members of the audience his material and himself must be connected in a cohesive and revelatory truism resonating beyond his character, beyond the joke, beyond the space. He must become entertain the collective unconscious.

While Freudian and post-Freudian ideas prove to be more appropriate for examining the details of the psychological processes that take place inter- and intra-psychically within the totality of the comedic performance, Jungian and post-Jungian theory explores the social and mythological aspect of stand-up comedy. This thesis applies a variety of Jungian ideas to the analysis of stand-up comedy: Individuation, the Self, the Persona, Enantiodromia, the Amfortas Wound, Temenos and the Trickster.

## 3.
### *3.1.  Individuation*

Jolande Jacobi defines individuation as a 'spontaneous, natural process within the psyche,' which is 'potentially present in every man, although most men are unaware of it' (Jacobi, 1973: 107).

Jung states that the individuation process is driven by the Self – the centre of the personality and is also a transpersonal centre. He writes in *'Psychological Types'*: Jolande Jacobi helps define the Individuation process as an individual uniquely placed to affect the mass.

> *'Only a man who can consciously assent to the power of the inner voice becomes a personality. And only a personality can find a proper place in the collectivity; only personalities have the power to create a community, that is, to become integral parts of a human group and not merely a number in a mass. For the mass is only a living organism that receives and bestows life. Thus self-realisation, both in the individual and in the extrapersonal, collective sense, becomes a moral decision, and it is this moral decision, which lends force to the process of self-fulfilment that Jung calls Individuation.*
> (J. Jacobi p 106. The Psychology of C.G.Jung. Routledge 1942)

Thus, individuation does not mean some kind of narcissistic loneliness, but always presupposes involvement with one's fellow human beings (CW7: 267).

Jung perceives individuation as the *'world-creating quality of consciousness'* (CW 14 par132) (which Edinger explores further;

> *"One is a separate, unique world of being there can be no norms, since a norm is an average of many. The individual psyche is and must be a whole world within itself in order to stand over and against the outer*

*world and fulfil its task of being a carrier of consciousness. For the scales to be balanced, the individual must be of equal weight to the world.'*

(E Edinger Anatomy of the Psyche p.9 Open Court 1991)

Individuation ' is a process of maturation and unfolding' (J. Jacobi p 106. The Psychology of C.G.Jung. Routledge 1942) activated within the individual upon self-reflection, but also as a member of the collectivity, and the wholeness he has achieved is in contact, through consciousness and unconscious with the whole world. Its ultimate aim is to create an independent thinking, unique individual who would at the same be "a member of collectivity".

The comedian's creative process itself, which is interactive, plays a significant role in his individuation. Individuation is a two-way process, which involves sharing and canalising personal psychic complexes into his own comedic material shared with the audience in a socially acceptable form. It is closely related to what Edinger termed 'canalization' (replacing 'sublimation'). Edinger defined canalization as:

> ... the conversion or transformation of *libido* as it performs various mental activities. The transfer of psychic intensities or values from one content to another. Canalization sets up a gradient so instinctual energies can do productive work. It does so via the *symbol*, which offers a steeper gradient than the natural one. The transformation of instinctual energy is done via an analogue of the object of the instinct: a psychic mechanism imitates the *instinct* and thereby captures its energy (like a power station at a waterfall). The first achievement of this by primitive man is magic.
>
> (Edinger, 1994: 81).

During the performance, the comedian is able to divulge his personal anxieties, neuroses, and, at times, wounds. The transference and counter-transference that takes place between the performer and audience is the pivotal transformational process. This is explored further in Chapter 6: Going on Stage: Inter and Intra-psychic matrix of the Comedian.

## 3.2. *The Amfortas Wound*

Jung acknowledged a connection between Wagner's *Parsifal* (1882) to the feeling type (Volume 6, *Psychological Types),* The concept of the Amfortas Wound is important for this thesis because it can be seen as a allegory for a 'question of attitude by which every activity, including the sexual, is regulated' (CW6: para. 373) The myth implies the dichotomy of instinctual urges – Freud's primary drive being an instinctual sexual drive, Jung called 'a nature bound compulsion. ' Whereas Jung argued that laying deeper in ones psyche more than primordial sexual instinct is 'attitude'. It is within the 'attitude' that transcendence can occur on a higher plane. "sexuality is not the point." "It was not sexuality that dealt him his wound so much as an attitude of nature-bound compulsion." (Jung, 1921: par.372). What lies behind sexuality and power is the 'attitude' to sexuality and power." (Jung CW6 Par373) Sexuality energizes our impulses and "glamorizes" in the original sense of the word: it lends an uncanny aura of power to whatever it touches' which was the fundamental point Jung was emphatically making to Freud in his letters. It is this profound distinction that permanently and irrevocably split Jung and Freud in 1913. It has been a division, which has affected psychoanalytic thinking for over a century. Both eminent psychological theoreticians chose a father and young man mythological relationship, reflecting their own psychology and familial complex, to highlight mankind's inherent 'sin' or 'guilt,' which has to be assimilated or transcended. Thereby, the myths can be viewed as the microcosm within the macrocosm of their philosophies. It is this 'attitude' to the 'sexual instinct or 'attitude' not just the raw instinct itself that the comedian is forced to reflect upon depending upon the audience as being a representation of their Self and society. It is an integral part of male individuation, and is therefore pertinent to our study.

Wagner's opera is loosely based on Wolfram von Eschenbach's poem *Parzival,* dated to the first quarter of the 13th century. In Wagner's version, King Amfortas was given guardianship of the Holy Spear, by his father, and is seduced by the witch Kundry. Klingsor, who castrated himself because he could not control his sexual impulses and hence was rejected from the Knights of the Grail, disguises Kundry as an alluring woman who seduced Amfortas. Klingsor grabs the Spear and stabbed Amfortas: this wound caused Amfortas both suffering and shame, and could not heal on its own.

In the last act, he is brought before the grail shrine and his father's coffin. He implores his dead father to grant him rest from his pain. The Knights urge him to reveal the Grail, but Amfortas refuses to do this. He asks the Knights to kill him in order to end his suffering. Parsifal, who had refused to yield the Holy Spear in battle, touches the king's side and heals him. The Grail is then revealed.

The Amfortas Wound can be regarded as a contemporary allegory for the crisis and for the general quandary associated with societal patriarchy and change to the role of the female in society. Pivotal to this thesis is the Amfortas myth amplifies Jung's basic tenet that the wound in the male psyche can only be healed through recognising the spiritual and empathic connection made on a numinous level.

> we get entangled in an insoluble contradiction, since the thing that harms is also the thing that heals. Such a paradox is true and

permissible only when one sees the opposites as united on a higher plane . . .
(Jung, CW 61921: pars. 372f).

The myth implies the dichotomy of instinctual urges. Jung states that healing of the personal or social rift can only take place in unison with a higher attitude – and this is exactly what is revealed in the Holy Grail legend. Jung writes: 'It is purely a question of attitude by which every activity, including the sexual, can be regulated' (CW16: para.373). It can be argued that stand-up comedy can be seen as the search for the Holy Grail capable of healing the performer's personal wounds as well as the wounds of his society. Humour becomes the tool with which the comedian can probe different aspects of his deeply buried, disowned contents of his personal wound; and it is during this process of exploring his pain that the audience relates to him. In a way, the audience and the comedian are united by the anecdotal expression of the comedian's pain, comparable to the compassion Parsifal felt for Amfortas.

Robert Johnson does not engage in intellectual detachment of many post Jungian theorists as too simplistic, that the 'story has presented the healing of the wounded feeling function in mythological language, and the actual transformation in one's life is likely to be less dramatic and not just one glorious moment....'

Here Johnson in simplistic terms, echoes Jung's chosen analogy of the Amfortas Wound as the wounded feeling function for the male psyche in his Psychological Types. (R. Johnson The Fisher King and Handless Maiden. Harper San Francisco p47, 48 1993)

Socially, it is important for the contemporary male to examine the complexity of his multi-layered personal, social, inter and intra psychic relationships, and the stand-up arena enables him to engage with his projections and enables de-integration and re-integration to occur. As Fordham explains:
*'States of integration and deintegration can be observed objectively in behaviour or subjectively as feelings of good and bad, love and hate....'* (M. Fordham Explorations into the Self p.31 Karnac Books 1985)

Stand-up comedians are able to create their own narratives and identify their neuroses through their work. This process of exploring the intimate contents of the male psyche enables the comedian to examine and influence the transformation of masculinity's role in contemporary society. I propose that the healing of the Amfortas wound by Parsifal is the metaphor for the potential healing of the wound in the male psyche. The masculine wound, which Jung touched upon during his exploration of psychological types, is the difference between thinking and feeling types. The male predominantly is the thinking type who is rational and active. The feeling type, which Jung attributes mostly to the female, is passive, empathic and communicative. Parsifal during the considering his mothers death awaked his conscience and feelings of respect to women reflected by his question, 'whom does the grail serve?' The comedian can reflect upon his actions and intentions by permitting the audience to be his conscience.

For the stand-up comedian, the personal is closely related to the collective and the two always communicate with one another: 'The dialogue on the personal level has led to the activation of the collective unconscious, whereby a direct experience of the transpersonal dimension becomes possible' (Edinger et al.: 91).

### *3.3. The Ego and the Self*

The search for the Self is part of the individuation process. Jung defined it as 'a sort of atomic nucleus about whose innermost structure and ultimate meaning we know nothing' (CW 12, para: 249). Jung, as Marcus West points out, regarded the Self as the centre of the psyche. It is the totality of the psyche. The Self is the archetype of wholeness, the regulating centre of the psyche. It is also the organising and guiding principle, steering the individual's development (West, 2007: 164). West writes that

> The self also represented, for Jung, the unconscious *goal of development,* a potential toward which the personality naturally unfolds. As the guiding principle of the psyche, Jung held that the self was never itself manifest, but remained an archetype, guiding the individual from the unconscious. Experiences representing or approximating to an experience of the self are imbued with a sense of *wholeness,* thought to represent the experience of integration of the different parts of the personality.
>
> (2007: 164-5).

The Ego is conceptually different from the Self. Jung writes: 'The Ego is, by definition, subordinate to the Self and is related to it like a part to the whole. Inside the field of consciousness it has, as we say, free will. […] It finds its limits outside the field of consciousness in the subjective inner world, where it comes into conflict with the facts of the Self' (CW9/II: para. 5).

Comedians are constantly in search of their unique comedic voice, or essence, which they achieve during the performance, when they are accepted and loved by the audience. During the stand-up performance the comedian gets a glimpse of the Self. It becomes manifest when the audience feeds parts of the personality back to the comedian, making him, or her albeit briefly, feel whole. For Jung, the encounter with the Self-archetype, whenever it happens, is similar to a numinous experience. It feels like an encounter with 'the will of God'. The term 'God' here being understood as 'the mighty daemon expressing a determining power which comes upon man from outside, like providence or fate, though the ethical decision is left to man' (Jung, 1951: para. 51).

The creative process that occurs during a stand-up performance involves very close interaction with the audience – which means that the emotional exchange between the viewer and the comedian is at its most intense. As the American comedian Garry Shandling notes, the result of this interaction is often very cathartic. It is, in fact, a form of therapy:

> I think it still helps me find who I am. I've honestly had my therapist say to me: 'The same way you are on stage, you should be able to deal with your life like that'. Which is, if you have somebody heckle you, you don't just stop and complain, you just take care of it. And he said that's how you have to live your life. So I think it's not unusual for actors or comedians to use the stage as a way of feeling free and good about their lives […].
>
> (Ajaye, 2002: 207)

## 3.4. *The Persona*

Jung defines the Persona as 'that which in reality one is not, but which oneself as well as others think one is. In any case the temptation to be what one seems to be is great, because the persona is usually rewarded in cash' (CW9/I: para. 221). The Persona is thus a mask, an artificial façade created and employed for the purpose of gaining social benefits. As Elie Humbert puts it, 'the Persona is charged with the task of inserting the subject into a social network of communication' (Humbert, 1996: 51). As she points out, '"Persona' originally referred to the mask actors wore in the theatres of antiquity. This mask made the actor's voice resound … while it allowed the audience to recognise the role that the actor played' (1996: 51).

It might be said that the comedian wears a mask on stage, and it is indeed rewarded in cash. This mask is usually an exaggerated part of his personality and it has the dual function of attracting the audience and protecting his inner vulnerability. His vulnerability can be expressed by extreme need to please the audience or by attacking the audience when they do not respond favourably. The humour style and attitude chosen by the comedian can be said to be their Persona because it becomes a layer of protection of the comedian's tender psychological core.

Comedians accentuate a part of themselves that become a part of their Persona. The material used often comes from the comedian's personal experience – but it is often exaggerated for comedic effect. If the on-stage Persona is very successful, the performer may become reluctant to take it off even off-stage. This is a psychologically dangerous moment because he may eventually lose the ability to differentiate between his real self and the artificial mask. What used to be a part of his genuine personality becomes a rigid, exaggerated, oversized mask.

In his book, *Comic Insights: the Art of Stand-Up Comedy* (2002), the comedian Frankin Ajaye warns his readers about the dangers of developing an on-stage persona – and about taking it too seriously. He advises budding comedians to 'be themselves' while on stage. In his view, genuine humour is based on genuine personality, not on an over-inflated, fake mask:

> Don't be concerned too much about developing an image or persona when you're starting out. In fact, never consciously try to create one if you are trying to do humour based on your true point of view of life, society, the world, etc. Whatever you are will emerge naturally, though it will be in reality somewhat heightened when you're on stage. On stage, you are you plus fifteen percent. Richard Lewis, Richard Pryor, Woody Allen, Elayne Boosler, Bill Cosby, Garry Shandling, and many others have very distinct personas and comedic images that have emerged over the years. These personas are very close to the person that they are when they're not performing.
>
> (Ajaye, 2002: 36)

Ajaye also advocates 'being yourself' because it is the best way to achieve a strong stage presence. In his view, this natural approach will bring the best response from the audience:

> Many comedians think [commanding your space on stage] means coming at the audience with rapid speech and an aggressive attitude. But that's not necessary. If you're soft-spoken or laid back, a good delivery, good timing, a strong point of view, and the words 'commitment and conviction' tattooed in your brain will help you create a strong stage presence.
>
> (Ajaye 2002: 17)

Some stand-up performers, such as the British comedian Jenny Eclair, have the opposite opinion about the comedian's behaviour on and off-stage, and on the size of their Persona. She admits to her ego being fed – through the Persona – by the audience's reaction, the elation and the success. The adrenaline, the psychological over-inflation, the sense of omnipotence become addictive, they become drugs. Eclair admits that withdrawal of these drugs leaves her depressed. Her on-stage Persona and actual personality are inseparable:

> I've had a few gigs at Hackney Empire when I've come off-stage feeling completely omnipotent. I'm ghastly to live with. I overdose on adrenaline sometimes. It's a downfall for a lot of comics. You get so hyped up that when you come down to reality, you can't actually deal with it. When I came back from Edinburgh, I took a couple of weeks off to be a mother again, and come eight o'clock at night on a normal night in, I thought, 'What do I do now? I've got to cook a meal, stay in? I missed that winding up, the gearing up before a gig. I'm only really happy when I'm working. Otherwise, I get so depressed that I have to go back to bed. I don't actually like it. My daughter is a great substitute. She's the only other thing, but I couldn't be domestic and just do that.
>
> (Cook, 1994: 187)

Speaking metaphorically, when the Persona grows too big, the comedian becomes 'full of hubris'. The mask becomes the attitude of a God. If the comedian over-identifies with that attitude, their (Jungian) ego becomes blurred. They have over-identified with their Self as God image. The whole operation – establishing a contact with the Self – in this case is not therapeutic. It is not about improving the dynamic of the Ego-Self axis – it is about remaining in the heightened state of hubris; identifying with God. The ego-self axis is a constant shift between the comedians drive to develop himself and how he develops his Self; at what expense. This oscillation must exist continuously or over-inflation can occur. The mask of God inflates 'reality'; the Persona, fed by the unconscious forces, gets out of control. Mario Jacoby writes about the dangers of over-identification with the Self: 'If the Self may be experienced as an image of God, the distinction between the Ego and the Self is extremely important for psychic health. For I am not God, and God is not I. An identification between the ego and the self means delusions of grandeur such as become manifest in certain psychoses' (Jacoby, 1985: 70). As Joseph Henderson argues, 'the Ego must continually return to re-establish its relation to the Self in order to maintain a condition of psychic health' (Jung, 1978: 75).

Without reflective and self-critical processes, the Ego is weakened and the Persona is over developed. The bridge between the Self and the Persona is established – without the balancing interaction of the Ego. Such a powerful relationship of two 'collective' entities overlooks the reality check of his life and his in this case of his identity. As Jacobi writes, paraphrasing Jung, regarding over- identification with the Persona 'would allow self-esteem to be fed by collective roles instead of being grounded in genuine personality' (1985: 88). This provides 'a state of alienation and depersonalisation that the individual has to compensate for by identifying with a collective role. His own ego is puffed up by the importance of the chosen role, it is "inflated"' (1985: 88). Also, 'identification with roles defined by society may not only procure the pseudo-satisfaction of a person's need for self-esteem – at the cost of his genuine individuality. There is also the danger that contents of an archetypal nature originating in the collective unconscious may lead to inflation' (1985: 88). This detachment from reality equals the (relative) loss of the Ego. A comedian can be seduced by the audience into being successful with a persona, which would be difficult to adjust or remove and consequently be trapped by his need for success rather than his need to be his-Self. He therefore may hinder or indeed forfeit his own development in terms of becoming individuated in order to maintain his successful or adored status. It may be said that Ajaye advocates keeping an eye on reality, being grounded in 'here and now'; being realistic – even on stage; to be able to control the Persona and the inflation of the ego. Ideally it is about being in control of one's creative process and not sacrificing one's own convictions in order to please the audience.

In conclusion, it is essential that the comedian is conscious not only of his material, but also of the psychological processes triggered in his psyche during the intense interaction with the audience. He should be able to laugh at himself – which, for the comedian, is a form of self-reflection. Only then would he be able to avoid the distortion of various psychic structures and relationships between them – particularly the power struggle between the triangular relationship of the Self, the Ego and the Persona where the Self is sacrificed for fame.

## 3.5. *Enantiodromia*

Jung proposed that psychic balance is consistently in question and various psychic agencies vie for power or primary position. He termed the transformation from one extreme to another enantiodromia and is very important for our analysis of stand-up comedy in relation to the psychological processes of individuation.

The comedian activates enantiodromia by focusing on various aspects of his life. Neuroses are injected into his material and then projected onto the audience – for instance, through the popular subject of personal relationships. This intra-and inter-psychic comedic material becomes a debate – and at times polemic – with the audience who might or might not show their approval. The comedian accommodates the audience's reaction (positive or negative) to his material; the reaction contemplated through the activity of enantiodromia and integrated into the Self in a form of reconciliation of opposites. The stand-up has a vital and critical voice that is free of pretence. The comedian observes and exposes society and social change, resonating with members of the audience as he is drawing disparate members together through his humorous commentary.

As Jung argues, enantiodromia is the play of opposites in the course of events – which reflects the view that everything that exists turns into its opposite: 'Construction and destruction, destruction and construction – this is the principle which governs all cycles of natural life, from the smallest to the greatest'. (CW6: para. 708). The comedian Roseanne confirms in one of her interviews that this interplay often occurs in comedic performances. A show can be 'like heaven and hell' and 'good and evil, that battle is always here' (Quoted in Ajaye, 2002: 190).

Humorous narratives can pose emotional ambiguity for the audience, and by laughing at something that is very personal or socially unacceptable (a taboo), the audience creates and supports an internal dialogue of the comedian through which conscious recognition emerges. For the comedian it is this recognition of a personal attitude, which has the potential to activate the transcendent function as a mediator between the rational and archetypal function of the psyche. It is the principle of enantiodromia that operates in this situation. The material at which the audiences laughs can, in some cases, create an enantiodromic reaction. The dynamic of enantiodromia as an internal regulator, is intrinsic to the individual's interaction, internally and externally, consciously and unconsciously, when ethical decisions are made. Upon activation, it can lead to the union of opposing forces within the performer and the performance. It can also make the audience member realise the power of the thought process within the humour.

### 3.6. *Temenos*

The comedy club becomes a holy place, or Temenos, for the stand-up comedy process and structure. In ancient Greece *Temenos* was a piece of ground surrounding or adjacent to a temple (Oxford Dictionary Online). Jung used *Temenos* as a symbol with multiple meanings to describe a number of psychological processes. For him – symbolically – *Temenos* is a place that *contains.* And it can contain a number of different things. For instance, it can be used to describe 'a sense of privacy that surrounds an analytical relationship' (CW18: para. 410). He also writes in *The Tavistock Lectures* that *Temenos* is 'a taboo area where [the man] will be able to meet the unconscious' (CW12: para. 63). The philosopher Mircea Eliade envisages *Temenos* as a 'territory of radical difference. […] the sacred has nothing to do with redemption and understanding. It is a space where the subject is altered and 'othered'" (Yarrow, 2007: 38). The anthropologist J. Huizinga calls *Temenos* 'a sacred space, a temporarily real world of its own' (Huizinga, 2002: 15).

The comedy club can be compared to *Temenos* for a number of reasons. First of all, it is a place where the comedian can express his thoughts and ideas – make them known to the world. His creative output has an effect not only on the audience but on the society as well. On the persona level, the comedian uses the space to reveal his personal wound, his unconscious and his conflicts. On the social level, he enters into a reciprocal verbal exchange with the audience and an archetypal connection is established as a result. As Philip Yarrow explains, 'the rationalistic or logocentric viewpoint of monotheistic theology perceives the sacred in transcendental terms as the space where God reveals himself through language' (Yarrow, 2007: 39). This is certainly true of stand-up comedy.

The comedy club is a space where transformation happens through language in both the performer and the audience. The audience is affected and potentially altered through the process of what Levy Bruhl called Participation Mystique which, 'denotes a peculiar kind of psychological connection with objects, and consists in the fact that the subject cannot clearly distinguish himself from the object but is bound to it by a direct relationship which amounts to partial identity. (Jung, [1921] 1971: paragraph 781). Although the term is criticised and disputed there is a connection within the comedy club between the audience and given stand-up comedians, which gives it validity. Humour gives performers permission to say whatever they want; it gives them a licence to explore their own unconscious; it gives them permission to push the boundaries – psychological, personal, social and political. The stage and the club becomes an entity where beliefs, attitudes, conditioning, structures, and pre-determined values are explored without boundaries. Taboos can be examined on stage and boundaries can be re-negotiated and returned to society with a new perspective. The audience take part in what Levi Bruhl called *participation mystique*

## *3.7. The Trickster*

The Trickster is the embodiment of the force that disorientates the established line of thought, compelling the psyche of the individual and the collective psyche to reconfigure its stance. The notion of the Trickster is pertinent to our argument because the comedian's material is transformative – Trickster-style – as it embodies 'the truth'. The joke, being sharp, provocative and often indecent, challenges the audience to change their view of the world.

There are many different definitions of the Trickster. For instance, Paul Radin defined it as 'creator and destroyer, giver and negator, he who dupes others and is always duped himself' (Radin, 1972: xxiii) while Karl Kerényi calls the Trickster figure 'the spirit of disorder, the enemy of boundaries' (Radin, 1972: 185).

Jung's essay, '*On the Psychology of the Trickster Figure*', discusses the different guises the trickster takes in literature, folklore and myth. Jung writes that this archetype is 'a faithful reflection of an absolutely undifferentiated human consciousness, corresponding to a psyche that has hardly left the animal level' (CW9/I: para. 465). The Trickster is connected with the divine – he is 'God, man and animal at once […] both subhuman and superhuman, a bestial and divine being, whose chief and most alarming characteristic is his unconsciousness' (CW 9/I: para. 472).

My argument is that it is not the comedian that is the Trickster – but the joke, the comedian's material. Like this, stand-up comedy can be seen as an inclusive form of rebellion; as institutionalised radical freedom. The Trickster does not respect boundaries like the joke slips into the psyche bypassing the critical faculty of the conscious mind. Laughter is created through the friction of disorientation; and this is how the trickster like function of the joke is born. The joke itself recognises a personal or social 'truth', which is then distorted and challenged. It challenges the expectations of the listener. The joke is almost like an attack; it is aggressive in nature; and the response to it is a form of spontaneous release. The comedian Jimmy Carr acknowledges the aggressive nature of the joke in his book *Naked Jape*: 'the truth is the joke is seldom, if ever, a victimless crime. Someone or something is always the butt of it' (Carr, 2006: 196).

The intention behind the joke is very important. The process that takes place during the stand-up performance is transformational both for the audience and the comedian – it can be said to be mercurial. Jung aligns the Trickster figure with the alchemical figure of Mercurius (Samuels, 1985: 242). Donald Kalsched defines Mercurius as both 'diabolical and symbolical'. As a threshold deity, 'he either dissociates or associates various inner images and affects. […] He is totally amoral, like life itself, instinctual, underdeveloped, a stupid blockhead, a practical joker, a hero who aids mankind and changes the world' (Kalsched, 1996: 40).

Edward Edinger explains in his book *Alchemical Symbolism in Psychotherapy* that Mercurius serves as a metaphor for 'the autonomous spirit of the archetypal psyche, the paradoxical manifestation of the transpersonal Self. To subject the Spirit Mercurius to *coagulatio* means nothing less than the connecting of the Ego with the Self, the fulfilment of individuation' (Edinger, 1985: 85). This definition links well with our idea of stand-up comedy as a potential process which enables individuation for the comedian and society. Like the Spirit Mercurius, the joke has both personal and collective links. On an archetypal level, it resonates with the cultural and symbolic parts of the collective psyche. It has to make sense collectively in order to be transpersonal and transcendent.

On the personal level, the joke transforms the comedian and individual within the audience; on the collective level it symbolises and vocalises the need for change in society and culture. In this sense, the joke-trickster is the reflection of our inner world, the world of the unconscious. It reflects the potential of the individual and the individual's social milieu. The performer is the mouthpiece of the trickster principle challenging social norms, regulations and mainstream values. The comedian's keenness to break taboos ensures the psychological health of society as he releases anything that is repressed and discusses any issues that are silenced. At the same time, the joke is profoundly individual. Members of the same audience will laugh at different aspects of the comedian's material and different parts of this material, however the punch line is aimed to reach the whole audience into one cohesive sound of laughter, but nevertheless can have differing understanding and resonance within each member of the audience.

The Trickster is also a healing archetype. The joke, despite its aggressive qualities, also has viable therapeutic qualities. One of the main arguments of this thesis is that stand-up comedy is a form of therapy, both for the comedian and society. Through its paradoxical structure and forceful mercurial nature the joke can undermine and overturn a long held believe and create a differing viewpoint. Jung writes in *On the Psychology of the Trickster Figure* that this archetype has a lot in common with the shaman and the medicine-man for he, too 'often plays malicious jokes on people, only to fall victim in his turn to the vengeance of those whom he has injured' (CW9/I: para. 457). He is the 'wounded wounder' who is the agent of healing and the sufferer that takes away suffering (CW9/I: para. 457).

Speaking metaphorically, the Trickster figure can be seen as consisting of two different archetypes: Mercurius, Hermes forming the Trickster. These three aspects of the Trickster figure are important for understanding the creative forces of stand-up performance.

Mercurius is the essence of the joke; it is also its 'feminine' aspect, the Eros. In alchemy, the supreme spirit imprisoned in matter when freed by the alchemist, Mercurius took his/her form in the hermaphroditic Philosopher's Stone but also stands for the prima materia and the opus. For Jung, Mercurius symbolised the unconscious Self. He/she also provided the alchemical counterpart to the all-good and therefore incomplete Self-symbol of Christ. The anima and Wise One archetypes flow together in Mercurius's androgynous symbolism.

A list of his aspects: all conceivable opposites; both material and spiritual; process by which lower/material is transformed into higher/spiritual; a trickster and God's reflection in nature; reflection of the artifex's mystical experience and opus; the self; the individuation process; the collective unconscious. As Christ is the archetype of consciousness, Mercurius is that of the unconscious.

Jung continues to define the feminine nature of Mercurius as 'the coniunctio of Sol and Mercurius is discussed, and an analogy is drawn to the Christ/Mary relationship. (C W of C. G. Jung Volume 14: Mysterium Coniunctionis)
Here it is announced the feminine values of Mercurius. The pregnant space incubates the paradoxical concepts.

Jung continues
*At the same time, he was "the universal and scintillating fire of the light of nature, which carries the heavenly spirit within it." This fiery spiritual seed impregnated*

*the Virgin, i.e. the feminine aspect of the hermaphroditic Mercurius. He was also synonymous with divine water, "the spirit of life, not only indwelling in all living things, but immanent in everything that exists." (Psychology and Alchemy, par. 528)*

This is the deep of the psyche being the spirit and light, which is ignited, and Hermes takes the inspiration to transform into the intellectual form (logos) of the joke.

Logos being the word, the masculine form. He is the bridge the structure and form bringer to the conceptual paradoxical nature of Mercurius.

Hermes 'who gave the world music and laughter' (p 41 The Female Trickster. RS Tannen Routledge 2007) Jung reminds us that Hermes was originally a wind god, and so was the Egyptian Thoth, who made the soul's breathe. (Para *Alchemical Studies*, par. 257). The name Hermes comes from ερμενηυς Hermeneus, which means "the interpreter." In Greek mythology, the job of Hermes was to be the messenger of the gods. In Greek mythology, Hermes was famous and known for his quality of speech, was a powerful speaker and could convince people. In other words, Hermes is related with the Word, or what in Greek is called λόγος, the Logos.

The trickster is the outer form, the presentation of the joke. It is the interwoven combination of the force of creation as intent structured within the comedic form into a transformative quality of the joke. The transformational quality of the joke is both personal and collective. It relates to the comedian and the audience and enables the comedian to be transformed as well.

The joke communicates with audience members as representatives of the community, revealing the false nature of social norms, questioning morality and civilization. The joke-trickster tests the limits of rules and laws, whether moral, political, social or perceptual. By bringing up and discussing complex and often controversial issues, the comedian triggers self-healing processes in the social psyche, represented by art of that time, as well as in the psyche of the individual.

Therefore as Jung reminds us that any "creative process, so far as we are able to follow it at all, consists in the unconscious activation of an archetypal image, and in elaborating and shaping this image into the finished work by giving it shape, the artist translates it into the language of the present and so makes it possible for us to find our way back to the deepest springs of life. Therein lies the social significance of art: it is constantly at work educating the spirit of age, conjuring up the forms in which the age is most lacking" (p. 82). *The Spirit in Man, Art, & Literature (Collected Works of Jung Vol. 15) by C. G. Jung (Author).*

This is related to the Amfortas Wound Myth because the joke – like the sword in the myth – both wounds and heals society by revealing its deepest repressed issues and inadequacies. In a way, the joke, regardless of its modality – whether it is social, political or personal – on stage transforms into a social commentary on current affairs. As William Doty reminds us, one of the mythological incarnations of the Trickster, Hermes, is endowed with the ability to improve the social life of man: 'In some of his many activities concerned with new social orderings and interrelations, Hermes recovers the sinews of Zeus' arms and legs after Typhon had cut them off, thereby immobilizing the god; joins the gods in overcoming the Titans and Giants, proves Phrixius innocent of Demodice's false accusations…' (Hynes and Doty, 1993: 223).

Professional comedians themselves confirm this oxymoron, simultaneously debasing the socially responsible nature of the Trickster. The joke is a symbolic intruder; it exposes or disorientates in order to reveal the truth. The joke breaks into our psyche and announces a profoundly altering viewpoint. For instance, Roseanne Barr (stage name – Roseanne) admits that, although the language of comedy is aggressive, this power is part of the 'attack' on any stale values individual members of the audience may harbour: 'You hit them [the audience] with it. If you look at the language of comedy, it's kinda like a violent attack on their consciousness in a way. I think we want to hit people in the head, so their head will open up. We know that people don't buy the crazy shit in the world because we don't' (Ajaye, 2002: 189). At the same time, this kind of verbal violence is the agent that breaks the false belief of cognitive dissonance; something that changes people and their environment, Roseanne claims: 'I think it's calling from a higher consciousness that shows through to the audience when they see your commitment to what you're saying' (2002: 189).
This view is echoed by another stand-up performer, Jim Barclay who says that his motto (or rather war cry before going on stage) was 'challenging and denting the audience's prejudices' – not laying on them my own, but challenging theirs' (Wilmut and Rosengard, 1989: 45).

The Trickster, in its joke form, is therefore a key part of stand up performance because it cuts through society's psyche, both the individual collective and cultural unconscious. The joke embodies the symbolism of the Trickster and it is quite paradoxical in its intentions – it is both playful and aggressive, wounding and healing, masculine and feminine. Like the Trickster, the joke has the miraculous ability to infiltrate boundaries – and when it does this, contrary, or at least unexpected, points in image and verbal form collide and laughter occurs.

## *3.8. Conclusion*

Key Jungian ideas illuminate the psychological and anthropological mechanisms behind the comedic performance. The comedy club can act as a container; it has to have something sacred about it in order for the transformation to take place. It is only though Jungian theories that we can recognise the mystical – or even ritualistic –nature of stand-up performance. Jokes including their creative aspect, their emergence in the psyche of the performer, other branches of depth psychology cannot exclusively explain the audience's reaction to them and the social and personal change they trigger. Certain elements of stand up performance for instance, *participation mystique* that is born when a large number of people laugh together at a joke – cannot be seen as an entirely rational mechanism. Laughter is beyond the idea of defence mechanism as it also contains transformational and transpersonal aspects. The 'joke as a healer' has a capacity to connect opposites echoing those in the human psyche. In the words of David L. Hart, the psyche 'discovers ways in which apparently conflicting symbolic content can be contained in a single structure' (Young-Eisendrath, 2002: 95). And this is what the trickster-joke does, uniting within itself old and new, darkness and light, the collective and the individual. The bedrock of tension, it leads to the reconciliation of opposites via the transformative power of the symbol and laughter. However, for Emma Jung in the Holy Grail the journey towards individuation, "for only in the individual are opposites reconciled and united." And that the myth "addresses the religious problem of modern man'. By addressing the question 'to whom does the Grail serve?" The comedian certainly reconciles opposites in the joke structure, but true healing for both himself and the collective occurs when the comedian recognises that he is serving a spiritual calling and not just his own ego.

# CHAPTER 4

## STAND-UP COMEDY AND THE FREUDIAN LEGACY

Freudian and post-Freudian theories are important for this study because they help us analyse in detail the comedian's creative process and the dynamic of his relationship with the audience. Jung's theories discuss the symbolic and transformational value of the performance. Freud's theories also reveal the stages of development within the deep analytical processes behind the comedian's desire to create, to relate and have a dialogue with the audience. Including the potential reason to become a performer might lie in the comedian's personal anxiety stemming from Oedipal crisis, projected into the world. The comedian also tries to manifest and re-create himself socially as well as personally – as Jaques Lacan's ideas are relevant. Freudian and post-Freudian theories illuminate the internal and external dynamic of the comedic performance and his engagement with the current social and political issues of his environment.

In this chapter I will engage a number of Freudian and post-Freudian ideas, including humour such as Freud's concepts of Oedipus complex and libido; Jacques Lacan's concept of symbolic order; Melanie Klein's envisioning of the relationship between the mother and the child; John Bowlby's analysis of attachment and separation; Heinz Kohut's concept of the Self and his analysis of narcissism and, finally, Donald Winnicott's and Christopher Bollas's theorising about mirroring and attunement, and the influence of these processes on the formation and development of creativity.

The principle aim of the chapter is to draw all these disparate theories together in order to show the complexity of stand-up performance as a therapeutic process in which the audience plays the role of the symbolic mother as therapist. This symbolic process provides the comedian with sufficient mirroring and attunement to allow him to deal with his personal problems. During the creative moment the comedian feel omnipotent and is encouraged to uphold the illusion of omnipotence. If the audience fails to provide perfect mirroring, the comedian may regard it as a form of aggression and attack the audience. Seen in this light, humour can be seen as both a defensive and an offensive mechanism.

# *4.*
## *4.1. Freud*
### *4.1.1. The Oedipus Complex*

The idea of humour being used as a way to challenge the social order, and the so-called civilized behaviour, is closely linked with Freud's Oedipus complex (first mentioned in *Five Lectures on Psychoanalysis,* 1910). By using humour, the (predominantly male) comedian attempts to displace the father figure in its many incarnations. He challenges several father figures at once: the internal father, other male comedians (by challenging them to a competition) and, ultimately, the social order.

Although the term Oedipus complex does not make its first appearance until 1910 Freud made the actual discovery of the Oedipus complex during his self-analysis – though the ground had been prepared by the analysis of his patients (Laplanche and Pontalis, 1973: 283). Freud writes in his essay '*A Special Type of Choice of Object Made by Men'* (1910), when the boy learns that his parents are not ideal beings and that they too have sexual intercourse, he

> …tells himself with cynical logic that the difference between his mother and a whore is not after all so very great, since basically they do the same thing. The enlightening information he has received has in fact awakened the memory-traces of the impressions and wishes of his early infancy, and these have led to a re-activation in him of certain mental impulses. He begins to desire his mother herself in the sense with which he has recently become acquainted, and to have his father anew as a rival who stands in the way of his wish; he comes, as we say, under the dominance of the Oedipus complex. He does not forgive his mother for having granted the favour of sexual intercourse not to himself but to his father, and he regards it as an act of unfaithfulness. […] As a result of the constant combined operation of the two driving forces, desire and thirst for revenge, phantasies of his mother's unfaithfulness are by far the most preferred; the lover with whom she commits her act of infidelity almost always exhibits the features of the boy's own ego, or more accurately, of his own idealised personality, grown up and so raised to a level with the father
>
> (Freud, 1960: XI, 171)

Simon Critchley points out that 'in humour the childlike super-ego that experiences parental prohibition and Oedipal guilt is replaced with a more grown-up super-ego, let is call it super-ego II' (Critchley, 2007: 102-103). Drawing on Freud's ideas, Lemma (2000) writes that it is during the Oedipal phase that the infant's appreciations of humour develop. Most of these researchers, however, did not analyse the Oedipal element of humour in detail but only mentioned that the Oedipus complex can be used as a means of explaining the human desire to create and perform jokes.

Although Freud did not directly write about the Oedipal colouring of jokes and humour, his analysis of jokes as a defence mechanism is steeped in the Oedipus complex. By making fun of prohibitions and serious things, the joker challenges the superego imposed on him by his parents as representatives of society and civilization. The world of stand-up comedy can be seen as a stage on which the Oedipus complex is played out. The whole process is very masculine. On the one hand, the performer on stage challenges assumptions, rules and rituals prescribed by the social system. Speaking metaphorically, in being disobedient and rude to the father (society), he challenges the patriarch. On the other hand, the audience becomes the symbolic mother who the comedian, ideally, tries to seduce. The symbolic mother is expected to mirror the comedian and the laughter reminds the comedian of similar exchanges in infancy. (Lemma, 2000: 57).

The release of the Oedipal tension depends on the success of the show and the reaction of the audience. In her book *Humour on the Couch: Exploring Humour in Psychotherapy and Everyday Life* (2000), Alessandra Lemma expounds on the role of humour in the resolution of the Oedipus complex. From her view, humour acts as a mechanism that manages the internal Oedipus complex. She writes that

> Healthy humour … rests on the capacity to tolerate antithetical ideas, to manage opposites. This capacity is won at a cost. We can have to tread the arduous route and endure dis-identification from our parents. This rests on a relinquishment of an exclusive relationship with both parents along with the acknowledgement that they have an exclusive relationship with each other. If the child negotiates the Oedipal stage in a relatively healthy way he acquires an internal model of an intercourse (between the parents), which is, on the whole, a creative activity.
>
> (Lemma, 2000: 57)

Lemma implies that the comedian learns to deal with the ambiguity and the ambiguous response. Her view is that a 'wise' comedian, whose Oedipal conflict has been resolved or diluted with the help of therapy, should look upon the audience as a symbolic mother and should demand undivided attention and acceptance from it. However, in reality this does not usually occur in stand up comedy, since the audience is ambivalent it creates an antagonistic and aggressive reaction in the comedian and he leaves the stage to retaliate (be funnier) next time. Most often than not, the comedian goes into an 'Oedipal overdrive' (he becomes angry and loses self-control) which may even result in an abusive verbal row with the audience. However, the dissolution of the Oedipus complex is still a possible long-term outcome.

Another Freudian concept I would like to use in relation to stand-up performance is the genital stage. According to Freud, the genital stage constitutes the final phase of Oedipal development. This stage can be defined as a 'stage of psychosexual development characterised by the organisation of the component instincts under the primacy of the genital zones' (Laplanche and Pontalis, 1973: 186). This stage is also characterised by 'a distinction between Oedipal demands and the degree of biological development reached' (1973: 187).

In my view, stand-up performance can be seen as a re-enactment, or symbolic realisation, of the genital stage. During the performance the comedian acts out the undeveloped stages and concludes with the genital phase. By re-enacting it, the performer receives an opportunity to ease the Oedipal tension (the immediate outcome) or dissolve the Oedipus complex altogether (the long-term solution).

Stand-up performance can be regarded as a 'live' creative process of high emotional and cognitive intensity. Moreover, this intensity is aggravated by the fact that the process is interactive. That is why all the deep-seated emotional issues are often triggered during the performance. According to Freud, jokes drag the repressed material from 'the realm of the unconscious' (Freud, 1960: 258) and re-activate the jokes' ancient dwelling place that is the comedian's childhood (1960: 210).

To conclude the section, the Oedipus complex can be viewed as an important aspect of the comedic performance because it addresses the primary Oedipal relationship in the comedian's psyche; and also highlights the unresolved stages of the Oedipus complex. The comedic performance also offers an opportunity for the dissolution of the complex, and the comedian may or may not use this opportunity.

### *4.1.2. Freud's Concept of libido*

Freud's concept of libido is also crucial for my argument. As Freud defined it in *Group Psychology and the Analysis of the Ego* (1921), libido is 'the energy regarded as a quantitative magnitude of those instincts which maybe comprised under the word "love"' (Freud, 1960, Vol. 18: 111). It is also 'the dynamic manifestation of [the sexual instinct] in mental life' (Freud, 1960, Vol. 18: 111). Seen from this perspective, the comedian sublimates his sexual energy and aggression in his performance, and transforms them into jokes. The comedian uses the framework of stand-up performance to express his creative aggression and individuality in a relatively safe environment.

Jung's definition of libido famously differed from that of Freud. Jung used the terms 'energy and 'libido' interchangeably. For him, libido was not necessarily about sex, or sexual excitation – it was more about the amount of energy a person possesses. Jung writes in *Psychological Types:*

> By libido I mean *psychic energy.* Psychic energy is the intensity of a psychic process, its *psychological value.* This does not imply an assignment of value, whether moral, aesthetic, or intellectual; the psychological value is already implicit in the determining power, which expresses itself in definite psychic effects. Neither do I understand libido as a psychic force, a misconception that has led many critics astray. I do not hypostatize the concept of energy, but use it to denote intensities or values.
>
> (Jung, CW6: para. 778)

I suggest that both Freud's and Jung's definition of libido are displayed by the comedian during the performance. The sexual and spiritual energies are expressed physically and verbally in the performance where both definitions have a transformational quality; the *dromenon* (the Greek word for 'ritual') means 'something performed'. This combination of the term libido can be named 'comic performance libido'. This libido is presented in the stance of the comedian who can prowl along he perimeter of the stage in a manner similar to a caged lion. Or coquettish like a female primate waiting to succumb to alpha male advances. Whichever presence the stand-up adopts or portrays it has both the seductive and creative elements emitted through his movements. It can be termed as the mating ritualistic movement of the stand-up comedian.

It can be argued that this combination of the sexual, spiritual and the creative causes a frisson between the comedian and the audience, and thereby interactivity is born which is pivotal to the process of the comedian's self-realisation.

## *4.2.  Lacan – Signified and Signifier*
## *4.2.1.  The Phallus*

According to Lacan, the Phallus is the signifier (Lacan, 1998: 89). This concept of the signifier goes back to the French linguist Ferdinand De Saussure who proposed that the linguistic sign consists of two parts: the signifier (form; word) and the signified (content, subject). Saussure argued that the relationship between these two parts is not fixed but arbitrary. For instance, when we hear or see the word 'cat' without the cat itself being present, we all imagine different cats. The signified is always personal and the signifier represents the 'linguistic glue' that holds together the social order. The difference between Saussure and Lacan is that, for Saussure the signifier and the signified are mutually interdependent while, for Lacan, the signifier is primary and produces the signified: 'The more the signifier signifies nothing, the more indestructible it is' and also 'it is these indestructible signifiers which determine the subject; the effects of the signifier on the subject constitute the unconscious, and hence also constitute the whole of the field of psychoanalysis' (Evans, 1996: 186). Lacan used the term 'signifier' to denote a range of linguistic and symbolic phenomena united by their 'phallic' properties: words, units smaller than words (morphemes and phonemes), units larger than words (phrases and sentences), as well as non-linguistic things such as objects, relationships and symptomatic acts (Evans, 1996: 187).

According to Lacan, signification is an aggressive process during which the signifier 'strikes the signified, marking it as the bastard offspring of this signifying concatenation' (1998: 89). Signification, as described by Lacan, can also be seen as a metaphor of the sexual act. The signified is thus defined, raped and stifled by the signifier during the process of signification (the sexual act). The subject, Lacan argues, 'designates his being only by barring everything he signifies, as it appears in the fact that he wants to be loved for himself; a mirage that cannot be dismissed as merely grammatical' (1998: 89).

Thus, Lacan's ideas are firmly grounded in sexual dichotomy. Signification is an intrinsically male process – and, in order to perform it, one must have phallic properties. He writes that 'the man finds satisfaction for his demand for love in the relation with the woman, in as much as the signifier of the phallus constitutes her as giving in love what she does not have' (1998: 90). Meanwhile, if a woman wants to take a proactive role in the signification process, she must reject her femininity: 'In order to be the phallus, that is to say, the signifier of the desire of the Other, ... a woman will reject an essential part of her femininity, namely, all her attributes in the masquerade' (1998: 91).

This directly relates to the psychological dynamic between the comedian and the audience. The comedian creates and owns the word – and then directs it towards the audience. The audience is the Other that has to be seduced and impregnated with the signified that is close to the comedian's own vision. So, in a way, one could say that, in Lacanian terms, laughter is like orgasm. The comedian's word becomes the Phallus that cuts through the audience, which metaphorically represents the feminine. The listeners are seduced; they fall in love with the comedian; they are supposed to give themselves to the performer. During the entire signification process they remain passive yet tantalised and responsive.

The audience, who can be seen as the female as the receptor, is also supposed to be attuned enough to the comedian's internal processes and have instinctive knowledge of his life in order to respond favourably to his joker. This means that what the audience imagines when they hear the signifiers and signified within the joke, closely match those owned by the performer. Female stand-up comedians, and their 'phallic' and creative processes will be dealt with in a separate chapter (Chapter 7).

## *4.2.2. Phallus as the Signifier and the Symbolic Order.*

The idea of the Phallus as the signifier, which bars and controls the signified is closely linked to Lacan's concept of the Symbolic Order. This concept was inspired by Claude Levi-Strauss's idea that the social world is shaped by certain laws that regulate kinship relations and the exchange of gifts (Evans, 1996: 201). Evans writes that 'since the most basic form of exchange is communication itself (the exchange of words, the gifts of speech), and since the concepts of law and structure are unthinkable without language, the symbolic is essentially a linguistic dimension. […] The symbolic is the realm of the Law which regulates desire in the Oedipus complex' (1996: 201-202).

Comedy, whose primary weapon is the word, can be said to belong to the realm of the patriarchal specifically to the Symbolic Order. Jimmy Carr echoes this:

> Are men better at telling jokes than women? Well, perhaps – the aggressive, point-scoring aspects of stand-up comedy certainly seem to come naturally to them. But then men are also better at football, fighting and forgetting significant dates. These special masculine talents are undoubtedly partly chemical, a side effect of that red fog of testosterone that enshrouds the male brain. Bu there's a large degree of cultural conditioning at work, too. A patriarchal society moulds men into hearty jokers and claims this as a virtue. The impulse to tell jokes seems to spring in large part from a certain competitive, attention-seeking quality which contemporary Western culture still tries to breed out of its womenfolk, despite the valiant efforts of Germaine Greer and the Spice Girls.
>
> (Carr, 2006: 167-168)

In *The Seminar. Book I. Freud's Papers on Technique* (1953) Lacan refers to Symbolic Father as the Name of The Father. The boy has to identify with the father symbolically in the final stage of the Oedipus complex, which gives rise to the formation of the ego-ideal. Thus, the boy completes his passage into the symbolic order, becomes like the father – avoiding castration and annihilation by the father (Evans, 1996: 81). Lacan distinguished between the Symbolic Father (the base of the symbolic order), the imaginary father (the construct imagined by the child), and the real father (the biological father) (Evans, 1996: 61-63). In relation to stand-up comedy, the male performer may be regarded as attacking the Symbolic Father (or a constellation of fathers) and defending himself from castration at the same time.

Although the comedian operates with the word – and thus acts within the realm of the symbolic – it can be said that he also re-works the patriarchal structure by attacking it from within. Lacan states that the Symbolic Father is also the dead father, the father of the primal horde who has been murdered by his sons (Evans, 2001: 62). The comedian uses language (Lacan's *langage*) – the father's weapon of choice – to attack the Symbolic Order from within. In appropriating language, the comedian alters the order and opens up a new perspective on the world. It is not only the social order (Symbolic Order, the law) that is being challenged by him, but also the linguistic pattern itself.

Many comedians cite the father – whether real, symbolic or imaginary – as the bedrock of their creative conflict. Becoming a comedian is often has an element of rebellion in it. For instance, Dominic Holland says about his relationship with his parents:

> I had a very funny upbringing – very Catholic, very disciplinarian father. He was a lecturer in French at London University. Now he's retired. He was very strict and quite draconian. He didn't like me living with my girlfriend. We're a very traditional family. My two brothers are both lawyers; my sister has a Masters in Philosophy. Now she's a town planner. I've got an MBA, so we're all very education-orientated. I'm the only person who's taken a novel career path.
> 
> (Cook, 1994: 77)

Another comedian, the American George Carlin talks about his problems with authority – the Symbolic Father, 'I'd been thrown out of three or four schools, I had quit the Air Force, I'd got kicked out of the altar boys, the Boy Scouts – anything where there was a lot of authority, I was very soon gone. But I had this dream of getting into the movies, so I assumed that you had to play their game. So there I was in a suit and tie with a mainstream attitude' (Ajaye, 2002: 82).

Alexi Sayle made a profound impact in the comedy circuit in the early 1980's railed against the patriarchal social structure by having a skin-head hair cut 'identified with the working class as 'those people who work for a living and have surplus value extracted from them' and admits he used to do comedy 'to make trouble.' (Wilmut. P Rosengard. Methuen Press 49/50 :1989).

## 4.3. *Melanie Klein and the Object Relations Theory*

One of the most prominent features of the comedian's relationship with the audience is its emotional intensity. From my view, the mystery of this intensity can be explained by ideas borrowed from Klein's object relations' theory. My proposition is that during his stand-up performance, the comedian perceives the audience as the 'mother', and seeks to establish a relationship with 'her'. The connection with this kind of mother figure can turn out to be either good or bad.

According to Klein (1935), the infant possesses a number of psychic defence mechanisms for dealing with bad part-objects such as unreliable breasts. The infant regards bad objects as 'internal prosecutors' (1988: 116-17). The infant's ways of dealing with them include introjection, projection, expulsion and denial of external reality (1988: 117). Stand-up comedians also tend to react aggressively to any verbal challenge from members of the audience in order to avoid real or imaginary failure. These instances are a replay of Klein's theory of the depressive position (1935) – a defensive state in which the child dreads persecutors ('bad objects') and tries to ward them off by attacking them (1988: 117).

### *4.3.1. Audience Responsiveness: The Good Breast and the Bad Breast*

Klein also theorised that children internalised different parts of the maternal body and then used them as metaphors in their psychological life. Klein writes that, for the man, the breast is not a merely physical object: 'The whole of his instinctual desires and his unconscious phantasies imbue the breast with qualities going far beyond the actual nourishment it affords' (Klein, 1997a: 180). The breast represents 'maternal goodness, inexhaustible patience and generosity, as well as (………..) creativeness' (1997a: 180).

These breasts are part of the object world of the child (Klein, 1988: 141). They play an important part in the formation of the ego (Klein, 1988: 50) and symbolise, respectively, the caregiver who keeps the child well fed (literally, physically, emotionally, attention-wise), or the one who lets the child 'starve' (again, literally or metaphorically). Thus, the breast is an object, which the child internalises regardless of its modality. Because the baby's survival depends on the amount of attention the caregiver is willing to give it, the relationship between the 'breast' and the child is very intense. In this early connection, predominantly oral in character, originates the child's subsequent ability to adapt to and interact with the external world (Klein, 1988: 59).

In the context of stand-up comedy, the audience is expected to be the good mother and the good breast, and to offer them validation of their existence by accepting their creativity. Non-approval of creativity usually triggers aggression, withdrawal or over-compensation on the part of the comedian. Using the Kleinian theoretical framework, it can also be said that the comedian, like a baby, is greedy for attention and approval. Most comedians go on stage as a solo performer because they know that whatever response, good or bad, they extract from the audience (the symbolic mother), belongs entirely to them. Their 'greed' is so voracious even a bad response belongs to them. They own and interject or internalise the good and although they deflect the bad, they have still absorbed the, albeit negative, attention. The comedian is greedy for attention and confirmation. Klein writes:

> Greed is an impetuous and insatiable craving, exceeding what the subject needs and what the object is able and willing to give. At the subconscious level, greed aims primarily at completely scooping out, sucking dry and devouring the breast: that is to say, its aim is destructive introjection; whereas envy not only seeks to rob in this way, but also to put badness, primarily bad excrements and bad parts of the self, into the mother, and first of all into her breast, in order to spoil and destroy her. In the deepest sense it means destroying her creativeness.
>
> (1997a: 181)

If the audience is creative, too reflective or too critical, there is no space for the comedian's creativity. The aim of the performer is to subdue the audience, to manipulate it into submission and acceptance. The stand-up must be heard and if the audience (mother) is too powerful and hence becomes the neglecting, self-absorbed mother; the stand up will do anything within his range of material to attract their attention event if it does fill the performer with guilt shame or remorse. The stand up in this case may become aggressive and attack or choose material which is does not fit his true performance self. If it is not responsive, or is too proactive/creative itself (for instance, when the comedian is challenged by members of the audience), it becomes the bad breast, which has to be punished for its lack metaphorical milk – acceptance, praise and love. Like the notorious Kleinian breast, the audience is not always reliable. Sometimes it provides the comedian with the love and attention he craves, and sometimes it goes cold and unresponsive (withdraws the breast). The comedian feels something like this: 'how *dare* you fulfil your own needs instead of mine? Give me your milk (the metaphor for attention), if not I am going to attack you and I will make you give it to me'.

Seen in this light, the comedian wants to attract the audience's attention in order to keep his creativity alive; it is as if the audience feeds him with their laughter. Klein theorises: 'For the talent to develop ... in fixation to the primal scene (or phantasies), the degree of activity which is so important for the sublimation itself, undoubtedly also determines whether the subject develops a talent for creation or reproduction' (Klein, 1988: 103). In another of her essays, *Envy and Gratitude* (1957), she argues: 'we find in the analysis of our patients that the breast in its good aspect is the prototype of maternal goodness, inexhaustible patience and generosity, as well as of creativeness. It is these phantasies and instinctual needs that so enrich the primal object that it remains the foundation for hope, trust and belief in goodness' (Klein, 1997a: 180). Moreover, as many comedians, including Charlie Chaplin (1964), have observed, humour is born out of the sense of loss, and exists for the purpose of helping human beings deal with this lamentable state. This certainly taps into Klein's idea concerning the depressive and his attempt to reconnect with 'lost', 'disintegrated' and 'broken' objects (1997a: 144).

It also runs parallel to the image of the wound and the stand-up performance, as humour becomes a radical method of dealing with the wound a means of both sublimating and compulsively recreating the trauma, which Freud termed Zwang. Zwang being the compulsion to repeat the trauma or neurosis Freud also called it the Fate Neurosis like the Oedipus Complex where there is an internal force, which is repeated, but the individual struggles against it. (LaPlanche and Pontalis 1973:77) The American stand-up comedian Garry Shandling explains the origins of his creative inspiration: '…so much of humour comes from pain. So, unfortunately, I still tune into my pain and write funny stuff because I can tune into my pain. […] I think the average person probably is in pain in life, but they cover it, so you don't know they're depressed. Artists who are expressing their pain are at least not in denial' (Ajaye, 2002: 208).

Psychologists and psychotherapists researching humour have also adopted the breast element of the object relations theory. For instance, Chris Bollas (1995) writes that the mother-baby relationship is one of farce – not only because the mother's behaviour towards the infant is full of mimicry, vocalizations and all sorts of comical exaggerations – but also because the mother is full of good milk and good humour (quoted in Barron, 1999: 39-40). According to Bollas (1995), the mother can be regarded as the first clown. Lemma also observes that 'the shared laughter rekindles the pre-verbal memory of similar exchanges in infancy, when the mother's smile and face lit up and conveyed that there was nothing to fear, that we were understood and loved' (2000: 57).

The Bad breasts, such as hecklers, are punished by comedians in a variety of ways they have to be robbed of their dignity and perceived power. Hecklers dare to divert the attention of the audience from the performer onto themselves. This is similar to what Klein describes as 'sadistic impulses directed against the mother' 'I found that aggressive impulses and phantasies arising in the earliest relation to the mother's breast, such as suckling the breast dry and scooping it out, soon lead to further phantasies of entering the mother and robbing her of the contents of her body' (1997a: 142). The comedian Arnold Brown provides a good example of such aggression when he reminisces of an incident he had during his performance at the Tunnel Club: 'I believe there is a dark, violent side to me – and this is why I do comedy. At the Tunnel Club, most of the audience were behind me, and this guy at the front seat started shouting, 'You're rubbish!' It wasn't the odd heckle – it was every other second. I was so angry that I grabbed him and got him in an arm lock. I actually got a laugh from it. I help him, and carried on doing my act, and the audience half-forgot him' (Cook, 1994: 218).

The British comedian Mark Thomas provides another example of rage at the bad breast. When he was compering in a workingmen's club in Kensal Green, the club treasurer heckled him. This incident triggered a cycle of rage and abuse from both sides:

> As the evening continued I was getting progressively more and more belligerent. I went on stage and said: 'right! How many of you lot are in short-term housing? How many of you are in squats? How many of you are in council house flats? How many of you have moved into the area? I want to find the new money and the old money, and I want to find those who haven't got any money'. Half the audience were Ladbroke Grove squatters who'd bunked in with mates who were helping out with the catering. They started cheering, and the regulars started going mad. One of the waitresses started heckling. I grabbed the fire extinguisher and fired it at the front table. All these side salads went scooting off everywhere. The treasurer turned my mike off, and it turned into a running battle.
> 
> (Cook, 1994: 222)

Some comedians even enjoy battling against the bad breast – or dealing with it in a more mature way, which does not involve immediate destruction. For instance, Rob Newman describes his attitude towards hecklers:

> I've always loved heckles, I've always welcomed them – and I've always enjoyed playing around with them. At the Alley Club [*which Newman run for a year*] it was hecklemania – not like at the Tunnel. There it was brutal – it was about trying to destroy the comic. Only twice have I asked the hecklers for a fight, and that was because I wasn't really being me. Doing Comedy of Hate, you have to be larger than life. [...] The thing I love most is coming off the script, and you can't do it if you're in a super-aggressive mode. I have comics who take a heckle as an affront to their authority. You've got to work with the heckle, you've got to say yes to it.
> 
> (Cook, 1994: 217)

By contrast, when the audience acts as a good breast, it is successfully internalised and its responses are utilised for the purposes of self-therapy. The comedian is euphoric and elated, he feels on top of the world. Speaking metaphorically, he feeds on the attention and laughter offered to him by the listeners. And he does not need to share his happiness, success and achievement with anyone.

According to Klein:

> the good internalised breast acts as a focal point in the ego, from which good feelings can be projected on to external objects. It strengthens the ego, counteracts the processes of splitting and dispersal, and enhances the capacity for integration and synthesis. The good internalised object is thus one of the preconditions for an integrated and stable ego and for good object relations.
>
> (1997a: 144)

The good audience is the submissive audience – the audience that accepts the comedian and his creativity as they are. They do not question or criticise his creative output. The ideal audience should not be subtle in their responses – they should express their emotions openly and positively – which is similar to the mother mirroring the child. For instance, the so-called theatre audience may like what is happening but will not show their approval of the performance – this is not good for the comedian's self-esteem because he needs to see and monitor the listeners' reaction all the time.

### 4.3.2. *Trauma and Phantasy*

Also important for my analysis of stand-up comedy is Klein's concept of acting out: which is re-dramatising, re-living the trauma and acting out this trauma over and over again. Klein uses this concept to describe the relationship between the patient and the therapist – but it can also be applied to comedy as a form of therapy. In acting out, he, the patient, has to 'deal with conflicts and anxieties stirred up in the transference situation' (Klein, 1997a: 55). During this stage 'the patient may turn away from the analyst as he attempted to turn away from his primal objects; he tries to split the relations to him, keeping him either as a good or as a bad figure: he deflects some of the feelings and attitudes experienced towards the analyst on to other people in his current life...' (1997a: 55-56). Similarly, performers project their inner experience onto their immediate environment, including the audience. This is a creative moment. They recreate their inner life in a humorous anecdotal manner.

Closely linked with the audience, as a mother metaphor is Klein's idea of *phantasy*, which can be defined as a form of therapeutic play. Phantasy is both activity and its products (Klein, 1988: 23). Klein's own treatment of her little patients consisted of triggering their phantasies (with the help of toys), and then observing and examining them. This is really similar to triggering a psychotherapeutic creative process and analysing its contents. Lemma notes that Klein's method was 'a prototypical example of the sublimated activity which represented the symbolic expression of anxieties and wishes' (Lemma, 2000: 47-48).

Seen in this light, the comedian's union with the audience can be represented as a kind of *phantasy* of the ideal primal relationship. The performer phantasises about the ideal audience and the ideal (and plentiful) love they give him. It is as if he or she replays this relationship during the performance. The comedian also plays out his own anxieties and phantasies during the performance in the hope to healing or modifying them.

To recap, several of Klein's ideas, including phantasy, the depressive position and the concept of the good/bad objects, can be used to analyse the comedian's intensive, tense and sometimes even aggressive relationship with the audience.

## 4.4. *John Bowlby and Heinz Kohut – Attachment and the Formation of the Self*
### *4.4.1. Bowlby*

Attachment theories are pivotal to our argument. In his article The Evolution and History of Attachment Research (1995) Grossman explains the importance of attachment for the individual as a foundation of all future relationships:

> Attachment is not one relationship among others; it is the very foundation of healthy individual development. More, it is the precondition for developing a coherent mind, even if it is, finally, insufficient by itself for understanding the whole mind. Scientifically, attachment theory has done nothing less than bridge the gap between individual experience and objective research.
> (Grossman, 1995: 116).

In this respect, Bowlby (1973; 1979) can assist us in the construction of our argument. Attachment is defined by Bowlby as 'a form of instinctive behaviour that develops in humans, as in other mammals, during infancy, and has as its aim or goal proximity to a mother-figure' (Bowlby, 2012: 106). In his essay *Separation and Loss Within the Family'* (1970) Bowlby writes that, while attachment behaviour is directed towards the child's actual parents, 'it nonetheless continues to be active during adult life when it is usually directed towards some active and dominant figure, often a relative but sometimes an employer or some elder of the community' (2012: 106). The audience becomes a psychological extension of the mother figure. The comedian needs to positively attach himself to the audience to have a reinforcing reaction. In *'Childhood Mourning and Its Implications for Psychiatry'* (1961). Bowlby theorises that 'in infants and young children the experience of separation habitually initiates defensive processes which lead to yearning for the lost person and reproach for desertion both becoming unconscious' (2012: 69). In this sense, the desire to become a stand-up comedian can be regarded as originating in the disruption of an emotional bond or bonds while the desire to win over and retain the audience can be seen as an urge to recover the lost person. 'If all goes well – Bowlby writes – there is joy and a sense of security. If it is threatened, there is jealousy, anxiety, and anger' (2005: 4). This can be used as a metaphor for the stand-up performance because, while on stage and seeking a secure connection with the audience, the comedian feels emotionally fragile and vulnerable. The perfect connection brings with it the feelings of being loved and even 'omnipotent'. However, when things go wrong, the comedian feels deflated and depressed. The lost person is not a concrete person or a real lost carer in the comedian's life but rather a symbol of the lost mother, a symbol of the primal unity, something that stands for the individual's ideal paradisiacal relationship with the world.

The performance offers the comedian an opportunity to establish a relationship with the audience, which is short-lived but very intense. The performer does not see the audience as a conglomeration of individuals but regards it as a whole: a mother figure. The audience are already in a positive attentive anticipatory mood. There are five stages to successful attachment.

1. Seduction: The comedian has to respond to the audience's positive attitude and further seduce the audience as him being worthy of their positive attitude.
2. Interest: He has to be interesting to the audience and make them laugh.
3. Trust: Trust is beginning to build. He has to fulfil commitment to the audience expectation of consistent interaction. The interaction is reciprocated from one to the other. The audience wants the comedian to be funny. The stand-up offers his creativity and the audience responds by laughing. The comedian has engagement and bonding occurs where the audience are prepared to forgive the stand-up for not making them laugh but they like him anyway.
4. Engagement: Continued engagement through further humorous stories whereby the audience has to respond favourably. The audience needs to be aware that he is responding to them, this will show in his timing and tone of his delivery. Much like the playful interaction between mother and child. The comedian then has to further add a funnier story or anecdote to inspire the audience to react.
5. Turning Point: Total engagement. It is his finale and the audience will respond accordingly if totally engaged by the comedian. If she (the audience) is not engaged then the comedian has to work harder to find the turning point where the commitment and trust of the stand-up has been made and in Bowlby's terms a 'secure base ' has been established. Unlike the mother child didactic the stand-up has to try very much harder to establish a secure base with the audience. But the rewards of doing so are immediate and oceanic.

During the performance the comedian strives to engage the audience, aiming it to be accepted and creating empathy.

Bowlby's ideas on aggression (1958) and secure base (1988) are also pertinent to our argument. Aggression is also a reaction to loss – real or perceived. In '*Effects on Behaviour of Disruption of an Affectional Bond*' (1978) he writes that 'behaviour of an aggressive sort plays a key role in maintaining affectional bonds' (2012: 85). Bowlby writes in '*Psychoanalysis and Childcare*' (1958) writes that 'an aggressive child is acting on the basis that attack is the best means of defence' (2012: 13). Also children become aggressive when they can't express their own will.

This directly relates to the stages of attachment for the performer-audience relationship. Comedians feel the need to express themselves – and in the process of self-actualisation they confirm their own will, the right to exist. Comedy club is a space where verbal aggression is permitted. The comedians use aggression – mostly subconsciously – as a defence mechanism. The principal aim is always to elicit a response from the audience, whether positive or negative as long as there is actual feedback. In any case, the audience must not remain passive – it should either love or hate the comedian. The comedian's behaviour as regards expression of aggression may depend on the act that had gone before them or something that had happened in their private life prior to the show. An example of this is provided by the comedian Jeremy Hardy in Jeremy Cook's book *Ha Bloody Ha: Comedians Talking*:

> Once I followed a singer who'd been given a really hard time by the audience. I was so angry, and I hated the audience so much, that I went on and attacked them. I maintained an attitude of antagonism throughout. I did my forty-five minutes with complete loathing for them. They were a bit baffled, because they felt they were justified in hating that singer, and they couldn't see why I was upset on her behalf.
>
> (Cook, 1994: 209)

Hardy also explains why he sometimes becomes angry with members of the audience and how his behaviour is shaped by the audience's responsiveness or non-responsiveness. What he describes here sounds like defensive measures aimed at preventing narcissistic injury:

> I've provoked people who I probably should have left alone. I had a drunk guy who was asleep in the front row, so I started doing some stuff about the fact that he was asleep. I wanted the audience to know that he was already asleep, so they didn't think I'd put him to sleep. And then I thought it'd be fun to try and get the audience to wake him up. So we all woke him up, but he was so drunk that he wouldn't shut up all night, and it became very irritating. I thought, 'Oh God, I should have left him alone'.
>
> (1994: 208)

The comedian's unconscious aim is to 'unite' the audience into an object, which they can control and manipulate into demonstrating the expected response. Aggression is one of the tactics used. Another comedian, Steve Hunt says: 'It's almost unheard of for an entire audience to be hostile, and if a small group decides to, you can cope with that because at least it's a response' (1994: 213). The audience, as a maternal object, can respond to verbal and emotional aggression of the performer because it feels guilty, shame, annoyance and even responsible for the comedian's emotional states. The viewer, united with other viewers, is expected 'to contain' the comedian by giving them the opportunity to discover their true 'self' in the process of the performance. Any aggression and anger aimed at the audience during the performance have as their final goal acceptance and containment two of the components of self-acceptance. It is as if the comedian is pushing the boundaries by asking 'How much do you love me?'. Meanwhile, the audience is fragmented in its thinking 'Am I good enough?' 'You're not good enough,' 'you have made me feel bad,' 'you are bad' and the connection has disintegrated. The comedian would have to begin again to re-build this connection.

If aggression can be seen as metaphorical emotional violation of the audience, 'seduction' is a milder way of establishing what Bowlby terms (1973) 'secure base' – an attachment situation aimed at providing the individual (child) with a safe emotional environment. Before displaying any aggression in jokes (directed against the symbolic father), the comedian has to establish a secure emotional connection with the audience (the symbolic mother). Once this connection is established, either by aggression or coercion, the comedian feels safe and accepted. The best comedians seduce the audience and thereby they connect with the audience.

In this sense, Bowlby's theories explain certain tactics applied by performers to the audience for the purpose of binding the audience together and making them response in predictable ways. This can even be seen as a form of psychological conditioning on behalf of the comedian.

### *4.4.2. Heinz Kohut*

According to Heinz Kohut – who primarily worked on the issues of narcissism and the self – humour is indelibly linked to narcissism and primary omnipotence. In *The Analysis of the Self* (1971) Heinz Kohut links creativity and humour via the concept of narcissism (Segal, 1995: 62). His argument is that 'the creative individual has the child-like capacity to play imaginatively with that individual's surroundings, because such a person tends to be less psychologically separate from the surroundings. The creative work becomes part of the self (1995: 62). What is more, humour as a transformation of narcissism (1995: 62). Humour makes people reframe painful feelings and inoculate them in a creative fashion. Stand-up comedy, in particular, allows the performer to convert the personal pain into something socially acceptable, and even into an attractive commodity. As Julia Segal writes, 'pain is not directly observable in the way that behaviour is (1995: 222). Comedians may be said to rationalise their pain, the feelings; and to re-imagine, re-fantasise it in a new way; shape and mould it into a performance. They project their pain onto an experience and the audience's reaction only becomes a problem when the comedian is rejected. Fantasy, in terms of imagination, is about adding a new dimension to your life; it is bridging the gap between reality and human desires; the ideal version of ourselves. It fills the void; it also acts as a replacement for the missing components in people's lives. Kohut argues that

> The capacity for genuine humour constitutes yet another important – and welcome – sign that a transformation of archaic pathogenetic narcissistic cathexes has taken place in the course of analysis of narcissistic personalities. The humour of which the narcissistic patient becomes capable is, I believe, the complement to another favourable result in the course of the analysis of these patients: the strengthening of their values and ideals.
> 
> (Kohut, 2001: 324)

Mario Jacoby writes: 'Kohut …postulates the existence of a 'narcissistic libido' that forms and transforms to eventually stimulate the maturation of the personality in the course of a lifetime. Under favourable conditions, this process of maturation results in qualities he describes as empathy, creativity, humour, and wisdom' (Jacoby, 1999: 112).

Seen in this light, performance becomes a form of object-relation. The audience can be seen as a self-object, the mother, for the comedian who, like a child, tries to establish himself securely. Kohut writes:

> The child does not build up an inner sense of self-confidence; it continues to need external affirmation. […] But … we do not see merely fixation on a small child's need for mirroring – the traumatic frustration of the normal need intensifies and distorts the need: the child becomes insatiably hungry for mirroring, affirmation, and praise. It is this intensified, distorted need which the child cannot tolerate and which it therefore either represses (and may hide behind pseudo independence and emotional coldness) or distorts and splits off. […]
> In the narcissistic transference, the infantile need for self-object is remobilized.
> 
> (Kohut, 2011: 558)

The comedian as a narcissistic injury regards rejection by the audience; the response to which might take the form of 'fight' or 'flight'. Kohut also writes that human creativity follows the necessary pattern of intense and quiet periods: 'one might say that a phase of frantic creativity (original thought) is followed by a phase of quiet work (the original ideas of the preceding phase are checked, ordered, and put into a communicative form, e.g., written down), and that this phase of quiet work is in turn interrupted by a fallow period of procreative narcissistic tension, which ushers in a phase of renewed creativity, and so on' (Kohut, 2011: 816). Creativity becomes a form of therapy for the comedian because it allows him to explore, recreate and fantasise about his inter- and intra-psychic structure on stage.

Moreover, according to Kohut, pleasure-seeking and self-expression tendencies in individuals are not incompatible. They often coincide and assist in the creation of a psychological equilibrium in human beings. There is certainly no conflict between them, and they do not exclude each other. In other words, the artist's narcissistic tendencies constitute an important part of his life: 'there appears to be no major conflict between the pleasure-seeking and the self-expression agents of the personality. One might be inclined to assume that the absence of conflict is due to the fact that that these two major strivings are of equal strength, that equilibrium of forces exists' (2011: 760). This concept is certainly applicable to many comedians who suffer from depression and drug addiction. At times their indulgences are denoted as self-absorption, however they could also be avoidance. (Depression is discussed further in Chapter 7) Their creativity goes hand-in hand with problematic behaviour (both on and off stage) and even (rarely) suicide.

Yet, stand-up comedy as a live experience can have a socially responsible motivation. The reason for the comedians to go on stage, create jokes and engage the audience is short-lived but intense relationships do not always have narcissistic roots or lead to vanity and self-love. Many comedians often feel the need to be useful they feel the need to change the world. While the pleasure-seeking man' is narcissistic in that he cannot create but only absorbs the psychic energy of others. By contrast, there are some comedians who are eager to both publicise themselves *and* change the world. Comedy is about transforming the world, as well as establishing oneself. Performers of live comedy push the boundaries of the world. Their genre gives them the opportunity to challenge taboos in order for the audience to review and adjust them. Comedians always check with the audience whether they have overstepped an important boundary or a taboo. For instance, they might joke that they have slept with their grandmother, and then ask the audience: 'Have I gone too far?'

There are certainly parallels between Kohut's vision of the audience's reasons for enjoying comedy, and our idea of the audience's reaction to the jokes created on stage. The audience seeks to be transformed, not just entertained. Good stand-up comedy has the potential to enable the audience to be self-reflective. The comedian has to offer the audience something that is relevant to their everyday experiences.

Meanwhile, the people in the audience seek self-renewal by reflection, by going through someone else's creative process and then absorbing its results.

For instance, the American comedian Bill Hicks is often described as rebellious and scandalous. Andy Fyfe writes in *The Telegraph:*

> In Edinburgh, he reduced an audience of 300 to hysterical tears, with an assault on the modern world that was as brutal as it was brilliant. The first Gulf War? "That wasn't a war. A war is two sides fighting each other. Iraq: 150,000 casualties. USA: 79. Does that mean if we had sent over 80 guys we woulda still won?" Abortion? "Pro-lifers, don't link your arms around clinics. Link them around cemeteries. Let's see how committed you really are." The Media? "By the way, if anyone here is in advertising or marketing, kill yourself. Seriously, there's no joke coming, you are Satan's spawn, filling the world with bile and garbage. Kill yourself now; it's the only way to save your souls. Now, on with the show...
>
> (Fyfe, *The Telegraph*, 12 May 2010)

Many comedians also see themselves as being socially responsible, and think that their creative endeavour is the result of social responsibility. Some of them even have strong political views and, as a result, their material is politicised. For instance, the eccentric stand-up comedian Jim Barclay used to open his performances at the Comedy Store by openly proclaiming his political views: '...now, is that everybody? Good evening, ladies and gentlemen. My name is Jim Barclay, and I am the wacky and zany Marxist-Leninist comedian; and it's my job to come on here and tell you jokes which precipitate the downfall of capitalism and bring an end to tyranny and injustice wherever it rears its ugly head, so'ere we go with a starter for ten' (Wilmut and Rosengard, 1989: 27).

Another comedian, Jack Dee, speaks of the importance for the stand-up comedian of reaching out and engaging all strata of society during the performance. According to him, the performer should always bear the social in mind when writing and compiling the material:

> There's no point being a comedian if you're going to deliberately appeal to your peer group. There's a certain amount that will always make your peer group laugh and you have direct access to that. You can talk about taking drugs and being a student – to a certain extent, you've got a ready-made set. But when you actually appeal to people from a completely different background and age to you, then you're being funny – you're doing it.
>
> (Cook, 1994: 194-5)

Some stand-up comedians do not aim to be openly political but still want their jokes to be socially committed. Ben Elton says:

> Irishmen are not stupid, and it's not funny to say they are – you can pretend for ten minutes and after that your cover's blown. Women's tits are not funny and it's not funny to say they are. So where do you look? You look around you, inside your heart and in what you're doing – that's where the comedy is. And inevitably that becomes social – you have to take a line, and my line is socially committed; but it's not because I want to be political, it wouldn't be funny. For example, I'm not preaching about the little squirrels who don't have a home because MacDonald's have cut the trees down to grow the grain to feed the cows to make the hamburgers – it's *funny* that this organisation that has a clown giving blind children money as a logo is in danger of unbalancing the entire eco-structure of the planet!
> (Wilmut and Rosengard, 1989: 93)

To use Kohut's terminology, the 'guilty narcissist' in stand-up performers feels responsible for his own behaviour as well as for the behaviour of people in his community, and therefore exposes and challenges dangerous behavioural patterns. Comedians often attack and provoke the social order – even knowing that it may result in repercussions – because challenging authority is part of being socially responsible. By doing this, they also announce their position in the world and achieve a new status.

## *4.5.   Mirroring, Attunement and Shame*

Mirroring and attunement theories developed by the British independents such as Donald Winnicott are also of utmost importance for the analysis of the comedic performance. In this sub-section we will link the concepts of mirroring and attunement to the concepts of shame and object control.

### *4.5.1.   Mirroring and Control*

As discussed, the contact the performer establishes with the audience as an extension of his relationship with the mother reflects the performer's confidence and ability to establish secure connections. It can be said that the comedian regards the audience's reaction to his skills in melodramatic terms: 'It's either they love me or I die'. This directly relates to the British paediatrician Donald Winnicott vision of the early mother-baby bond and his concept of the 'good enough mother'.

Winnicott writes in *The Maturational Process and the Facilitating Environment* (1965):

> The good-enough mother meets the omnipotence of the infant, and so she repeatedly. A True Self begins to have life, through the strength given to the infant's weak ego by the mother's implementation of the infant's omnipotent expressions.
>
> The mother who is not good enough is not able to implement the infant's omnipotence, and so she repeatedly fails to meet the infant gesture; instead, she substitutes her own gesture which is to be given sense by the compliance of the infant. This compliance on the part of the infant is the earliest stage of the False Self, and belongs to the mother's inability to sense her infant's needs.
>
> (1990: 145)

The False Self, according to Winnicott, is a form of ego-distortion, which corresponds to social compliance and social masks. It can be healthy or expression of healthy (polite and mannered social attitude) or unhealthy (a set of superficial social masks concealing profound fragility) (1990: 143). By contrast, the True Self is the healthy aspect of the ego – the genuine character core. From the True Self 'come the spontaneous gesture and the personal idea. The spontaneous gesture is the True Self in action. Only the True Self can be creative and only the True Self can be real' (1990: 148).

Seen in this light, the audience, as good mother, allows the baby to express himself creatively on stage. If the audience fails to engage in the 'two and fro' aspect of the performance (joke followed by laughter), the (male) comedian may become offensive. Offence is also his arrogant way of showing power. Failure to connect is regarded by the performer as a form of neglect and possible passive aggression. The mother is therefore seen as bad, neglectful, and deserving a verbal attack. The good enough audience is supposed to love the comedian anyway – regardless of what he says, how good he is, or who he is. This loves takes the comedian to the state of omnipotence; to the stage where he is able to address his fragmented areas and re-build himself from scratch psychologically. By contrast, failure to establish a perfect connection with the audience is felt by the comedian as a lack of opportunity to exercise his creativity, to display and confirm his True Self – which is responsible for the feelings of 'reality' and 'existence'. Unable to display his True Self, the performer metaphorically 'dies on stage'.

It can be said that the mirroring exchange should be regarded as the core narcissistic dynamic in which 'a subjective element is safeguarded *within* a holding maternal structure' (Wright, 2009: 5). The audience is asked to 'hold' the fragile psyche of the comedian. Kenneth Wright writes that 'in the absence of inner maternal holding, every contact with an external form (symbol, view, interpretation) risks repeating the original trauma of impingement…' (2009: 5). At the same time, Wright argues, creativity can be seen as a way of re-creating the lost connection with the primary caretaker in childhood; as a replacement for the lost warmth, understanding and feeling of attunement and connection to the mother (2009: 69). For instance, the creative artist is someone who 'has suffered a relative deficiency in mirroring and attunement – perhaps a disruptive loss of the mother's responsiveness – which has made him feel that security lies in becoming one's attuning 'other' (2009: 69). Hence creativity fills in the gaps of the neglecting mother or the unresponsive mother. Wright gives as an example the poet Rilke whose mother used to dress him as a girl to make up for the disappointment of having a son instead of a daughter. However, 'Rilke succeeded in keeping himself alive and discovered in himself a means of creating and finding the forms that he needed. His poetic calling can be seen as acknowledgement of his most important task: to create and recreate the responsive mother he had lacked' (2009: 69).

As far as recreation of the maternal figure is concerned, stand-up comedy is even more complex. The specifics of stand-up comedy lie in emotional and special closeness of the entertainer to the audience; in the immediacy of mirroring responses that the comedian anticipates and receives from the listeners. What the comedian tries to connect to is his sense of self. Comedy performances can become a healing component for him. It is a way of getting in touch with one's lost or broken self, or creating the new self; as well of his newly acquired role in the world. It is also about trying to elevate one's status – 'the more you love me, the better I become'.

### *4.5.2. Transitional Objects in Comedic Performance*

The success of this venture depends on the quality of the audience's responses. It can be argued that the comedian's material becomes the transitional object, which keeps the entertainer's broken self alive while 'the mother' is absent. It saves the comedian from total depression and keeps the anxiety in control. From Winnicott's view, the baby endows transitional phenomena with special significance because they symbolically stand for the missing mother. Therefore, they have special meaning. Wright writes:

> Typically, the transitional object is the comforting bit of blanket that the infant mouths and caresses. Winnicott called this the 'first *not-me* possession' but he also saw it as a special object, which the infant had imaginatively *created*. This root of creativity is central to his theory of personal development for in his view it underpins the quality of later experience. Only when the baby is allowed such an early experience

can the world be endowed with personal meaning, and only then can there be creative involvement with it in later life.

(2009: 39)

For the comedian, it is about putting everything that is 'the most pronounced part of me' into words and symbols; into jokes. As Wright notes, Winnicott's transitional area lies between the communication of raw emotion (e.g. baby crying) and the full development and recognition of symbolic expression:

> Transitional functioning allows an emotional experience to be 'held' (contained) within a sensory form or concrete object; the particular object is emotionally invested because it *evokes* the needed experience through its analogical structure. Thus, an observer can see that the baby's comforting bit of blanket is *like* the mother's skin in being soft and warm. For the baby, it creates the illusion of the mother's skin, and thus facilitates the *illusion* of the object's presence *while not confronting the reality of its absence*. Such transitional concrete 'symbols' provide a first means of holding on to experience in its absence by re-creating a simulacrum of it; the object 'holds' the missing experience, obliterating or 'softening' its absence. In this sense the transitional object is a primitive form of mental containment.

> Two tentative conclusions can be drawn from this: first, it is only possible to feel *in touch* with feelings that have been contained within a form or an object; and the second, feelings can only be *contained* in so far as the means to grasp them symbolically, or pre-symbolically (transitionally), are available. *Transitional* containment is the key to emotional survival; *symbolic* containment is the key to holding feelings in mind and getting to know what they are like.

(2009: 21)

The performer as a transitional object that is expected to demonstrate a range of expected reactions can, also regard the audience, and its reactions. The object 'contains' the comedian during the performance while he is trying to replay and re-live the early emotional and psychological dramas. During this 'mirroring' stage the stand-up comedian goes back to the pre-Oedipal stage. The process is both regressive and progressive. On one level, the performer hopes that the audience will be loving. If they are not, the detachment/rejection drama is re-played. This is an important point for the comedian because he will be pushed into dealing with rejection and the shame that comes with it. This is exacerbated by the fact that they will have to deal with shame and helplessness in an exposed environment and immediately.

The moment of rejection is when all projections in a relationship between objects are withdrawn. This moment is emotionally dangerous as it may provoke emotional violence triggered by the sense of shame within the comedian. The audience's reaction is a projective form of confirmation of the comedian's existence. For instance, Jimmy Carr says about the audience: 'The great attraction of stand-up as a balm for the fragile ego – as opposed to, say, writing a book or appearing in a radio play – is the instantaneous nature of the audience's feedback. Do they love me? Yes, they must do – they're laughing' (Carr and Greeves, 2006: 114). Carr also famously said that 'you're only ever as good as your last joke. Not even your last show – your last *joke*' (2006: 115).

Rejection by the audience is regarded by the comedian as the failure of the transitional object to work; as another loss of the mother figure. When the creative person seeks mirroring and attunement from the audience, he actually seeks to repair the damaged primal relationship. Creativity, through an emotional dialogue with the audience, allows the comedian to re-organise his world anew; to regain the control over their internal and external world. For instance, the comedian George Carlin states that, 'the thing that most comedians need to remember when they go on stage is that they're really the boss. But my feeling is you gotta believe in yourself, and know what your attitude is what your observations are based on. (Ajaye, 2002: 85).

The comedian's aggressive reaction to being rejected by the audience can also be explained using the concept of shame. Shame is a realisation that one is a separate individual – not omnipotent but left to his own devices, abandoned by the 'primary carer'. Shame is a reaction to not being understood, accepted and mirrored. When surrounded by like-minded people, we feel safe, understood, cared for. We feel omnipotent, in charge of things.

Denial of shame can account for the violent language comedians use to describe the process of performance. Jimmy Carr notes that the language of professional comedians is full of violent expressions and metaphorical references to death: '"He died on stage tonight" being the nadir, and "he really killed out there" the parlance of comedians evoking the pinnacle of achievement. Woody Allen once said that he preferred doing stand-up in nightclubs to TV shows, because "you've got all the time in the world to kill the audience … over the course of the show you can kill 99 per cent of them". Jimmy Carr's vision of this is even bleaker: It's as though a comedy club is the chosen arena for a fight to the death, where either the audience or the comic gets out alive – but never both (Carr, 2006: 115). Another comedian, Shelley Berman, notes that sometimes the comedian 'makes the mistake of developing hostility towards the audience – which is a common thing: You have to fight the desire to become hostile. The comedian who says, "These are the jokes, folks" is making a mistake, but we are all prone to make an error of this kind' (Wilde, 2000: 90).

Shame drives the creative individual to become an agent – to act, to do something, to leave his mark on the world. The biggest nightmare of the agent is the fear of exposure – fear of being a nobody with nothing to offer to the world: At the same time, the defining aspect of the active agent is the ability to deal with shame – the ability to act without fear, to attack, and to deal with the consequences of failure if the desired result is not achieved.

The comedian David Baddiel provides a good example of how a comedian feels when the audience is rejecting him:

> *I've been booed off twice, but only once after I was well established. I died terribly at the Comedy Store. My only excuse is that I hadn't slept the night before, and I went on at a time when the audience were completely gone. I remember people shouting and screaming and then hearing through the general roar of abuse, somebody shout, 'The walls are closing in!'. And it was true. I remember thinking, 'Is that a heckle or is it God commenting on the event?'. And that was when I decided to leave. It was a late night show on Friday, and I was doing the entire weekend – but I came back the next night, and did one of the best nights I've ever done. When you've been booed off, the next gig you do you're really wired for it, and it can be really a great gig.*
>
> *It's brilliant to go on next after someone dies. When I got booed off at the Store, Jack Dee went on next and absolutely stormed it. I was really friendly with Jack then and really pissed off with him for doing that. But I've done that as well. I've gone after comics who completely died, and thought, 'This is going to be an absolute stormer!'. And it practically always is. Most audience's bloodlust is satiated by one comic dying – except at the Tunnel.*
>
> (Cook, 1994: 159)

Failure of connecting with the audience feels, for the comedian, like the dissolution of basic trust. It can be seen as a form of separation anxiety. The comedian regards the rejection as a hard blow; as an attack on the core of his personality. The comedian often associates with his outer persona – his identity as an entertainer. He expects that the audience will confirm this ideal image of himself, which corresponds to what Kohut and Winnicott call 'the False Self'. It is as if he needs a label to define himself. This means that if his skills as an entertainer are not accepted, if he is 'no good' at what he does, he feels as if the 'caretaker' – into which role the audience is pushed – abandoned him for being an 'imperfect child'. Non-acceptance is felt by the performer as an aggressive act; as an attack on his integrity as an individual. Consequently, his identity is lost or dissolved and has to be rebuilt again, and the cycle is repeated. For instance, the comedian Jerry Seinfield writes that stand-up performers have 'embarrassment anxiety' and stage fright in the face or failure or survival: 'People think of comedians as people who are outgoing and comfortable in front of people, when in fact it's just the opposite. What you are trying to become skilled at is "embarrassment"' (Ajaye, 2002: 199). Rejection by the audience is unconsciously regarded by the comedian as a break of basic trust and a disappointment in the self-object.

> *According to Kohut, we need, during our whole life, to be safely held by the 'matrix of mature self-object relationships,' which is comparable to the oxygen required for out biological survival. Without 'empathic resonance,' without meaningful interaction with significant people in our social environment, we are bound to fall into an empty space.*
>
> (Jacoby, 1991: 146).

Rejection by the audience may shake one's internal world – but comedians tend to overcome the shame and come back stronger than before. Comedians who manage to survive on the circuit get their fair share of being loved, supported and mirrored. The American comedian Franklyn Ajaye argues:

> *'As you continue to perform, your routines and jokes will have the stamp of your "uniqueness". People will not only laugh at your material, they will be fascinated at the workings of your mind and look at the subjects you cover in a different way. Then when they think about that subject, they will think about what you said. Soon, they'll want your "take" on things, and eventually in their minds your material and point of view will become indelibly linked'*
>
> (Ajaye, 2002: 11).

Lack of mirroring leads to regression as the performer is reverted into the state of being neglected, unaccepted and unnoticed. It reminds him about the threat of psychological annihilation, the state of non-existence. The comedian Richard Lewis explains it in this way: '…we feel we need too much attention, we're babies, we're introverted, we're convoluted. […] Like a lot of comics, we can be on and feel accepted, and other times we can go into a shell and want to shoot people' (Ajaye, 2002: 136).

Thus, the comedian's relationship with the audience is characterised by a complex emotional interaction that involves mirroring, attunement, shame and the desire for control. Failure to establish a connection with the surrogate 'mother' results in a mini narcissistic crisis while a successful connection confirms the comedian's sense of existence and self-worth.

## *4.6. Conclusion:*

Freudian and post-Freudian theories illuminate the process of the performance and interacting with the audience because they identify the psychic agencies activated with the immediacy of this process as well as with the element of interactivity that is present therein. They also deal with the emotional content that is derived from the psychosexual aspect of the relationship between the performer and the audience. They can be employed to analyse issues such as anger and aggression (narcissistic injury) that the performer may feel and express towards the audience; elation which comedian's feel when they are 'mirrored' (accepted by the audience), omnipotence through being loved and adored by a group of people, depression and fear of annihilation of the self (a reaction to rejection by the audience). These concepts explain the mechanisms of the complex, intense relationships that happen during live stand-up performances between the man on stage and the people in the auditorium.

# CHAPTER 5

## A JUNGIAN THEORY OF COMEDY

This chapter offers a new perspective on the comedian and the joke. This new approach to humour is heavily influenced by Jungian and post-Jungian theory, and utilises the concepts of individuation and alchemy to argue that the comedian reflects and influences social processes in the humour he generates.

Arthur Asa Berger reminds us in his book *An Anatomy of Humour* (1999) that there are many theories of humour, all of which approach the subject from different perspectives (Berger, 1999: 3). The most famous one is probably Freud's concept of the joke as a sort of defence mechanism, masking our aggressive or sexual impulses; arising from the need to comply with the civilised norms of behaviour. In this sense, humour deflects our instinctual energy, as well as inoculates it by turning it into something more socially acceptable. Humour also serves the function of exposing the shadow, thus overlaying its destructive potential into a positive force.

Humour is a phenomenon that combines the paradox of the sadness in the recognition of realistic personal limitations and the joy of awareness as experienced by others. As Alessandra Lemma writes in *Humour on the Couch* (2000), Freud's later conceptualisation of humour brands it as 'the triumph of narcissism', that is, 'a reassertion of narcissism via adaptive regression' (Lemma, 2000: 33). In other words, 'humour allows the individual to triumph over the forces of repression or the pain of reality' (Lemma 2000: 33). As a result, 'a psychoanalytic perspective highlights humour's psychically integrating function bringing together the contradictions and conflicts that are an unavoidable part of being human. The humorous vision facilitates a psychic elaboration and mastery of unpleasant and discongruent conflictual situations or emotions' (2000: 34-5). Freud's conclusion was that 'jokes are from their nature to be distinguished from the comic and only converge with it, on the one hand in certain special cases, and on the other hand in their aim of obtaining pleasure from intellectual sources.' (Freud, CW 8: 208).

Semiotics offers us another perspective on humour. The semiotic theory of humour (and jokes) argues that humour is best discussed in the context of 'communication, paradox, play and the resolution of logical problems' (1998: 4). Semiotics deals with the correlation between signs and their meanings, as well as with the systems of signs and the meanings they generate in various sign combinations. For instance, the American psychiatrist William Fry writes in his book, *Sweet Madness* (1963): 'during the unfolding of humour, one is suddenly confronted by an explicit-implicit reversal when the punch line is delivered. The reversal helps distinguish humour from play, dreams, etc. [...] but the reversal also has the unique effect of forcing upon the humour participants an internal redefining of reality. Inescapably, the punch line combines communication and meta-communication' (Fry, 1963: 158). There is also the incongruity theory which argues that the main technique of all humour is thwarted expectations, and it's this sudden change that we enjoy and at which we are prepared to laugh: '... we have to recognise an incongruity before we can laugh at one' (Berger, 1998: 3).

W.C. Fields was famous for delivering the incongruous:
'Do you believe in clubs for young people?'
'Only when kindness fails.'
(Routledge, Language of Humour A.Ross:7:1998)

Many comedians today use 'the incongruous' in their one liner jokes.
John Moloney
'I wasn't always this fat; I used to be 7lbs 6oz"
(Live at Jongleurs 1998)

Alison Ross, in her book Language of Humour demonstrates the differing linguistic models used in humour.
Structural phonology is the ambiguous use of words, which sound the same and have many meanings.

*What's black and white and red all over? A newspaper.*
(Routledge, Language of Humour A.Ross:9:1998)

Morphology is where words are transposed into another meaning.
*'What is a baby piglet called?'*
*'A piglet.'*
*'What is a baby toy called?'*
*'A toilet.'*

She continues to the more sophisticated analysis of humour which she termed; Conversational Implicature.

> A. *'I didn't sleep with my wife before we were married, did you?'*
> B. *'I don't know. What was her name?'*

This becomes humorous when written and spoken. There are many structures of jokes and more are formed during the creation of humour. The linguistic deconstruction of structure is a method to find the punch line in comedy.

However, it is the stand-up comedian who forms the creative input of content within the semiotic structure.

All these theories are not mutually exclusive. They can be combined to provide a fuller view of the joke's meaning and its effect on the audience. For instance, Berger reminds us how both the psychoanalytic and the semiotic approach argue that people often perceive jokes unconsciously rather than consciously, and a range of factors dictates their reaction to them, including social, political and anthropological. Each of these dimensions, however, boils down to the issue of the tension between the individual and civilisation.

Inherent in all humour is the juxtaposition of the expected i.e. the cultural norm and conjoined with the unexpected, i.e. the individual interpretation, which will give the tension intrinsic of the unexpected.

# 5.
## 5.1. *The Supra Joke*

A Jungian approach to the joke and humour states that the comedian and the joke are inseparable; it is their union, which makes transformation occur. The joke has to be adapted to society and society's expectations. We cannot have a joke without society. The Jungian theory of comedy stresses both the effect of the joke on society and its role in the comedian's personal development. Should the comedian understand the self-analytic effect of his stand-up process to be the catalyst for his individuation, he can in turn trigger and influence the individuation of society as a whole. In the Jungian analysis of the joke we should take into consideration the transformative aspect humour and laughter, both for the comedian and his society. Moreover, a Jungian vision of humour does not contradict Freud's analysis of jokes. It approaches it from a different; more optimistic angle as it also takes into consideration the social and political change that humour brings to society as a whole not just for the individual. In this sense, the Jungian approach to humour has social and anthropological properties.

In order for the comedian to individuate on stage he needs the audience as a participant in the dialogue. The comedian and the audience jointly own the joke. In order to be born, the joke needs to be absorbed and reflected by external participants. By itself, without the audience, the joke does not exist because it is a combination of the personal and the social; of the individual and the collective. Likewise, humour is as much an individual as it is a collective phenomenon. It only exists for a group of people, as part of society. The comedian creates the joke not only to reflect upon his or her own problems, but also to discuss the problems that are pertinent to a particular society. Sometimes a joke becomes so attuned to the problems of the community in which it is born that it becomes a Supra Joke. This happens when the comedian and the audience are one; the comedian in effect becomes the spokes person for this section of his society. In order to become a Supra Joke, comedic material needs the following specific qualities:

1. Social relevance: it has to reflect the current social and cultural issues. A comedian has to be aware of cultural tension and inherent political and social themes that he can reflect and transform. He has to be self aware to know what who he represents sociologically and personally. He has to detach himself and become an observer with a social conscience.
2. Novelty: It has to be a revelation for the public
3. Transformational qualities: it has to make the unconscious material conscious, and to transform the 'dark matter' of hidden social issues into comedic material.
4. Therapeutic qualities: the transformed material has healing properties as the issue is announced, and dragged out of the shadows. The healing properties are the amplification of the problem being socially recognised, yet not announced. Here Chris Rock takes his role as host of the Oscars and brings the difficult issues to the public domain in a humorous manner. The juxtaposition of humour with social awareness makes awareness palatable and healing touching the sensitive with the occasion and his personal attitude and structure to comedy with profound affect.

To quote Chris Rock at the 2016 Oscars

> 'Theres' all this controversy. There are no black nominees. People say to me Chris you should quit, you should quit. Why is it only unemployed people who tell you to quit something. No one with a job ever tells you to quit. Then I realised they're not going to stop the Oscars if I quit. It will happen anyway. And the last thing I need is to loose another job to Kevin Hart. ………………….. the big question why are we protesting this Oscars it's the 88$^{th}$ academy awards, which means the whole no black no nominees thing has happened at least 71 other times. You gotta figure it happened in the 50's the 60's, in the

60's Sidney didn't put out a movie. And black people didn't protest do you know why we had real things to protest at the time. We were too busy being raped and lynched to care about who won cinematographer. When your grandmother is swinging from a tree its hard to worry about who best documentary foreign short………………………………………..

In the inmemoriam package is going to be black people shot by the cops on their way to the movies. Yes there I said it……………………………..

We want opportunity, we want black actors to get opportunities?
Chris Rock: (2016) YouTube https://youtu.be/kqhVNZgZGqQ

- Making the illegitimate legitimate: taking the edge off otherwise concealed, inappropriate and controversial subjects by presenting them in a humorous manner.

To create a Supra Joke, the comedian, who is continuously inspired by personal events, needs to present both the archetype and the actuality; as well as connect the personal and the collective. Within the collective archetypes, our personal interpretation and cultural aspects also impacts on the tone and specific characteristics of that primordial image.
Jung writes:

> The meeting with oneself is, at first, the meeting with one's shadow. The shadow is a tight passage, a narrow door, whose painful constriction no one is spared who goes down to the deep well. But one must learn to know oneself in order to know who one is. For what comes after the door is, surprisingly enough, a boundless expanse full of unprecedented uncertainty, with apparently no inside and outside, no above and no below, no here and no there, no mine and no thine, no good and no bad. It is the world of water, where all life floats in suspension; where the realm of the sympathetic system, the soul of everything living, begins; where I am indivisibly this *and* that; where I experience the other in myself and the other-than-myself experiences me.
>
> (Jung CW9/I: para. 45)

The joke is thus capable of transferring itself, rather like water, from the personal level to the collective very quickly. It can reach the deepest layers of society's psyche. One can adapt Jung's essay on Nazi Germany from Andrew Samuel's book 'The Political Psyche' to understanding the deep psyche of society.

*We are living in times of great disruption: political passions are often aflame, internal upheavals have brought nations to the brink of chaos…This critical state of things has such a tremendous* influence on the psych life of the individual that the analyst… feels the violence of its impact even in the quiet of the consulting room…The psychologist cannot avoid coming to grips with contemporary history… Andrew Samuels takes this quote by Jung about the impact of politics on society and its impact in the therapy room today as it was then. Samuels continues to elaborate the relationship between politics and depth psychology and in turn ' the political development of the person. ' Politics is the governance of society and as such the 'Political Psyche' implies a 'Social Psyche.' The method by which we govern society has a structure, which becomes inculcated within our deep psychological structure. Politics being one component of the Social Psyche.

> *Politics concerns the way in which power is held, or deployed by the state, by institutions, and by sectional interests to maintain survival, determine behaviour, gain control over others and, more positively perhaps, enhance the quality of human life.*
> (A.Samuels The Political Psyche. Routledge 3 : 1993)

This is because we are never fully ourselves, separated from our society; we are never fully separated from the collective unconscious. Jung argues:

> The collective unconscious is anything but an encapsulated personal system; it is sheer objectivity, as wide as the world and open to all the world. There I am the object of every subject, in complete reversal of my ordinary consciousness where I am always the subject that has an object. There I am utterly at one with the world, so much a part of it that I forget all too easily who I really am. 'Lost in myself' is a good way of describing this state. But this self is the world, if only a consciousness could see it. That is why we must know who we are.
> (CW9/I: para. 56)

The stand-up must engage with the audience, and at the same time distinguish himself from it. It is in that moment that he creates the profound explosive impact of the Supra Joke.

Deliso Chaponda, a black comedian from Malawi, generates supra jokes. This monologue is from the *Comedy Night* (BBC):

> *My name is Deliso Chaponda. I'm from Malawi. I've been living in the UK for seven years and I still don't fit in. England legitimately is a nation of complainers. Everybody hates their jobs they hate the weather, the biggest complaint is financial crisis. I'm from Africa,*

*what are you talking about?' How dare you over-privileged b\*\*\*\*\*\*\*\*\* call that a crisis! Where's UNICEF, where's Bono? You can tell me it's a financial crisis when there's planes over London and they're throwing fish and chips out of the window. A lot of people ask me why England a lot of people ask me why the UK, you could have gone to the Bahamas you could have gone to France, why the UK? Truth is, I moved here because there's a group called the BNP. It's like a right wing party, and they put out a newsletter saying that immigrants are taking all their good jobs and all their good women, and I thought – wow that sounds great to me!*

(www.bbc.co.uk/programme/p028jqdn)

Supra Jokes are often controversial – this is how they make an impact. Once we have a universal joke, it means that part of society is becoming more aware and potentially unified in their ability to make the necessary changes. When society becomes unified by a controversial joke, it matters whether it made people laugh or choke with anger. They can be shocked, disgusted, delighted or enlightened. This process can even be called Supra Individuation. It does not necessarily have to happen via delight and laughter – it can also happen via negative feelings such as shock.

Supra Jokes are so powerful that they expose the subjects which society otherwise prefers to keep hidden; under lock and key of censorship. As will be discussed later in this chapter, they emerge as a result of the alchemical interchange of energies of the performer, the audience and society. The joke has to be the arrow, which drives through all assumptions expectations and beliefs, and twists it into a new concept with humour. The audience laughs and thinks about the concept behind the joke. This challenges their beliefs and assumptions, leaving the remnants of transformational attitude to become embedded within the psyche.

It is not surprising that many Supra Jokes come from Afro-American, West Indies or comedians of African descent particularly in the USA as they feel different, are and have been treated differently and are keen to challenge the assumptions and societal expectations about their race. Particularly since the race issues in the USA are very volatile and consistently brooding within the political and social structure. A good example of such a joke can be Chris Rock's politically incorrect and challenging monologue about self-racism:

*Now we've got a lot of things, a lot of racism in the world right now.*
*Who's more racist? Black people or white people?*
*Black people.... You know why? Cause we hate black people too*
*Everything white people don't like about black people*
*Black people really don't like about black people*

*There some shit goin on with black people right now*
*There's like a civil war goin on with black people*
*And there two sides....*
*There's black people, and there's niggas*
*And niggas have got to go*
*Everytime black people wanna have a good time*
*Ignorant ass nigga fuck it up*
*Can't do shit, can't do shit, without some ignorant ass nigga fuckin it up*
*Can't do nothin*
*Can't keep a disco open more than 3 weeks*
*Grand opening, grand closing*
*Can't go to a movie the first week it comes out*
*Why cause niggas are shooting at the screen*
*What kind of ignorant shit is that*
(YouTube https://youtu.be/f3PJFOYE-x4)

Another example of a controversial Supra Joke is Gina Yashere's monologue about being stopped by the traffic officer: 'I think I'm the only black person in America that is not afraid of the police. In fact I pull them over. I do. I did it recently. I said – "Excuse me, officer, I can' t help but notice that you have been following me for eight miles". And the accent confused him. He was like that: "Oooh, I'm sorry, mam, I thought you were black"'.

Andi Osho, a black female comedian of Nigerian descent, tackles the controversial subjects of race and depression:

> Let me just check all the black people in the house make some noise. […] As a black comic, you see a sea of white faces staring at you, and it feels like an auction.
>
> Things have gone politically correct. My friend has had a baby who had s*** around her face and she said to me: 'Can you pass me the muslin?' I'm not allowed to say that because it sounds like 'Muslim'. Paralympians are great role models. They're so brave. Look at the black people running! They're just so fast and none of them being chased. We should do that next time.
>
> Do you know what I propose? They should add disabilities, they should add non-physical ones.
>
> Depression that's a disability. They should get a guy sitting in a sandpit at the end of the long jump crying, 'what's the point'?
> (https://youtu.be/ezW_4RjLPuQ?list:)

Other comedians who successfully create the Supra-joke deal with sensitive issues or anomalies within our society, Paul Merton, a UK comedian approaching the theme of mental health continues the point of depression by combining truth with humour in his jokes. It is this element of personal revelation, mixed with self-deprecating and self-unveiling vulnerability that also adds to the humour. In this way, the comedian is no longer on a pedestal but one of the audience. His pain echoes the pain of the audience, and the frisson of honest despair wrapped within the humour creates the Supra Joke:

> One day they said to me 'There's a trainee psychiatrist. Can he have a bit of practice, a bit of an interview?' Sometimes a sense of humour is not necessarily your best friend, it's misinterpreted, and towards the end of the hour I got a bit bored, and I thought I would liven it up a bit. I said: 'You haven't asked me about my father. He said 'why should I?' I said 'Because he's the Duke of Edinburgh'. He said: 'That's very interesting, I'll write that down'. I said: 'No don't write it down, it's a joke'. He said: I've got to write it down because you said it'. I said: 'No, don't write it down'. He said: 'I've got to write it down'. I thought: 'Fuck, I'm here for another month!'
>
> (https://youtu.be/58sXGK3Ejac)

Tanya Lee Davis is a 3 foot 6 inches comedian. She has had a number of shows, including '*Abnormally Funny*' and '*Little Comedian, Big Laughs*'. Her jokes often touch on the public's reaction to disability and all kinds of difference: 'Don't feel sorry for me 'cos I'm ginger, I spend most of my day watching people watching me. I love children, I love their reaction. What happened to you, were you in an accident? No, I didn't eat my vegetables when I was your age you little shit'.

Bobby Mair is another generator of Supra Jokes who likes the idea of producing scandalous, insulting and rude texts. Here he talks about 'family issues' in his trademark loud and controversial way:

> I really want Justin Bieber to sing at my funeral just that for my friends at the funeral my death is the second worst things that's happening there. Like People genuinely want you to feel sorry for this kid 'cos he was raised by a single mom. What's way more depressing than these two miserable people getting a divorced? It is two miserable people staying together and raising the comedian you see before you. You know why I moved here? So that the physical distance between me and my family matched the emotional one. […]
>
> I'm adopted and so I've never met my mum and I don't know what she does for a living, and that makes it really hard for me to enjoy a

lap dance. Some men want a beautiful stripper, I just want one who didn't have my nose.

(Russell Howards Good News
https://youtu.be/eLChjMragEg)

Mair is not afraid to talk about politics either:

> I have a theory I think. Every person in the Middle East should vote at the next US elections. Think about it. Every person. 'Cos it really fucking affects them like more than anyone else in the world. It affects them 'cos if you're a guy in Nebraska, it's just a figurehead you blame your life on. There's no connection. If you are Ahmed in Afghanistan, who gets elected gets to determine the size of your next family reunion or how many paralympians you're going to have.
>
> (Russell Howards Good News
> https://youtu.be/eLChjMragEg)

Similarly, Ian Stone, one of the most controversial comedians on the UK circuit, is not afraid to mention subjects that would normally be silenced:

> 'I am a Jew. If I was a practising Jew, I would find a Muslim and occupy their seat. I say 'occupy'; but if there are any Americans in, I mean liberate, obviously.'
> (http://Infiniteexcursions.wordpress.com/category/stand-up-comedy/)

Often comedians tap into the psyche of their society even before that society is ready to accept the truth. For instance, in 1997 the then-obscure comedian Jerry Sadowitz made a joke about Jimmy Saville being a paedophile. Due to its scandalous nature, the joke was soon hushed up and the album containing it was also withdrawn. These are Jerry Sadowitz's words: 'there have been serious allegations of child abuse in Cleveland. To my mind there is only one way to find out whether this is true or not and that's to . . . CALL IN JIMMY SAVILE! You can't afford to f*** about! Bring in an expert! Am I right? A friend of mine reckons Jimmy Saville is a paedophile. Rubbish — he's a child-bender! That's why he does all the f****** charity work: it's to gain public sympathy for when his f****** case comes up' (Samuel, 11 October 2012, *Mailonline*).

This is a Supra Joke at play. Its predictive nature can cause a positive or negative reaction, but it is always powerful.

## 5.2. *The Supra Comedian*

Comedians that use Supra-jokes are the ones that initiate social change; they bring into the open the complex and taboo subjects which, are otherwise avoided, in the everyday context. Self-deprecating jokes and detachment from the subject is key to the Supra-comedian. This ability is key to becoming a Supra-comedian, for they see themselves as part of their society, they are prepared to laugh at themselves as well as laugh at the social processes in which they participate. The individuation process is about linking oneself to the people around you, and seeing oneself within the political and social processes. As a result, to engage in a joke often means making light about oneself. Not everyone who tells jokes is able to individuate and to self-reflect via this process. In a way, a strong drive to make jokes, to write comedy or to perform stand-up is also associated with the powerful desire to understand oneself and to introduce change into one's community.

Not all successful comedians are Supra-comedians, although they share some of the traits. The Supra-comedian has to be experienced. The Supra-joke is a powerful message and it requires a strong person to deliver it. The Supra-comedian is like an alchemist who dares to walk into the world of darkness, extract the hidden material and transform it into comedic gold. This dark material, the stuff of the Supra-joke, would become dangerous and brooding if not transformed into a comedic text. The Supra-comedian brings back the equilibrium, and they also find hope for their society.

In order to do this successfully, Supra-comedians should have a definite, clear, original and powerful comedic voice. They know that the audience will love them. It is only out of this confidence that they can deliver the Supra-joke, and it is by creating the Supra-joke they become the Supra-comedian. They know that they stand-alone when they deliver their message,
'It is almost as if loneliness is the price demanded by the Gods of those with whom they share some especially occult understanding. Loneliness becomes the school in which one is forced to learn to bear 'one's uniqueness as an individual' (C.G.Jung *Memories, Dreams, Reflections*, p327)

They should be able to differentiate themselves from others, to see themselves clearly as individuals. As a result, they are not easily influenced and question everything. Jung writes in *The Red Book* (2009): 'if we do not differentiate, we move beyond our essence, beyond creation, we fall into non-differentiation, which is the other quality of the Pleroma. We fall into the Pleroma itself and cease to be created beings. We lapse into dissolution and nothingness. This is the death of the creature. [...] Hence the creature's essence strives toward differentiation, and struggles against primeval, perilous sameness. [...] This principle is the essence of the creature' (Jung, 2009: 347).

The Supra-comedian is that very 'creatura' who strives to stand out of the collective and to differentiate via jokes. Their humour is not prescribed, it is created anew, and is a unique product delivered in the unique manner. They stand apart from the other comedians. Some audiences are ready to hear the Supra-comedian. The public have accepted him as a performer; he is 'good enough' (to use Winnicott's term). And he has found, as Bowlby has named, it his 'secure base' in his own performance and comedic skills. The Supra-comedian has a unique attitude and personality he can be controversial, but compelling.

Personality is key of the Supra-c omedian's success and to his 'Supra' status. Jung stated that 'personality is the supreme realisation of the innate idiosyncrasy of a living being. It is an act of high courage flung in the face of life, the absolute affirmation of all that constitutes the individual, the most successful adaptation to the universal conditions of existence coupled with the greatest possible freedom for self-determination' (Jung CW 17: para. 289). It is the expression of the psychic structure of the comedian in terms of storytelling, which captures the audience. They identify with the comedian. The compelling difference is his vision of the future or his vision of the individual within the collective.

The Supra-comedian has a unique ability to instinctively perceive and construct a differing transformational view based on reality, intuitively forging the collective truth of society and the collective unconscious into a humorous narrative. It is within the collective unconscious that the archetypes reside, are understood and manifest their energy. It is the Supra-comedian who brings the paradox of the collective unconscious to light and transforms the ego. He becomes more than an 'artist' who composes the language of laughter. He becomes the leader who is brave enough to say something that others are reluctant to say – or even don't see at all. Supra Comedians are almost elevated to the status of heroes. In fact, they are called 'comedy gods' on the circuit.

The Supra-comedian is able to highlight through their compelling humorous rhetoric anomalies, which paradoxically, have the healing qualities that the truth brings.
The Winnicottian transitional space, 'if lived long enough, leads to the emergence of the "True Self" which is the spontaneous self that loves paradox and humour and transcends itself through enjoyment of a cultural (symbolic) life.' (Kalsched.1996:145)

Yet, off stage, Supra-comedians are ordinary people. If they elevate themselves, they will lose their transformational qualities, and people won't trust them to be transformative. They must have 'feet of clay', in order to be transformational. 'His legs of iron, his feet part of iron and part of clay' (Daniel 2:31-33) That's why many of their jokes are self-deprecatory. By announcing their own shadows, they relate to the audience and remain human. This is exactly what Eddie Izzard, Chris Rock,

George Carlin, Bill Hicks, Trevor Noah, Ellen DeGeneres and Woody Allen do when they performing.

The Supra Joke is the result of a highly charged creative act. As Anthony Storr puts it in *Churchill's Black Dog*, 'The creative act is essentially integrative. Opposites are united; disparate elements are reconciled' (Storr, 1994: 266). Following Jung, Storr also writes that creativity is an independent force, difficult to handle but also self-rewarding:

> One feature of the highly creative is the zeal with which they pursue their chosen avocation. Creative ability is not simply a question of being endowed by Nature with superior gifts. It is not rare to encounter people of extremely high intelligence who, nevertheless, are not creative. They seem to lack the driving force, the compulsive urge to discover, which characterises men and women of genius. Although some geniuses achieve immediate recognition, innovators are often reviled. Many creative people labour for years in obscurity, or are only recognised posthumously. Although the desire for fame and prosperity is certainly one motive impelling most creative endeavours, it is not the only motive, nor, I believe, the most important. The act of creation, whether in the arts or in the sciences, is self-rewarding, quite apart from any worldly success which it may bring.
>
> (Storr.1994: 264)

Inspiration and illumination are often associated with madness but also with creativity. It is beyond the ego and ownership of the individual. It is this numinous instinct that comes from the collective unconscious embedded within the psychic structure of the comedian, which is administered in Supra-comedy. The comedian of this calibre takes the material to a different level; he or she elevates it, at the same time making it more accessible to the general public.

By speaking about the topical subjects, the Supra-comedian also deals with his own personal issues, and his neuroses attached to those issues. As a result, he reveals moments of inspirational thought within the confines of humour, which can be used to liberate the comedian of its power and affect. Humour also regulates the comedian's ego, as he must constantly bring himself down to earth to interact with the audience. His true transformational quality comes in that moment of equality of becoming one with the audience and engaging in the moment of revelation, which can only come from a true connection. This does not occur at every performance. This true spiritual encounter happens when the performer has a 'dialectic relationship going between the ego and Self. So that we do not suffer alienation from the Self or too much identification with it…….in which the tension between psychic opposites leads to the symbol, a 'living third thing' intermediate between the mystery of life and the ego's struggles'. (Kalsched, 1996:144)

Supra-comedians are not afraid of introducing controversial and downright rude subjects into their comedic routine. For instance, Bill Hicks talks about a subject that is sacred for Americans, the JFK assassination:

> Boy, I love talking about the Kennedy assassination, man. That's my favourite topic. You know why? Because to me it's a great example of, er, a totalitarian government's ability to, you know, manage information and thus keep us in the dark any way they … Oh, sorry. Wrong meeting … Ah [beep]. That's the meeting we're having tomorrow at the docks.
>
> I love talking about Kennedy. I was just down in Dallas, Texas. You know you can go down there and, ah, to Dealey Plaza where Kennedy was assassinated. And you can actually go to the sixth floor of the School Book Depository. It's a museum called … The Assassination Museum. I think they named that after the assassination. I can't be too sure of the chronology here, but …
>
> Anyway they have the window set up to look exactly like it did on that day. And it's really accurate, you know. 'Cause Oswald's not in it.
>
> Yeah, yeah, so wow, that's cool. Painstaking accuracy, you know. It's true. It's called the 'Sniper's Nest'. It's glassed in, it's got the boxes sitting there.
>
> https://youtu.be/1LcvNM7oc7k

The Supra-comedian always chooses topical subjects. For example, in one of her speeches, Ellen DeGeneres discusses the pace of contemporary life:

> Our attention span is shot. We've all got ADD or OCD or one of those disorders with three letters because we don't have time and patience to pronounce the entire disorder… That should be a disorder right there TBD Too Busy Disorder.
>
> What's with this sudden choice of disorders we've got now when I was younger we just had crazy people, just crazy people. All the commercials on television now are for anti-depressants for Prozac or Paxil and they get you right away. Are you sad? Do you get stressed? Do you have anxiety? Yes, yes I have all those things I'm alive. I don't wanna take a pill. Go to Africa go follow a bushman around he's being

> chased by a lion that's stress. Your not going to find a pygmy on Paxil, I'll tell you that right now.
>
> https://youtu.be/_W9JZkHdCdA

The Supra-comedian realises that he has the power for more than just humour. He carries the projections of a disenfranchised society. He is the voice of the struggle of the ordinary man against the patriarchal power although he uses the accepted patriarchal system to change its direction. In a way, the supra comedian is a therapist for his or her society integrating the Jungian principles of confession, elucidation, education and illumination. Jung wrote in 'The Aims of Psychotherapy': 'My aim is to bring about a psychic state in which my patient begins to experiment with his own nature – a state of fluidity, change, and growth where nothing is eternally fixed and hopelessly petrified.' (Jung, CW 16: para. 99).

Similarly, the Supra-comedian has to be fluid to resonate with his ever changing and evolving audience. He gives 'everyman' that he engages with an opportunity to review his life in comfortable, non-confrontational events, and to find his own understanding of the changes that are occurring. The present contradictory nature of the political-social-economic systems can confine the individual's development instead of enhancing it. The Supra-comedian announces these dilemmas and authenticates their existence. His role by has social, political and personal associations to it. Without his social role he would be an entertainer even on a greater and higher scale, but nevertheless without the developmental influence socially, collectively and individually. The Supra-comedian is identifiable through his playful nature as the most gifted of all comedians, but he must be authentic. He must be true to his onstage personality, or he will lose effect.

While society is becoming increasingly cerebral in its evolution, it needs a mirror to reflect its core issues, changes and challenges. The comedian can make observation and analysis of situations, which cannot be made by an individual who is being navigated by social and personal requirements. It is the comedian who stands on the periphery of society and comments. His material and thinking is counter-cultural. He disintegrates and reintegrates structures, religion, social norms, ethical boundaries inter and intra-personal relationships, by picking topical social issues to re-contextualise into a humorous anecdote. While disturbing all these elements, he in turn disrupts his own psychic system, which he evaluates at the same time; hence he can activate the individuation process.

### 5.3. *Supra -Jokes, Alchemy and the Transcendent Function*

The creation of Supra-jokes can also be regarded from the perspective of alchemy and transformation. This approach to humour is radically different from that of Freud and the post-Freudians, who regard jokes as a defence mechanism; as something retrospective and looking backwards, rather than as something that can transform the life of an individual or his society. Jung defined the transcendent function as 'the cooperation of conscious reasoning with the data of the unconscious' (Jung, CW 18: para. 1554). In his view, 'this function progressively unites the opposites' (Jung, CW 18: para. 1554). He also argues that this psychological process 'facilitates the transition from one attitude to another' (Jung CW6: para. 828).

Essentially, the Supra-joke performs 'the transcendent function'. For instance, when one is torn between opposites, one has to transcend them. One has to transcend one's conflicts to accommodate the opposing forces in life; to make them work for you rather than against you. It is a decision-making process, and it is vital to the process of individuation. Without the transcendent function, people would be torn between the extremes, forever unable to make a choice, particularly in a complex situation. It is the expression of the comedian's own collective unconscious, along with the audience and their collective unconscious that pushes towards the transcendent mechanism in-joke form, which is the Supra-joke. As Jung suggested:

> From the activity of the unconscious there now emerges a new content, constellated by thesis and antithesis in equal measure and standing in a compensatory relation to both. It thus forms the middle ground on which the opposites can be united...............the ego, however, torn between thesis and antithesis, finds in the middle ground its own counterpart, its sole and unique means of expression, and it eagerly seizes on this in order to be delivered from its division.
> (Jung CW 6: para. 825)

Jung also notes that the transcendent function is linked to the alchemical, the transformative process:

> If the mediatory product remains intact, it forms the raw material for a process not of dissolution but of construction, in which thesis and antithesis both play their part. In this way it becomes a new content that governs the whole attitude, putting an end to the division and forcing the energy of the opposites into a common channel............... The standstill is overcome and life can flow on with renewed power towards new goals time and dissolution; and its configuration by the opposites ensures its sovereign power over all the psychic functions.
> (CW6, para. 827).

The 'mediatory product' Jung mentions is the controversial material which would later become the joke. In Jung's view, the necessity to expose the conflicts, and then unite the opposites, comes automatically from the unconscious. It is as if the unconscious detects the problematic areas, and offers solutions in the form of creative activity. The comedian with his unique perspective wrestles with the two opposing views that he is able to observe. His painful contemplation, anxieties and personal vulnerabilities are woven in the fabric of the Supra-joke, which is the vehicle for the transcendent function. When delivered, it transforms the attitude of society towards a particular social issue. The job of the comedian is to be transformational; and the Supra-joke is socially transformational as well.

The birth of a joke (and particularly the Supra-joke) is also an alchemical process. Jung did not regard the alchemical process literally. (6.2.1)

## *5.4. Comedy as Alchemical Composition*

Metaphorically speaking, live comedy is, to some extent, an alchemical composition. Jung defines the alchemical process as 'a process of chemical transformation', which consists of four stages: *melanosis* (blackening), *leucosis* (whitening), *xanthosis* (yellowing) and *iosis* (reddening) (CW 12: para. 333). The goal, in the writings of different medieval authors, is either the white or red tincture, the philosopher's stone, the panacea, golden glass or malleable glass (CW12: para. 335). The form and shape of the final substance does not matter, however, because – as Jung and von Franz argue – alchemical transformation is a metaphor for the process of individuation.

The key argument of this thesis is that stand-up performance is a process towards individuation for the comedian. Comedians may be said to be addicted to showing they are individual, unique and separate and the heightened mental states that come with it. Individuation may come from their resonating with the audience during the performance when the audience in turn has resonated with them creating an oceanic feeling of connectedness. The state of euphoria is pivotal to individuation. Moreover, Jung argues, individuation – like alchemical process itself – is a seemingly unending and interminable process: 'the way is not straight but appears to go in circles. […] the process of development proves on close inspection to be cyclic or spiral' (CW12 : para. 34).

This can certainly be applied to stage performances because the comedian changes in the process of interacting with the audience. The comedian's individuation happens in dialogue with the audience. The comedian is addicted to the stage because the individuation process is interminable. To use the alchemical metaphor – to make something from nothing gives the comedian a sense of vitality. The comedian reconnects with the unconscious. The creative urge impacts both his physical and psychological energies. This causes a sense of euphoria in the comedian.

Euphoria has a dual effect. The audience expects to laugh and this predominantly occurs through receiving a new emotional perspective on the world – which, by definition, presupposes engagement into intra-psychic exchange with the comedian. Because of the interactive nature of the process, to the comedian it feels as if there is a union of energies.

Alchemy is a powerful metaphor to use in relation to the live creative process. For the comedian, the gold is the joke. The alchemical process only occurs when the comedian successfully relates to the audience. The comedian's material has to make sense to the audience and to appeal to everybody in order for the whole of the audience to laugh. The material has to be pertinent to that audience. It has to relate to their immediate understanding of the world. The audience becomes one, it becomes a chorus; it becomes united in their understanding and acceptance of the joke. The task of the comedian is to unite the audience and to ensure that it is not fragmented. The joke creating a means of unity in itself is the comedy gold.

This is how this metaphor unravels: several ingredients are needed for the creation of comedy. These ingredients are the comedian's personality, the energy drive, the warm attitude towards the audience and the accessibility of language - all of which are then united in the joke and the performance. The American comedian Roseanne explains how this kind of creative impulse works: 'It's just trying to put everything in its place. I think that's what we comedians try to do – to organise the world according to what we feel is right' (Ajaye, 2002: 189).

The comedian's personality and his confidence are probably the most important ingredients in the alchemical process because of his appearance and behaviour on stage depends on whether the audience will like him. Whether the connection between him and the audience will be established at all. Being on stage for the comedian is almost like a child attending a new school. It is about establishing your position in a new social hierarchy and making a connection with a group of new people. It is also about psychologically, and even physically coping with this new, complex situation.

During the performance the comedian organises the audience; he is in control. He unites the world around him and weaves its elements into something new. He re-constructs the space around themselves and thus, metaphorically, re-creates the world. This is a complex and fragile process because anything can emotionally influence a comedian before a performance, and he will come on stage anxious, angry or tense, which means that he might start taking his anger out on the audience. As far as the public image is concerned, the comedian's task is two-fold – to establish his position both among the comedic brotherhood and amongst the audience.

The American psychiatrist Silvano Arieti uses the metaphor of alchemy to describe human creativity in three stages, which corresponds to my three-stage process ('before', 'during', 'after') of live creativity: 'For the primary process, all that glitters is gold. It will be the labour of the secondary process to discover that all that glitters is not gold. The tertiary process will do at least one of the two things: either it will create a new class of glittering objects, or, by bestowing the glittering on other substances, will beautify them artistically, as gold can do (Arieti, 1980: 453).

Thom F. Cavalli writes about the essential connection between humour and alchemy: '… an ounce of humour is good for the soul. A well-crafted joke cracks open a truth we've all known but were unwilling to openly admit. This element of humour is a function of the trickster' (Cavalli, 2002: 86). To this Cavalli adds that 'humour has a way of turning situations upside down and thereby creating new connections. Sometimes the alchemical vessel needs a good shaking to break up the mindless routines that drain its lifeblood. Laugh with, not at, your habitual way of doing things' (2002: 202).

A phrase by itself is not necessarily funny – what makes it funny is the way it is delivered and the way the audience accepts it. The timing of the delivery is also important. The material should be easily digestible. The joke consists of the juxtaposition of the old theme with something new. The comedian has to be conscious of the audience all the time and to adjust his delivery to the audience's mood. It is only on stage, at one given moment, that he can change something in his material.

The comedian as alchemist takes everyday material (*prima materia*) and translates it into a modern language that is simple enough to be understood by the audience. In his interview with Larry Wilde, Woody Allen emphasises the point that an alchemical unity between the performer, the material and the audience is more important for the success of the venture than a perfect text. He says:

> Just don't make the mistake of falling into the material trap. To the degree you are a funny person, that's how much you'll succeed … not what kind of material you have. When I first became a comedian, I thought, gee, I write funny material, I bet I could get up and just read this to people and they would laugh. I tried that. I took the sheets of paper out in the nightclub and it meant nothing to the audience. They wanted something else entirely. What they want is an intimacy with the person. They want to like the person and find the person funny as a human being. The biggest trap comedian's fall into is trying to get by on the basis of their material. That's just hiding behind the jokes. It's not getting out in front of the audience and opening themselves up. It's all so ephemeral. Such a thin line of luck and intangibles. There is

> no real advice anybody can give on to what to do to become a comedian. The whole thing is such a rare combination of hereditary and environment and the audience that night and the temperature and the headlines in the papers and…
>
> (Wilde, 2000: 27-28)

Live creative processes can be regarded as on-stage individuation – the comedian's personal development can only happen in alchemical union with the audience. At the same time, the connection with the audience should not be fake otherwise the performer will not achieve the addictive feeling of elation that makes him seek encounter, with the audience over and over again. His task is to capture the alchemical golden moment. His relationship with the audience must ring true, both to him and the audience.

The on-stage individuation process gives the comedian an illusion of alchemical wholeness, a feeling of bliss and happiness. Sherry Salman writes that, in Jungian psychology, the notion of 'contradictory opposites lying side by side, albeit partially repressed, revisions our picture of mental health, and relativizes feelings of inferiority and pathology. Wholeness rather than perfection is the goal' (Young-Eisendrath and Dawson, 2002: 67).

United with the audience because he managed to capture its mood and say something that is relevant for the 'common people', the performer feels temporarily whole and happy. During the performance, comedians achieve temporary glimpse of wholeness, which they miss when they come off stage. They were 'at one' with the audience, and they want to recreate this state of unity, understanding and acceptance. As they go off stage, the feeling of elation dies, and they go back to feeling inadequate. This addictiveness to stage points at the compulsive element of the short-lived individuation process, the compulsive nature of which can lead to individuation.

In my recent interview with the British stand-up comedian Sean Meo that took place on 13.03.13, I asked him about his creative process and his motivation to go on stage. The key words he used in his reply were: power, addiction, fame, fortune and money. He kept saying that creativity starts at the basics and it is a very simple process: it is all about getting a piece of paper with nothing on it, writing a few lines on it, reading it out loud and making the audience laugh. Meo compares the process of creating jokes to 'being in a cave full of dark material trying to find nuggets'. This is about the alchemical process as well – making something out of nothing; transforming dark matter into something more valuable.

Meo also mentions that, although challenging, this is a very emotionally satisfying process. It gives one 'sense of well-being' because 'you might fuck up in a lot of areas of life' but stage always feels good and addictive. He also says that, although, he often cannot focus his attention when dealing with other areas of his personal and professional life, he always manages to focus on ensuring a good performance. He says that he just loves this process – for him, it is like a drug, he compares addiction to stage to 'needing a fix'. This includes the audience response and the feeling of power over the audience. He feels both happy and privileged to do that.

Stand-up comedy is different from any other form of art because the change from love to absence of positive (or even any!) reaction may happen in a matter of seconds. The comedian does not know when this happens, or even what causes it. The atmosphere in the audience is always electric, and easily swayed by the smallest and most insignificant incidents.

The performance is the most intense stage of the comedian's creative process. It triggers a range of inter and intra-psychic processes. Moreover, these processes are often closely linked, and indistinguishable from each other, because interaction with the audience is direct, explicit and dynamic. The comedian's emotional and intellectual reactions are directly shaped and influenced by the audience's reaction. For the comedian, live performance is a good opportunity for the comedian to form a connection with the audience, and thus individuate. Jung defines the individuation process as driven by the self – the centre of the personality. He writes in '*Psychological Types*':

> In general [individuation] is the process by which individual beings are formed and differentiated; in particular, it is the development of the psychological *individual* as a being distinct from the general, collective psychology. Individuation, therefore, is a process of *differentiation*, having for its goal the development of the individual personality.
>
> (CW6: para. 757)

However, individuation does not mean being separating oneself entirely from society, but identifying one's idiosyncrasies and as a separate but integrated being. This process is about becoming yourself yet remaining embedded on your community and giving something back to it:

> Individuation is always to some extent opposed to collective norms, since it means separation and differentiation from the general and a building up of the particular – not a particularity that is *sought out,* but the one that is already ingrained in the psychic constitution. The opposition to the collective norm, however, is only apparent, since closer examination shows that the individual standpoint is not *antagonistic* to it but only *differently oriented.* The individual way can

never be directly opposed to the collective norm, because the opposite of the collective norm can only be another, but contrary, norm. [...] Individuation, therefore, leads to a natural esteem for the collective norm, but the orientation is exclusively collective the norm becomes increasingly superfluous and morality goes to pieces. The more a man's life is shaped by the collective norm, the greater is his individual immorality.

(CW6: para. 761)

This is pertinent for our analysis of inter-and intra-psychic processes that occur on stage. The performer goes on stage in order to understand himself, to assert and affirm his or her personal narrative. The comedian Garry Shandling explains that the live creative process is cathartic and life-changing for the performer:

...I think it's incredibly cathartic for me. I think it still helps me find who I am. I've honestly had my therapist say to me, 'The same way you are on stage, you should be able to deal with your life like that'. Which is, if you have somebody heckle you, you don't just stop and complain, you just take care of it. And he said that's how you have to live your life. So I think it's not unusual for actors or comedians to use the stage as a way of feeling free and good about their lives and in the moment. It's an interesting experience. Am I making any sense?

(Shandling, 2002: 207)

On the one hand, a solo performance certainly feeds the 'individual' part of the individuation process. On the other hand, one cannot go on stage and talk about one's problems as if it were a therapy session – regardless of what the audience thinks. 'Being yourself' is not necessarily funny. Individuation is not a selfish process. Linking to the society – and the audience – is a challenge. Personal transformation can only happen in close dialogue with the community and society.

The comedian's individuation can only take place in dialogue with the audience. The comedian Jerry Seinfield expresses a similar view when he says that the comedian's long-term goal is to 'become yourself' (Ajaye, 2002: 198). This is not easy because

...as human being, you are always changing. There's always others things that you want to talk about, and feel you're able to talk about, but I don't believe in searching for it. That leads to hooks and personas instead of human beings and three-dimensional people on stage, which I believe an audience enjoys seeing more than anything else. So I would say a person should write everything that they think about, and they'll naturally enjoy talking about a percentage of these things. Then they'll naturally start to edit out those things they don't feel comfortable about. But that takes time.

(Ajaye, 2002: 200)

Individuation, however, is not only personal – it is also social. The audience individuates together with the comedian. The alchemical process certainly concerns both sides. Members of the audience may have a particular thought pattern or a set of rigid ideas. The task of the comedian is to challenge these rigid ideas as well as any conformity and tendency towards artificial 'normality' the audience may have.

The alchemy of individuation, taking place during a live comedic performance is a two-way process during which the comedian and the audience alter each other psychologically as well as challenge each other's personal, political and social views. The flow of the material originates in the comedian, then is absorbed by the audience, and then is re-absorbed by the comedian in a changed way. The end of the process alters the original material altered to suit both the performer and the audience. The comedian's creativity, and the audience's ability to be receptive, play a key roles in the success of the venture.

Thus, the magical connection with the audience, which ensures the successful oscillation and transformation of material, forms the base of any successful comedian's performance. For instance the American comedian Shelley Berman explains that one should always look out for changes in the mood of the audience: 'You go out and tell the jokes, but you know from the first minutes a little bit more about the audience you are going to play to. You can tell, but the joke itself is not a barometer. You get an attitude, but that does not help things, it does not change things. It will determine the way in which you will execute some of your work but it does not determine the words you'll use or the language' (Wilde, 2000: 88).

Jung concept of the container and the contained, developed by Winnicott into his principle of 'holding' is associated with a marriage can be aligned with the comedy club setting. The container is the Comedy Club, with its inherent structure, including comedians, which, as Jung tells us, 'seeks harmony and unity', whereas the contained is the audience seeking integration (CW 17: paras. 332-333).

Esther Harding writes about the container and the contained: '… there is need of a vessel to contain the materials that must be fused together and transformed. These terms – vessel, material, fusing, transforming – are all alchemistic in origin' (Harding, 1973: 422). Harding also writes that medieval alchemists looked for ways of uniting the materials, from which the 'immortal stone' was to be created. The materials were falling apart, and the alchemists needed a vessel, or a metaphor of a vessel, in order to bring them together:

> They realised that they needed a means to join the constituents of their stone in such a way that they could never again be separated. As their custom was – they were often called natural philosophers – they looked around in nature to see whether they could not uncover there a secret way of uniting things and to adapt it to their purposes. They found various examples of such a process, three of which impressed them especially, indeed fascinated them; that is, these processes became to them symbols simply showing forth the unseen workings in the unconscious. They meditated on these natural transformations, trying especially to imitate them in their art, seeking thus to produce the miraculous effects they desired. These phenomena were the hatching of a chick, the baking of bread or cake, and the marriage of male and female.
>
> (1973: 422)

The alchemical individuation, the result of which is live creativity, is a complex, unpredictable and intense process. Humour enlightens by challenging the stale concepts. It is almost as if the comedian is in an intense state of anxiety with the audience, who as the symbolic mother maybe disapproving. The comedian knows that he might be attacked, which will involve thinking on one's feet and reacting instinctively. The inexperienced comedian is ill-prepared for these moments of attack. He or she has not fully established the performance rhythm; has a lack of understanding of his or her personality; and is unsure about how to shield himself, either psychologically or verbally, from the emotional attack coming from the audience. By contrast, the experienced performer has built-in mechanisms to instinctively protect himself from attacks of various kinds, including attacks on his own personality or material. He knows his rhyme, and is flexible in delivering his material. He is also confident in his ability to manipulate the audience and to respond to it, as well as in his stage persona (which must incorporate parts of his own character). Any seasoned performer has experienced most responses and therefore knows how to react to this particular type of audience.

## 5.5. *The Comedian as a Trickster and the Alchemical Transformation*

The comedian publicly exposes social deformities, political unrest and cultural anomalies within a framework that has been encouraged and sanctioned by society. As such, he or she performs the function of the trickster.

The figure of the trickster is an embodiment of the polar opposites of nature and morality. He can represent the divine and bestial, obscene and decent, violent and tender, dismissive and uncaring, loving and hating all these conflicting attributes can be contained within one individual. He is the epitome of the human condition and, when explored in exaggerated form it creates tension and humour. The audience's reaction to both him and his exploits 'is prevailingly one of laughter tempered by awe' (Radin, 1969: xxiv). Radin also adds that 'if we laugh at him, he grins at us. What happens to him happens to us.' (1969: xxv).

The comedian and a trickster principle, has the potential to expose the inferior function of the audience, which Von Franz states is, 'the fourth door of your room is where angels can come in but also devils!' (Von Franz, 1979: 82). Jung reminds us that in medieval history, there is a description of the devil as *simia dei* (the ape of God), which encompasses the playfulness of its meaning. It is within that unconscious realm that the archetype of the devil dwells who is not only a representation of evil, but as a playful shape-shifter, 'half-animal, half divine' who can tease the individual into the grip of the shadow.' (CW 9/I: para. 255).

The trickster is the reflection of our inner world, the world of the unconscious. Radin says that the trickster 'can only become meaningful and intelligible'; if the audience attempts, 'to solve his problems inward and outward' (Radin, 1969: xxiv). Members of the same audience will laugh at different aspects of a comedian's material. For each person, there is a different realisation, and each decade delivers a new approach to comedy, just as different cultures laugh at different aspects of the same joke (Jung CW16: para. 323).

Members of the audience can relate to the archetype of the trickster who raises issues in his/her relationships. It is in the humour of the telling of the intimate events between the comedian and their spouse, in particular, that the audience finds transference.

## *5.6. Conclusion*

In conclusion there is superior stand-up comedian who conveys the transformational message and the incisive joke, which in its own right creates a disturbing unique and significant affect on the audience. Its power may not be immediately recognisable, except for those who are prepared to participate in the enjoyment of the insightful material and its master.

This process is a representation or carrier of the collective or individual member of the audience's unconscious conflicts. The audience member may temporarily need to see the comedian as a saviour in order for both transference and conscious recognition of their projections to occur, which can lead to the activation of the transcendent function.

# CHAPTER 6

## CREATIVITY AND THE COMEDIAN

The comedian is constantly creative and is updating his material whilst live on stage. His jokes are born in action. Creativity of this specific 'active' kind is the key ingredient of the comedian's performance. It is also related to the comedian's relationship with the audience. The audience becomes the performer's supplier of attention and love, and the comedian's behaviour depends on the audience's readiness to supply him with positive emotional reactions. The absence of these reactions tends to colour the comedian's creativity with a tinge of aggression and anger. This chapter analyses the nature and genesis of the comedian's 'live' creativity. It will compare Freudian and Jungian definitions of creativity and determine their relevance for our analysis of live comedy.

*6.*
### *6.1. Comedic Creativity from a Freudian View*

Freud discussed creativity in a number of his works in which he psychoanalysed famous painters as well as works of literature. The idea was to expose the personal, sublimated content hidden in the work of art. Freud defines sublimation as 'conversion of psychical instinctual force into various forms of activity' (Freud, 2002: 22). For instance, in his essay about Leonardo Da Vinci, '*Leonardo Da Vinci: a Memory of His Childhood*', he links Da Vinci's childhood memories to the imagery he would later generate as an artist. In this essay Freud is confident that psychoanalytic techniques of analysing imagery can be used to fill the gaps in our knowledge of the artists' psychobiography. For instance, he argues that Da Vinci's dream of being visited by a vulture can be analysed and explained:

> ………as we now posses in the techniques of psychoanalysis excellent methods for helping us to bring this concealed material to light, we may venture to fill in the gap in Leonardo's life story by analysing his childhood fantasy. […]

> If we examine with the eyes of a psychoanalyst Leonardo's phantasy of the vulture, it does not appear strange for long. We seem to recall

> having come across the same sort of thing in many places, for example, in dreams; so that we may venture to translate the phantasy from its own special language into words that are generally understood. The translation is then seen to point out to an erotic content.
>
> (2002: 33/76)

Jung criticised this approach for being too reductive. The idea that all aesthetic and spiritual results of creative activity in human beings have their roots in the basic side of human nature did not appeal to him. Jung wrote that, in his analysis of dreams and creative activity, Freud confused the two things that should not be confused: signs and symbols. He substituted symbols with signs. Signs being an indicator of activity or future activity and symbols being representation of a type of behaviour rather that the actual behaviour. As Jung states: ' A sign is always less than the thing it points to, and a symbol is always more than we can understand at first sight'. (CW15 Man and Literature 1966)

Comedian Arthur Smith asked:
'I wonder if there are enough traffic cones in the country for every student to own one?'

For Smith the cone was a symbol of fun for the student, it represented being able to relinquish responsibility and have a foolish time. If it were a sign it would mean that wearing the traffic cone should avoid him as cones denote giving space to area, or cordoning off an area.

Moreover, Freud saw the creative work of art as an escape from reality and a flight into the artificial world of phantasy as an abnormal gesture. For him, an artist is akin to a neurotic in his denial of reality. The artist is therefore spending time on something that can be regarded as the psychological remnants of childish play. For instance, Freud wrote:

> An artist is once more in rudiments an introvert, not far removed from neurosis. He is oppressed by excessively powerful instinctual needs. He desires to win power, wealth, fame and the love of women; but he lacks the means of achieving these satisfactions. Consequently, like any other unsatisfied man, he turns away from reality and transfers all his interest, and his libido too, to the wishful constructions of his life of phantasy, whence the path might lead to neurosis.
>
> (SE, XVI: 376)

This essentially means that Freud sublimated human creativity to infantile greed, sexual impulses and desire for power. The artist is a childish dreamer who turns away from reality because he is not mature enough to accept it. Instead, he loses himself in play and phantasy.

To counter this radical view, Jung argues in '*Analytical Psychology and Poetry*':

> The essential thing in Freud's reductive method is to collect all the clues pointing to the unconscious background, and then through the analysis and interpretation of this material, to reconstruct the elementary instinctual process. Those conscious contents which gave rise to a clue to the unconscious background are incorrectly called *symbols* by Freud. These are not true symbols, however, since according to his theory they have merely the role of *signs* or *symptoms* of the subliminal processes.
>
> (CW15: para. 105).

Freud's view of humour is directly linked to his concept of creativity. From his view, jokes exist as outlets for human instincts – and particularly for sexual and antisocial urges. For instance, when one unconsciously wants to insult another person – one can transform his aggressive feelings into a joke. Thus, a negative emotion is transformed into a form of creative activity, and the content is supplied by the situation itself. The insult does not take place because of propriety and aesthetic culture, but the psyche still seeks pleasure – and it reshapes this pleasure into a more socially acceptable form: 'Let us now suppose, however, that the possibility is presented of deriving a good joke from the material of the words and thoughts used for the insult – the possibility, that is, of releasing pleasure from other sources which are not obstructed by the same suppression' (Freud, 2001: 136).

The Freudian theoretical framework is apt when applied to the stand-up as comedians act out their aggression towards other people on stage. For instance, a comedian may subconsciously harbour murderous intentions towards his father or fight a powerful urge to rape a woman. Instead of doing these horrendous things, he fantasises about them – and then sublimates these fantasies in his material.

Contentious and literal as it sounds, there are certainly examples of psychological literalism and direct treatment of material on the comedic circuit. For instance, the American comedian Louie Anderson says in an interview: 'I think a lot of my act is working out the problems I've had with my family, my father in particular. And I think it really makes a difference. And I think it's healthy and helpful' (Ajaye, 2002: 54).

On the other hand, Freud's view of humour and creativity is still reductive and simplistic. He takes creativity back to sexuality and the Oedipus complex. When comedians joke about their parents – particularly the father – they can be said to be expressing their aggression towards the powerful parent. However, it is not as simple as this. The audience does not come to listen to a man moaning about his parental problems. The stage is not just a therapeutic setting. Live comedy is the kind of creative process that engages the audience directly. It is transformational both personally and socially. This transformational process is almost alchemical in that the comedian converts his issue into something that has wider resonance than just 'Oedipal moaning'.

Live comedy has to seduce and attract the audience – its aim is to make a connection with the listener. This involves transcendence of the personal and creation of an intermediate product – something 'more general' to which the audience can relate.

Jaques Lacan's idea of three psychological orders, Imaginary, Symbolic and Real is also interesting as far as psychoanalytic approaches to creativity are concerned. The Imaginary order directly relates to the creative life of man. It is opposed to the Symbolic and the Real.

The Imaginary is the first of the three orders. It comprises imagination, feelings, dreams, deception, creativity and seduction. Laplanche and Pontalis write that the concept of the imaginary can be grasped initially 'by the reference to one of Lacan's earliest theoretical developments of the theme of the *mirror stage*. In his work on this topic, Lacan brought forward the idea that the ego of the human infant – as a result, in particular, of its biological prematurity – is constituted on the basis of the image of the counterpart (specular ego)' (Laplanche and Pontalis, 1988: 210). From the intersubjective point of view, this is a dyadic relationship in which the subject is merged with the object – with the mother or any other primary carer. This relationship is 'based on – and captured by – the image of a counterpart (erotic attraction, aggressive tension). For Lacan, a counterpart (i.e. another who is me) can only exist by virtue of the fact that the ego is originally another' (1988: 201).

The realm of the Imaginary is pre-Oedipal; it is a happy time for the subject because he or she can experience *jouissance* (or pleasure and enjoyment – it stands for Freud's pleasure principle). Pleasure comes from 'owning' and being at one with the object – the mother. As Dylan Evans explicates:

> (……)the prohibition of *jouissance* (the pleasure principle) is inherent in the symbolic structure of the language, which is why '*jouissance* is forbidden to him who speaks, as such' (E, 319). The subject's entry into the symbolic is conditional upon a certain initial renunciation of *jouissance* in the castration complex, when the subject gives up his attempts to be the imaginary phallus for the mother; Castration means that *jouissance* must be refused so that it can be reached on the inverted ladder … of the Law of desire' (E, 324). The symbolic prohibition of

enjoyment in the Oedipus complex (the incest taboo) is thus, paradoxically, the prohibition of something which is already impossible; its function is therefore to sustain the neurotic illusion that enjoyment would be attainable if it were not forbidden. The very prohibition creates desire to transgress it, and *jouissance* is therefore fundamentally transgressive (see S7, ch,15).

(Evans, 1996: 92)

According to Lacan, a human life is punctuated by a series of losses – all reflecting the loss of the primary object that comes with the arrival of the Symbolic order. Lacan designates lack of an object (1996: 96). Meanwhile, the subject is addicted to the time when it could experience *jouissance* without the constraints of the Symbolic order. This is how desire is born. Desire (*desir*) for Lacan is a continuous force experienced compulsively – it is the desire for the (lost) object. Desire, Evans explains, is 'the surplus produced by the articulation of need in demand; 'Desire begins to take shape in the margin in which demand becomes separated from need' (E, 311). Unlike need, which can be satisfied and which then ceases to motivate the subject until another need arises, desire can never be satisfied; it is constant in its pressure, and is eternal. The realisation of desire does not consist in being 'fulfilled', but in the reproduction of desire as such' (1996: 37). In addiction, desire is born out of competition – what makes the object desirable 'is not any intrinsic quality of the thing in itself but simply the fact that it is desired by another' (1996: 38).

Desire is thus addictive and compulsive; it exists as an inexplicable force that takes the subject back to the now non-existent *jouissance* – the pleasure which had been forbidden by the Symbolic order. It can be said, using the Lacanian loss-desire paradigm that the comedian's addiction to stage and to performing is a form of compulsive desire for the audience (the metaphorical mother).
Lacan says:
"Desire full stop is always the desire of the Other. Which basically means that we are always asking the Other what he desires" (*My Teaching*, p.38).

From Lacan's view point the comedian is only successful when he fulfils the 'other''s or 'audience' or 'mother's needs. He cannot exist alone.
The stand-up comedians' main tool is language – which, according to Lacan, is the principal instrument of the Symbolic order. However, they use this tool in a transgressive manner, thereby challenging the symbolic order – the bearer of the law and language. This unusual, creative application of an otherwise standardised and rigid mechanism cause outbursts of laughter in the audience. Like this, comedic language is a paradoxical and self-contradictory (as well as self-renewing) phenomenon.

Using Lacanian terminology and concepts, it is possible to theorise that the (male) comedian cannot escape the Symbolic order, which he joined when he was a boy. There is no way back for the adult man; and he cannot regain the lost *jouissance*. However, he can cause *jouissance* in the audience by verbally challenging the symbolic order (the social order), and thus causing the audience to laugh. The comedian himself does not laugh – he absorbs (via mirroring) the audience's pleasure, which he knows he has caused. Thus, he reclaims and re-experiences the powerful emotions otherwise inaccessible to him, as they had been barred by the Symbolic order. Within the Oedipal paradigm, the comedian does not risk castration because his tool – the spoken word – belongs to the realm of the Symbolic.

However, he finds an alternative way of challenging the symbolic father by mis-using language and therefore undermining its rule-making and law-supporting properties. The law-giving father does not always recognise that the comedian has used his rule-implementing instrument in order to abuse the father. Like this, the comedian engages the 'mother' (audience) in a mutual, incestuous pleasure exchange, and the father cannot recognise the dangers that this exchange implies for himself or the Symbolic order both as the patriarch and the masculine.

It can be said, using Lacan, that the comedian becomes addicted to the process of receiving *jouissance* from the audience. It is as if he has a desire for the audience's reactions, which lead him back to the Imaginary. Therefore, he challenges the symbolic on three different levels: first, by misusing language (thus causing the symbolic to laugh at itself), secondly by provoking an outburst of *jouissance* in the audience; and thirdly by enjoying *jouissance* 'unlawfully' via the audience. The desire to be on stage, receiving attention and feeling your own power, is addictive because one can express one's own creativity, as well as absorb the visible results of the creative process. The American comedian Jerry Seinfield explains in an interview the origins of his desire to become a comedian:

> I was about eight years old. I was sitting on my stoop with a friend of mine. We were having cookies and milk and we were talking and fooling around. I said something really funny and he laughed and spit the cookies and milk all over my face and hair and clothes. And I thought I would like to do this professionally. That moment of getting a laugh is when you know. Everybody has that in their life at some point or other, but when you feel that you can do that it is so powerful and addictive and fun. You just don't want to do anything else.
> (Wilde, 2000: 328)

Humour forces other men to engage with them. It is the best weapon not only comedians but also men per se have for challenging the patriarchal society (or the Symbolic, to use Lacan's term).

Having lost the paradisiacal state of being at one with the object, the artist keeps seeking psychological states in which he can experience it again. Thus, the creative artist rather like a child seeks *jouissance* when he is making a new object – a painting or a text. The creative process itself is very much like the encounter with the imaginary, and therefore generates jouissance for the artist and those consuming the work of art. The value of the work of art lies beyond the Symbolic and leads directly back to the Imaginary.

However, even though certain elements of Lacan's theory can be pertinent for my analysis of the immediate ('live') relationship between the comedian and the audience, overall I regard Lacan's body of theory too constricting, pessimistic and purely reflective. Creativity is bound to have a more positive stance – as a transforming and forward-looking process.

The British psychotherapist Melanie Klein regarded the creative process as inseparable from the impulse to destroy. Thus, in the psychic life of human beings creativity plays reparative and restorative roles. It has to do with guilt that comes with the baby's recognition of its own destructive phantasies and aggressive intentions. Creativity is born out of the fusion of erotic and destructive impulses. The ability to fuse these impulses is a sign of health (1999: 70).

Klein traced the impulse to re-create childhood problems. For instance, she talks about the artist Ruth Kjar, a talented female painter, who felt unhappy and empty. She felt particularly sad about the sale of a painting, which had been previously lent to her by her brother-in-law. She could not bear to look at the blank space on the wall because the empty space on the wall made her feel depressed. It reminded her of her own inner emptiness. Eventually, her husband suggested that she try to paint something on the wall, and she did. Unbelievably, she painted a masterpiece:

> ……the portrait of an old woman and one of her mother. The last two are described by Karen Michaelis as follows: "And now Ruth cannot stop. The next picture represents an old woman, bearing the mark of years and disillusionments. Her skin is wrinkled, her hair faded, her gentle, tired eyes are troubled. […]
>
> The daughter's wish to destroy her mother, to see her old, worn out, marred, is the cause of the need to represent her in full possession of her strength and beauty. By so doing the daughter can allay her own anxiety and can endeavour to restore her mother and make her new through the portrait. In the analyses of children, when the representation of destructive wishes is succeeded by an expression of

reactive tendencies, we constantly find that drawing and painting are used as means to restore people.

(Klein, 1998: 217/218)

Klein then concludes that 'the blank space has been filled' and that Ruth's creativity is clearly the result of her destructive feelings towards the mother. At the same time, Ruth obviously felt guilty about this cruel wish, and found a way to 'restore' the mother she so wanted to annihilate. By painting the portraits, Ruth also wanted to restore herself since her brokenness and emptiness were clearly caused by the dysfunctional mother-daughter relationship.

In another essay, '*Love, Guilt and Reparation*' (1937) Klein expresses the view that feelings of guilt transform, into love on one hand and creativeness on the other. This, she says, is clear when one looks at how small children manifest their creativity. In children, the impulse to create is born out of the oscillation between fear and the ability to manage it; between being in and out of control over one's internal and external reality:

> In children, creative impulses, which have hitherto been dormant awaken and express themselves in such activities as drawing, modelling, building and in speech, which, by means of psychoanalysis fears of various kinds become lessened. These fears had brought about an increase of the destructive impulses, and therefore when fears are diminished, destructive impulses are also lessened. Along with these processes, feelings of guilt and the anxiety about the death of the loved person, with which the child's mind had been unable to cope because they were overwhelming, gradually diminish, become less intense and are then manageable. This has the effect of increasing the child's concern for other people, of stimulating pity and identification with them, and thus love altogether is increased. The wish to make reparation, so intimately bound with up with the concern for the loved one and the anxiety about his death, can now be expressed in creative and constructive ways. In psychoanalysis of adults, too, these processes and changes can be observed.
>
> (1998: 335-6)

In this sense, creativity in adults is no different from children. Mature creativity, from Klein's view, is a paradoxical psychological phenomenon, which, on the one hand, aims at destroying and damaging the object and, on the other, at repairing it through love. The Kleinian child – like the Kleinian adult – sees the world as a source of pleasure and satisfaction on the one hand, and disappointment and pain on the other. The centrepiece, however, is a sense of guilt, which the child experiences when it fantasises about destroying the very object that sustains his life and gives him pleasure. According to Klein, creativity is a later term for reparation of an object on which one depends for physical and emotional security. The baby recreates the object, which it mentally destroyed or attempted to destroy in a fit of narcissistic vulnerability, which has to be repaired in order to progress.

Examples of this attitude, as well as its link with live comedy, could be found in a number of comedians' interviews. For instance, in an interview with *The Guardian*, Frankie Boyle speaks about love and emotions in a rude and dismissive way. The interviewer, Rosanna Greenstreet, asks him a series of questions to which he gives short answers. When asked, 'Have you ever said "I love you" and not meant it?', Boyle replies, 'Only to my children'. Other examples of being embarrassed about expressing emotions include:

> **What do you owe to your parents?**
> Realistically, about five grand of babysitting money.
> **What or who is the greatest love of your life?**
> My kids. I think kids deliver on all the stuff romantic love only promises. I am in love every day.
> **What does love feel like?**
> It feels like a belt around my throat.
> **How often do you have sex?**
> I regularly have sex with someone I hate – or masturbation, as I call it.
> (http://www.guardian.co.uk/lifeandstyle/2012/aug/24/frankie-boyle-comedian)

The struggle between creativeness and destructiveness is clearly seen in the comedian's answers. To an extent, they sound crass and insensitive towards the children. At the same time, it is clear that what the interviewee rejects is not the children, or women, but the very idea of love as a state of being emotionally dependent on the other. Inevitably, love involves being vulnerable and potentially rejected or broken. It is much easier to prevent this by rejecting love and emotional dependency altogether. Yet, at the same time, this attitude is potentially destructive for the object. With the object gone, the baby feels lonely, guilty and even more helpless than before it had destroyed it. In this interview, Boyle seems to attack the very people he loves – yet he simultaneously (in fact, within the same line) repairs the damage he does. In his humour, the two processes – destruction and reparation – are almost indistinguishable from each other.

To use Kleinian views on creativity, aggressive humour exists somewhere on the border between creativity and destruction; between the self and the object. It is a war zone in which the bond between the comedian and the audience occurs in the process of oscillation between love and hate; between a desire to connect and a fear of losing yourself. This is confirmed by Bill Hicks, whose angry performances were a testimony to the existence of destructive creativity, in line with Klein's ideas. Andy Fyfe writes:

> Cowboy-booted, chain-smoking Hicks was the most significant American comedian of his generation, the natural successor to Lenny Bruce and Richard Pryor.
>
> He was rude, angry, uncompromising and saw within popular culture a conspiracy to dumb people down so that they could be more easily controlled. He died in 1994, at the age of 32, but still ranks high on most lists of the greatest comics of all time.
>
> (Fyfe, *The Guardian,* 12 May 2010)

Jimmy Carr also articulates this in his book, *The Naked Jape* (2006). He seems to regard the stage as an emotionally dangerous but exciting place, where intense aggression occurs between the comedian and the audience:

> Even if some laughs are bigger than others, there's no grey area in between getting a laugh and getting nothing. Live comedy audiences are ruthless and insatiable. If they smell fear you're done for. And you're only ever as good as your last joke. Not even your last show – your last *joke*. Every comic has a back-pocket full of 'bankers' – the funny lines that always get you out of trouble. But even one of those doesn't buy you very much time – thirty seconds of sympathy before they want the next one.
>
> This sounds brutal and it is. It's no accident that the language of professional comedians is full of violence and death – 'He really killed out there' being the pinnacle of achievement.
>
> (Carr and Greeves, 2006: 115)

Like Boyle and many other comedians, in his jokes Carr also scrutinises the issues of emotional dependency and the aggression associated with it. This is a joke that appears in one of his interviews for *The Mirror:*

> 'I hate those emails where they try to sell you penis enhancements. I got ten just the other day. Eight of them from my girlfriend. It's the two from my mum that really hurt'
> (http://www.mirror.co.uk/tv/tv-news/jimmy-carr-jokes-comedians-40-1323055)

Again, dependency on the object is associated with criticism, violence and emotional tension rather than with acceptance and love. In this case, the emotional and cognitive basis of the joke is rejection. It is a joke about mutual disapproval, dissatisfaction and disappointment. And without ambiguity it leads back to the original object – the mother.

Thus, Klein's link between creativity and guilt, and creativity and destruction, proves to be useful for our discussion of stand-up comedy. Fantasy of destruction provides a distance between the subject and the object; and subsequent reparation keeps the bond between the subject and the object alive. The dual process of creative destruction/reparation is important for the child's psychosocial development, and it is also very clear in the way people create and perceive humour and jokes. In fact, humour, with its existential and psychological edginess and the capacity for causing offence, is the perfect metaphor for the baby's attempt to simultaneously connect with the object and question its dependence on it. Comedians test the audience like the baby tests the mother – 'Let's see if they really love me' and 'Let's test the limits of their love'.

## 6.2. *A Positive View of Creativity in Comedy: Carl Jung, James Hillman, Otto Rank and D.W. Winnicott*

Freudian and post-Freudian theories imply that creativity means survival. The creative person is seen as traumatised and wanting to get rid of the trauma by replaying it in the safe form of a creative act. Freudian theory always attributes the creative power to the parents – they 'produce' the child both physically and psychologically. Thus, any creativity that is born out of the child – and the artist – is reactive rather than proactive. The child is not born with creativity but ends up feeling the need for sublimating the tension caused in him or her by a range of Oedipal issues. Creativity of any sort then becomes a kind of therapy, which, although devoid of a higher ('Godly') purpose, only serves to relieve the artist's psychological pain, as well as to mollify obsessive behaviours.

By contrast, Jung presupposes that creativity exists in human beings regardless of any personal issues experienced by them. Jung sees creativity as a gift from above; as a mark of uniqueness, of being 'chosen'. It originates in the collective rather than the personal unconscious and culminates in the Self. He also has a different view of the 'pain' constituent of creative life. Even though he recognises the pain element of creative existence, he stresses that this pain is an unpleasant but important element of the artist's life. Nothing is born without pain, creative work included.

In his essay about the child archetype, Jung argues that the motifs of abandonment, mistreatment, isolation and hardship of the miraculous child are valuable aspects of personality development Unpleasant feelings are necessary for developing the personality. He writes that 'the child is all that is abandoned, and exposed and at the same time divinely powerful; the insignificant, dubious beginning, and the triumphant end. The "eternal child" in man is an indescribable experience, an incongruity, a handicap, and a divine prerogative; an imponderable that determines the ultimate worth or worthlessness of a personality' (CW9/I: para. 300). Forced into isolation, the child seeks a way out of his miserable existence thus seeking and finding creative solutions to life's problems.

The creative person, who is rooted in his humble beginnings, and of insecurity and angst recreates and re-gathers the core self, the personality centre in the creative act. Thus, although the child's destiny has been pre-determined by gods or God (as it is in Christianity), the miraculous baby still has the right to re-make it's destiny by gathering and organising fragments of his experience. Thus, creativity is an important part of the individuation process.

The creative act, according to Jung, is a force of nature that 'achieves its end either with tyrannical might or with the subtle cunning of nature herself, quite regardless of the personal fate of the man who is its vehicle' (CW15: para. 114). The work of art is a 'living thing implanted in human psyche' (CW15: para. 114).

Interestingly enough, Freud's disciple Otto Rank is closer to Jung than to Freud in his views on creativity. As Rank states,' Jung's collective unconscious stands much closer to the soul-concept..........The soul, an ideology born of belief in immorality, produces new ideologies in order to maintain soul-belief" Like Jung, he thinks that being creative is a spiritual state that takes the artist beyond oral drives and basic needs. In his book *Art and Artist: Creative Urge and Personality Development* (originally published in 1932), Rank asserts that forming of the personality is the first manifestation of the creative impulse (1989: 37). Moreover, Rank – contra to his influential teacher – thinks that creativity has nothing to do with sexuality: '(…) the creative impulse which leads to the liberation of forming of the individual personality – and likewise determines its artistic creativeness – has something positively antisexual in its yearning for independence from organic conditions' (1989: xxiii).

Rank also links the emergence of individual creativity to the gradual development of individualism in the West in modern times:

> The individual artist, whose growth from the creative conception of a god has been sketched out, no longer uses the collective ideology of religion to perpetuate himself, but the personal religion of genius, which is the precondition of any productions by the individualist artist-type. And so we have *primitive art,* the expression of a collective ideology, perpetuated by abstraction which has found its *religious*

expression in the idea of the soul; *Classical* art, based on a *social* art-concept, perpetuated by *idealization*, which has found its purest expression in the conception of beauty; and, lastly, *modern art*, based on the concept of individual genius and perpetuated by concretization, which has found its clearest expression in the personality-cult of the artistic individuality itself.

(1989: 45)

Furthermore, Rank insists that 'in creation the artist tries to immortalize his mortal life' (Rank, 1989: 39). According to him, a work of art is a by-product of a whole range of impulses, including the individualistic desire to assert oneself and to ensure one's separateness from the crowd. One of these impulses is the urge to create one's personality – to be born as a separate person, which is also the urge to follow the 'creative will-principle' that is spiritual in nature. In other words, creativity becomes a form of individualist religion, which brings together the selfish-individualistic and collective aspect of the artist's life. Rank outlined in his analysis of the story of Faust as a symbol of individual creativity 'as it is for the filial era (filial era as the son's unwillingness to fulfil the duty imposed by his father (p46), Faust wins individual immortality through creative action that reconnects him with the community and his humanity. (O. Rank p56 Psychology and the Soul. John Hopkins University Press.1998)

Similarly, Jung regards the work of art as coming from an inexplicable spiritual source. Far from being the direct result of childhood problems, the psychological origins of a work of art are mysterious. Jung insists that the origins of creativity lie deeper than the artist's personal problems – they grow out of the collective unconscious. This living thing is an *autonomous complex,* a split-off part of the psyche. When launched, it can be so powerful that the artist may entirely lose control over his own psyche, and finds himself following the powerful creative impulse. When this happens, the artist's task is to shape and channel the impulse in the right direction and use its might and creative energy. The artist becomes a mere vehicle obeying the power of the creative force.

Moreover, because the impulse is born in the collective and not the personal unconscious, the artist may not recognise it as 'his': 'Depending on its energy charge, it may appear either as a mere disturbance of conscious activities, or a supraordinated authority, which can harness the ego to its purpose' (CW15: para. 115).

This can be related to the experiences of the stand-up performer on stage. Whereas Freud and Lacan are too limited in their views on creativity, Jung allows creativity to remain a force of its own; to live and breathe. Many comedians regard their creative process as something that happens by itself, independently from the performer. For instance, the American stand-up comedian Louie Anderson says:

> I haven't been able to figure out [whether comedy comes out of sadness or pain]. I think that comedy just comes out of you. And I think whatever kind of person you are, that's the kind of comedy that comes out. I think that half of how a joke is formed, is the right mixture of a lot of different things in the individual. It's like ingredients go into you, like maybe a rough childhood, an oversensitive heart, an intelligent mind, and then maybe a defiance and rebellion. And I think all those things go in the right combination, and then they come out as a joke or as a monologue.
>
> (Ajaye, 2002: 54)

Marie-Louise von Frantz writes that 'it is generally the creative artist who creates the future. A civilization, which has no creative people, is doomed. So the person who is really in touch with the future, with the germs of the future, is the creative personality' (Von Franz and Hillman, 1979: 11).

The archetypal psychologist James Hillman wrote extensively on creativity in different aspects of human existence. For instance, in *Re-Visioning Psychology* (1975) he argues that the psyche is creative and that contemporary obsession with 'scientification' of life stifles psychic images and restrains their flow (Hillman, 1992: 2). In *The Myth of Analysis: Three Essays in Archetypal Psychology* (originally published in 1960) Hillman writes that psyche is, in fact, a great creative achievement of human beings (1999: 20). Hillman follows Jung in his assessment of creativity and expands Jung's idea of the 'creative instinct'; the ability of human beings to actively change themselves and their environments. This instinct is not some kind of 'special gift' – it is present in everyone and manifests itself to everyone willing to explore one's own soul. Hillman writes:

> Jung affirmed often enough that the creative instinct is *sui generis* and independent of neurotic psychodynamics. It is not a gift or special grace, and ability, talent or trick. Rather it is that immense energy coming from beyond man's psyche which pushes one to self-dedication via one or another specific medium. Creativity impels devotion to one's person in its becoming through the medium, and it brings with it a sense of helplessness and increasing awareness of its numinous power. Hence our relation to creativity fosters the religious attitude, and our description of it often uses religious language. Our experiences of the force of individuality and its relentless pressure upon each soul to realise its potential are difficult to distinguish from

> experiences of the immanent Gods in their creator roles. For the Gods, too, are ectopsychic, 'beyond' the soul, neither wholly in it nor of it.
>
> (1999: 35-36)

The creation Gods are also the destroying Gods, Hillman adds (1999: 36). This is certainly true of comedic creativity, which is generally more destructive than the creative instinct in other arts. Comedic creativity can be definitely seen as being both positive and negative because during the performance the comedian attacks the audience, the people he uses in his jokes (including his family and spouse) and even himself. In fact, successful comedy is always aggressive. By its very nature, it is a very male art. A number of famous comedians (such as Frankie Boyle and Sam Kinison) have built a career on aggression and controversial behaviour.

Comedians also support the idea that creativity is closely linked to destruction – including self-destruction. The comedian Dana Gould says:

> Firstly, the same brain that makes the good stuff makes the bad stuff. Is it really so shocking that an engine that can propel a car from zero to 100 mph in six seconds can do pretty much the same thing in reverse? Comedians dwell on things. They ponder, stew, obsess and spin out scenarios for comedic effect. The more inventive the mind, the funnier the scenarios. The genius of a great comedian is the ability to stride onstage and make it look like all of those amazing ideas are flowing naturally, in the moment and off-the-cuff. But don't be fooled. A lot of after-hours thought, poured into notebook after notebook, goes into that stuff. Late nights alone with a hyperactive imagination, however, is also when you can get into a lot of trouble.
> (Gould, *The Rolling Stone,* 27 August 2014)

Gould adds that: 'Laughing and screaming are physiological cousins; both used by the body to release anxiety and tension. In terms of comedians, when the chicken-and-egg question of, "which came first, the sad or the funny" is raised, I can, with authority, say that the egg of acute anxiety begat the rubber chicken of inspired hilarity. In other words, I literally laughed to keep from crying. As do so many' (Gould, *The Rolling Stone,* 27 August 2014).

Similarly, speaking about the suicide of Robin Williams, the director Terry Gilliam insists that comedic talent is a miracle and a gift which 'does not come from nothing': 'When the gods gift you with the kind of talent Robin had, there's a price to pay. It comes from deep problems inside. A concern, all sorts of fears. Yet he could always channel those things and turn them into gold. I think that comes with the territory' (Youngs, *BBC News,* 12 August 2014).

Working stand-up comedians often describe their creative process as something that happens against their will by itself. It is the impulse and energy for creating and achieving individuality. For instance, Louie Anderson says in an interview:

> I think comedy just comes out of you. And I think whatever kind of person you are, that's the kind of comedy that comes out. I think that half of how a joke is formed, or how comedy is formed, is the right mixture of a lot of different things in that individual. It's like ingredients go into you, like maybe a rough childhood, an oversensitive heart, an intelligent mind, and then maybe a defiance and rebellion. And I think all those things go in the right combination, and then they come out as a joke or as a monologue.
> 
> (Ajaye, 2002: 54)

Speaking about the source of creative inspiration, the famous British comedian John Cleese says in an interview to an online magazine *Inc*:

> 'Creativity is not a talent; it's a way of operating'
> (http://www.inc.com/samuel-bacharach/leadership-tips-from-5-stand-up-comics.html).

Meanwhile, the British actor and comedian Ricky Gervais argues that it is important to find your own outlet of creativity, and furthermore importantly

> "You should bring something into the world that wasn't in the world before. It doesn't matter what that is. It doesn't matter if it's a table or a film or gardening--everyone should create. You should do something, then sit back and say, 'I did that,'" which supports Hillman's idea of the independent psychic force underlying all specific talents:
> (http://www.inc.com/samuel-bacharach/leadership-tips-from-5-stand-up-comics.html).

For Jung

> ' The creative process, so far as we are able to follow it at all, consists in the unconscious activation of an archetypal image, and in elaborating and shaping this image into the finished work. By giving it shape, the artist translates it into the language of the present, and so makes it possible for us to find out way back to the deepest springs of life.'
> 
> (Jung C.G. CW15. 1922:130.)

Whereas for Rank

> 'man's role as creator of culture, as does his ceaseless striving for new expressive means and symbols for myriad forms of self and of individualism in general;............... with the unfolding of the filial era, takes on the role of earthly, ephemeral, mortal soul-part, which can be immortalised in every changing symbolic expression'.
>
> (Rank, 1998:56)

This view also echoes Donald Winnicott's position regarding the nature of human creativity: it is a universal force that can manifest itself in a variety of forms depending on the individual as well as the environment. The important moment, however, is to find out what one's specific talent is. Then one can start utilising the powerful creative force that dwells in the psyche.

Some comedians like to explore scandalous subjects. For instance, Jimmy Carr has delivered a range of examples of aggressive and insensitive comedy. One of them was a joke about soldiers wounded in Afghanistan and Iraq:

> 'Say what you like about those servicemen amputees from Iraq and Afghanistan, but we are going to have a fucking Paralympic team in 2012'
> (http://www.guardian.co.uk/culture/2009/nov/05/jimmy-carr-paralympics-joke).

The joke did not go well with the public, and Carr ended up issuing a public apology.

The American comedian Sam Kinison also boasts an array of rude and insensitive material. This includes a joke about hungry children in developing countries:

> 'I'm like anyone else on this planet — I'm very moved by world hunger. I see the same commercials, with those little kids, starving, and very depressed. I watch those kids and I go, 'Fuck, I know the FILM crew could give this kid a sandwich!' There's a director five feet away going, 'DON'T FEED HIM YET! GET THAT SANDWICH OUTTA HERE! IT DOESN'T WORK UNLESS HE LOOKS HUNGRY!!!'
> (http://www.comedyontap.com/jokes/kinison/skjokes.html).

Probably the best (or the worst!) examples of insensitive comedy remains Jerry Sadowitz's infamous joke about Nelson Mandela. The joke was a result of a bet with his friend and fellow comedian, Nick Revell. Sadowitz came on stage and said:

> 'Nelson Mandela, what a cunt. Terry Waite, fucking bastard. I dunno, you lend some people a fiver, you never see them again.'
> (http://www.gqmagazine.co.uk/comment/articles/2010-02/02/james-mullinger-jerry-sadowitz).

Aggression and destruction, however, do not have to be always aimed at other people – in live comedy there is a good deal of self-aggression and aggression aimed at the nearest and dearest. A good example of this is Stewart Lee talking about his adoption and finding his real parents. 'I wonder whether I ought to get in touch with them, just out of courtesy. But on the other hand I read this book about it-and loads of people get in touch, and think it's going to be really great, and their mothers say, 'I had to go through the effort of getting rid of you in the first place, and now you've opened it all up again.' (p84 Ha Bloody Ha – W. Cook 1994)

Jung writes extensively in *Psychology and Literature*, *On the relation of Analytical Psychology to Poetry* and *'"Ulysses": a Monologue'* about the social uses of creativity. Quite in line with Jung's vision of creativity and its social significance (via the collective unconscious), Lawrence E. Mintz argues in his article 'Stand-up Comedy as Social and Cultural Mediation', that comedy is an inherently social phenomenon, and its roots are 'entwined with rites, rituals and dramatic experiences'. It is also 'the purest public communication, performing essentially the same social and cultural roles in practically every known society, past and present' (Mintz, 1985: 71).

The stand-up creative process may be inspired by childhood problems, but the urge to be on stage has many more layers and goes beyond psychoanalytic views on creativity. Comedy can be about revealing oneself – but it is also about transforming oneself as well as acting out of altruistic impulses. Far from being a confessional act in which the audience plays the role of the obedient, passive and loving mother, stand-up incorporates elements of intellectual, emotional and social transformation. Winnicott's theory of creativity was adjacent to his theories of personality development. A work of art is seen as a symbol of the artist's existence as an individual personality. Transitional objects – blankets, teddies and dolls – constitute the first expression of imagination at work; they are the first 'created', 'imagined' objects. Winnicott continues in *Playing and Reality* (1971):

> When symbolism is employed the infant is already clearly distinguishing between fantasy and fact, between inner objects and external objects, between primary creativity and perception. But the term transitional object, according to my suggestion, gives room for the process of becoming able to accept difference and similarity. I think there is use for a term for the root of symbolism in time, a term that describes the infant's journey from the purely subjective to

> objectivity; and it seems to me that the transitional object (piece of blanket, etc.) is what we see of this journey of progress towards experiencing.
>
> (Winnicott, 1992: 3-7)

Winnicott argues that living creatively is an important part of healthy living. A healthy individual is an individual who has the ability to express himself, it is not just a trait in uniquely talented people. For Winnicott, creativity encompasses a range of everyday activities including a garden, a costume or a meal cooked at home (1999: 65). The creative impulse is present in anyone – baby, child, adolescent, adult, old man or woman (1999: 69). In Winnicott's view, in his analysis of the great artists and authors, Freud and his disciples divert the attention from the main ingredient of the creative process: the creative impulse. Meanwhile:

> …it is inevitable that such studies of great men tend to irritate artists and creative people in general. It could be that these studies that we are tempted to make are irritating because they look as if they are getting somewhere, as if they will soon be able to explain why this man was great and that woman achieved much, but the direction of inquiry is wrong. The main theme is being circumvented, that of the creative impulse itself. The creation stands between the observer and the artist's creativity.
>
> (1999: 69)

Donald Winnicott wrote about the necessity to be shielded from the painful experience of reality (Winnicott, 1975[1951]). Fantasy not only provides a meaningful narrative, as Jean Knox puts it (Knox, 2003: 120), but also serves as a motivating and driving force. For stand-up comedians, their fantasy for recognition, expression and becoming as Jung called 'top dog' can be the drive necessary to go on stage and seek attention from the audience and to become successful or in their terms a star.

Winnicott almost accepts Melanie Klein's views on the subject of creativity as being a by-product of aggression and the subsequent impulse to restore and repair both the subject and the relationship. Gould writes about the connection between the child's fear of losing the mother and the birth of comedy, the emergence of comedic imagination. It is certainly born out of anguish, of the desire to recreate the parent and to laugh at one's silly panic about losing her. This, however, is not about happiness – this is about the ability to repair things:

> Being funny is not the same as being happy. This is an area to which I can speak with some expertise. False modesty aside, I have always been pretty funny. ………Why? Because of my "hyperactive

imagination." One day I came home from school and could not find my mother. ……….How did she know I was home? Because she heard me screaming.

Having my mother not answer when I called her name, at eight years old…… It meant something had happened. She had been taken away and I was now alone and defenceless in a hostile world. How would I eat? Who would take care of me? Was she dead? Who killed my mother?! Was I next?! Of course I screamed. I screamed and screamed and scr – "Oh, hi, mom. There you are. I was just wondering where you'd stepped away to. No, I didn't piss myself, I accidentally spilled a glass of urine on my underwear before slipping my pants on and it must have soaked through. Say, what did you make of the President's speech last night?"

(Gould, *The Rolling Stone*, 27 August 2014)

In fact, this reflects Otto Rank's argument that 'the act which we have described as the artist's self-appointment as such is in itself a spontaneous expression of the creative impulse, of which the first manifestation is simply the forming of the personality itself' (Rank, 1989: 37). In creating the work of art, the artist, in fact, creates or re-creates his own self; he re-forms and expounds his personality.

Thus, the artist – very much like the baby who is looking for ways to deal with the loss of omnipotence and perfect mirroring – creates a new object that can match the original lost object (the mother) – or even be better than the mother. Since the artist feels more in control and 'omnipotent' within the borders of his universe, he or she can produce 'an object that more fully contains and realises the artist's self' (Wright, 2009: 52):

With the help of this medium, and through the forms he creates, the artist retrieves elements of his subjectivity that were in danger of being lost. Within this new object – the art object in process of formation – he places these retrieved subjective elements within the forms of his own making. Thus an art work in progress is both maternal extension of the self, and a self in formation, within which the artist attempts integration with all the skill he can muster. The structure that results from this intuitive project (the art object) is in continuity with the fabric of the artist's self and resonates with it. It is a genuine mix-up of artist and object, though now with a separate existence in the real world.

(2009: 52-53)

Members of the audience seek to consume someone else's created symbols and transitional objects ('works of art') because they wish to experience 'contact with our own dormant sentience, and through it carefully contrived and resonant forms responding to it' (2009: 53). The audience has an impulsive response and re-creates feelings in response to the artists material…. as Wright confirms, 'this bears within itself the residue of living dialogue with the artist'. (2009:53).

This cluster of ideas certainly has validity for the stand-up circuit. Many comedians have spoken about the reparative function of their art. George Carlin says that the comedian is in charge and his material represents him. Moreover, it is good for the material to be organised into a coherent personal narrative: 'There's gotta be a kind of thread to your material because it represents you. It's nice to have a series of unrelated jokes, but it's better when they have a kind of segue' (Ajaye, 2002: 85).

Throughout this thesis I argue that creativity is compassionate, caring and healing, whilst being destructive. Jung's vision of creativity, stresses the importance of transformation and repair instead of treating all creative impulses as regressive and aggressive, which are also seen as reparative, but only if they are recognised as such. The aggressive act alone is not reparative, unless it is juxta-posed in a healing context.

Meanwhile, Winnicott's idea of the transitional object as being the bedrock of human creativity does not contradict Jung's views on creativity as being an important part of the individuation process. One might argue that the transitional object restores the artist's sense (or creates an illusion) of wholeness. The Jungian school aims for recognition of integration a particle of our Self through the artistic medium. Winnicott holds the artistic process in a transitional container in order to integrate it safely. Whereas Wright discusses whether the artistic material truly represents the artist. The artist will constantly re-form his art in order to mirror his true self. The process in the stand-up space is a vulnerable process as there is no third eye to measure or reduce the impact of the response towards the release and impulse of the comedian's creativity. His material is initially an un-diluted, un-edited expression of his unconscious self. In order to individuate he needs to reflect upon his impulsive expressions, disintegrating them and re-integrating them within a new paradigm in order to assimilate and quell the emotional cathexes.

Anthony Storr argues: 'the ecstatic sense of wholeness is bound to be transient because it has no part in the total pattern of 'adaptation through maladaptation,' which is characteristic of our species. Boeotian bliss is not conducive to invention: the hunger of imagination, the desire and pursuit of the whole, take origin from the realisation that something is missing, from awareness of incompleteness' (Storr, 1989: 197).

One can combine the concepts of individuation and artistry as transitional objects. In Jungian psychology, the Self is the image of wholeness. The artist recreates the Self by combining his personality with the transitional object; he reverts to the 'baby' stage when the world seems to be manageable and controllable by his primary carer. However, this is not a regressive action alone – it is part of the individuation process. The artist does not create his ideal world; instead, he, it can be said, is shaping his future while looking back and repairing his feelings to his past and re-integrating his past. Creativity is a paradox – just like the union of the opposites is a paradox. Storr writes:

> The path of individuation and the changes of attitude, which take place can be closely matched with accounts of the creative process given by men and women of genius. First, the mental state during which new ideas arise or inspiration occurs is exactly that which Jung recommended to his patients and which he called 'active imagination'. Although, occasionally, the germ of a new composition or hypothesis occurs in a dream, by far the greater number of new ideas occur during a state of reverie, intermediate between waking and sleeping.
>
> (1989: 199)

Storr also argues that 'creativity usually consists of forming new links between formerly disparate entities, the union between opposites described by Jung' (1989: 199). In other words, when people use art as a transitional object, they individuate and self-create: 'The end process of individuation shares with ecstatic states the experience of a new unity within, described by Jung as being a new reciprocity between conscious and unconscious. The sense of peace, of reconciliation with life, of being part of a greater whole, is closely similar' (1989: 196).

However, the sense of peace described by Storr is temporary, as the transitional object is a poor replacement of the original state of unity with the object. The unity of opposites, being a paradoxical idea, is never stable and never fully achievable. It has to be recreated anew all the time. The sense of wholeness that comes with stage/public success is also temporary. The comedian is compelled to go back to the audience in order to transform certain psychic agencies within himself; to redeem certain lost elements of his psyche. This process is never complete because 'ideal' individuation, as Jung postulated, can never be achieved. Comedians on stage seek wholeness and individuation in unity, with society and in relation to the audience. This union with the audience is almost alchemical, as the performer steps back in order to go forward.

Stand-up performers keep seeking emotional and intellectual dialogue with the audience because of the mysterious, numinous properties of the creative act. And just like the alchemical substance, the joke and laughter that come with it are fleeting, fluid and unstable. The performance has to be re-created on stage over and over again. Its form depends upon the comedian and his attitude towards the audience, towards his life at that time and also the audience's response to him. It may evolve to make it more current and socially and geographically relevant. The joke is not an item existing by itself – rather, it is born in relation to society and out of the comedian's attitude towards society.

## *6.3. Conclusion:*

The artistic process of creation has many valuable psychological processes manifesting in tandem and in opposition to each other. During delivery the material is also affected by the comedian's idiosyncrasies', including the audience reaction to him and the audiences interaction with each other. The variables are manifold and inconsistent. Hence the comedian has to constantly learn to deal with inconsistency and still be funny whilst adapting his creative humorous vision. His drive to express his creative vision within this medium is both elating and potentially depressing. However, the creative impulse alone is not enough for the comedian, he needs the audience to reflect and praise his ability or the impulse will potentially be rejected and the process for individuation cannot be activated in the form.

# CHAPTER 7

## GOING ON STAGE: INTER-AND-INTRAPSYCHIC MATRIX OF STAND-UP COMEDY

This chapter discusses the mechanics of the creative process of the stand-up performer. Using a combination of Jungian, Freudian, theories we will trace the trajectory of the comedian's creative act including three phases: preparation, on-stage and post-performance. I will explore the inter and intra-psychic processes and agencies activated at each of the comedian's three pro-active and re-active stages of creation, disintegration and re-integration of the material as reflection of his psyche Before, During and After the performance.

## 7.
### 7.1. *Before*

Most of the psychic processes involved in the preparation stage are intra-psychic, internal and profoundly personal. However, some of the processes also involve interaction with other people. Often the preparatory stage of performance is born out of interaction with others rather than being the result of intensive thought and lonely creative activity. The comedian may get inspired by his family situation or by the world around him. Incidents that happen in the comedian's life – the result of his exchanges with other people – may serve as an inspiration for the jokes. It is the creative urge that stands on its own and have its own merit. It is more than sublimation, it is a reflection of the comedians unique Self as a particle of his own development being reformed into a structure, which is enjoyable and can receive attention. Whereas sublimation is a channelling of a negative energy. The stand-up uses his material to reform his Self into a component or individual which is acceptable.

Negative experiences and the subsequent need for self-expression often trigger the creative process. American comedian Jim Carrey says: 'I don't think human beings learn anything without desperation. Desperation is a necessary ingredient to learning anything or creating anything. Period. If you ain't desperate at some point, you ain't interesting'. He adds: 'If you ain't in the moment, you are either looking forward to uncertainty, or back to pain and regret'.

All aspects and complexities of life can serve as the inspiration for the jokes: politics, personal life – or the opportunity to have freedom in a regulated, structured environment. Like any creative activity, joke writing is a meaning-making process. It is an opportunity to discuss oneself, an opportunity to announce who you are and to try out different aspects of your psyche.

The on-stage persona is an exaggerated form of one or the other aspect of one's personality. For instance, some people will go for their intellectual side, playing with themes and concepts; while others choose to joke about sex and discuss their sexuality. Usually comedians choose the subject with which they are the most fluent and find the easiest to engage with the audience.

If they've never been on stage, their creative process involves creative self-discovery and searching for the psychological goldmine that can be explored and exploited. It may vary according to the experience of the comedian. The task of the comedian is to find something unique, something topical as well as something that has personal significance for himself. This process involves playing with ideas. It is the journey of the conceptual distortion. It is also a world-organising and meaning-making process bringing together random thoughts and ideas, and lining them into a conceptually and creatively coherent whole.

Much of intra-psychic inspiration comes from the performers' childhood experiences and from their personal drive to make a mark on the world. For instance, the British comedian David Baddiel says:

> Comedy is about retaining the child within you. Most comedians have it in them more than other people. It's not just about finding it – you can't help it, it's just there, and for some reason it's stronger than it is in other people. You haven't grown up……….
>
> The reason I do this job is because I've got a deep confessional drive – my comedy seems to be all about confession. It's probably something to do with the fact that when my younger brother was born he was very much the mum's favourite – and although I wasn't neglected, I feel that there was a time when I wasn't being noticed as me. I remember as I was growing up, I was desperate to tell people about myself and for them to notice me and know who I was – totally. And that seems to be what I'm still doing as a stand-up.
>
> (1994: 71).

Many comedians emphasise the influence of parent-child relations on their choice of profession, as well as the importance of various incidents that happened to them in childhood.

Often comedians talk about how poverty and social issues influence them as individuals and as performers. For instance, Arnold Brown reveals the 'lack of ambition', in his working-class family and how he felt out of place in his social background:

> My mother and father weren't at war with each other, but they used to bicker over everything. My father ran a fruit shop. We were upper working class. ……..I was slightly ashamed of my background and I felt alienated by being Jewish in Scotland. It was very rare that a non-Jewish person would come into the house. It sounds like apartheid, but that was the way it was. It was almost a ghetto mentality.
>
> I came from an uncultured background. There were no books in the house. I remember going to a Jewish student society. The speaker said, 'As I read in the *Observer*…'. I'd never heard of the *Observer.* We used to get the *Sunday Post,* which was called the *Empire News* at the time. I'd go out with my father and buy ten Woodbines, a bottle of Irn Bru and a copy of *Empire News.* There was no television, no telephone, no fridge. That was my culture.
>
> (Cook, 1994: 81)

Not all of the formative experiences are negative. Some comedians feel inspired by the complexities and intricacies of interpersonal experiences. British comedian Charlie Chuck explains that his profession is rooted in his father and granddad's 'silliness' and light-hearted attitude to life:

> My dad brought me up with good morals – he never used to swear. When he used to lose his temper, he used to shout, 'Balls!' And then he'd always laugh afterwards – he'd always see the funny side of it. My mum was as daft as a brush. She used to teach me gibberish. Her dad, My granddad, used to have a bowler hat and briefcase and clog dance in the pub.
>
> He'd always had this silliness, and my mum used to teach me: "I won't stand such diabolical insolence from an incompocerous piece of crumption such as you!". So her nuttiness and my dad's straightness is where I get it from. One minute I can be telling pearls of wisdom, or I can talk off the wall and talk absolute gibberish. That's what's funny – that has them in hysterics. But it's only that. There's nothing else. It's total vaudeville.
>
> (Cook, 1994: 83)

Reminiscences and memories are decisive for live creativity, but they need the personality along with individual comedic components to develop and deliver humour. Comedy also has a very powerful intra-psychic aspect. Comedians can be inspired by encounters with other people, and jokes are born out of the tension of these encounters. It is always permitted for a comedian to self-deprecate their own religion and their own race. The comedian's identity is embedded in their community, family and culture. Jokes and performances, therefore, are born out of inter psychic encounters with cultural representations as well as with particular people. He thinks of what is happening outside and brings in what he regards as most important and relevant. His inside world mirrors and echoes the 'inside' dilemma. Issues such as ethnicity, gender and sexuality are pertinent. During the occurrence the comedian has the emotion but not the words, he has the intensity of feeling but not the vocabulary. Translating the emotions into jokes constitutes an important phase of the pre-performance process.

It is also important part of the intra- psychic aspect of the preparation process for the comedian to ensure that he is able to create a link between contemporary issues and local events in order to relate and make a connection with the audience. The comedian's task is to build a psychological bridge between his inner world and the outer world; between his own and the audience's problems and interests. In transforming his inner world into the comedic word, he also exposes and re-interprets the issues relevant for society.

The Jewish comedian Ian Stone often jokes about his Jewish appearance as well as about more serious political issues such as the Holocaust or blaming the Jews for crucifying Jesus. He makes relevant and important links between his internal world and the world outside. He is dealing with his inherited Judaism more than with the current political events. He is trying to reconcile his present social status with the status inherited from his biological family. The bridge is an attempt to reconcile his own identity issues (rejection) with his status in the present culture.

Most importantly, identity and appearance are the first things that the audience notice in a performer. They are the intra-psychic bridge. It is crucial for the comedian to make the audience identify with him. The comedian often self-deprecates in order to draw the audience into the performance and make them empathise with him. He has to invest into his material and think of what kind of jokes and linguistic modalities ensure him a fluid and recognisable connection and thereby the attachment process can begin.

External influences: creative, political, social or cultural - are therefore an important part of the creative process in general and its preparatory, pre-performance phase in particular. The American comedian Richard Jeni says on the issue of being influenced by the outside world: 'if a young comedian is really trying never to be influenced, I think they're doing themselves a disservice. Would you be a novelist and say, "I'm deliberately not going to read any of the great books"? Would you be a scientist and say, "I don't want to know what anybody else is working on"? In one sense there is no truly original idea. All you have is a set of pre-existing ideas combined and filtered through you' (Ajaye, 2002: 108).

Comedians make links all the time with the external world that are reflective of what is happening in their internal world. When asked how he came up with the title for his latest show, the American comedian Richard Lewis replied:

> I asked Ringo Starr, who I know and call Richard (which is his real name). I said, "Richard, I'm thinking of going back on stage, and I'm scared, and a little miserable about having to do it again, but I think I want to do it. I'm thinking of calling it Magical Misery Tour, to parody the Magical Mystery Tour. You think I have to ask Paul and George?". I felt like such a jerk. I mean, these cats are worth $500 billion, like they give a shit. And he says, "I doubt it".
>
> (Ajaye, 2002: 140)

Through this anecdote Lewis is exposing his lack of status and his acceptance of his internal state along with his self-deprecating tone. External influences are undoubtedly crucial for the comedian's success. His personal experiences are condensed into anecdotal form injected with his unconscious issues and personality tones, which they peel off in layers in front of the audience. Yet, at the same time, they have to link the personal to the social as well as to the audience's interests and culture. The game of being a stand-up is to pinpoint the different cultures in the room and to be verbally adept to identify with the audience.

## 7.2. *During*

The intra psychic and inter psychic processes during this stage are often intermingled. The intra-psychic components of the performance trigger inter-psychic events. Comedians can be agitated by a personal event prior to the show, which can resonate with the audience producing a defensive attitude. This in turn can impact on the flow of the comedian's delivery. The two processes are very much related and often merge completely. The comedian is absorbing the audience's reactions and simultaneously thinking about his response to them as well as to the success of his performance. Since he is very concerned with his success at this stage, he keeps thinking about the public's reaction to his jokes. He needs to monitor it and, if necessary, modify his behaviour and performance. His acceptance by the audience depends on the successful connection with it – and this is a very important aspect of the intra psychic process. The performance starts within, flows into the audience, is then re-absorbed by the comedian who – armed with his knowledge of the audience – prepares the next wave of jokes. After re-absorption, the material transforms internally. The 'during' stage of the live creative process is then doubly intensive because it involves several types of processes merging, intermingling and working together.

### 7.2.1. The Comedian's Individuation Process on Stage

One of the key arguments of this thesis is that comedians can individuate on stage together with their audience. In order to go through this kind of comedic individuation, the comedian should be able to possess the ability to self-reflect and to self deprecate. As Mario Jacoby writes:

> Time and again we may observe that people suffering from typical 'narcissistic vulnerability' just 'do not understand jokes'. They tend to suspect that other people's utterances are meant as an insult to their own person. One would need to treat them with the greatest care, as if walking on eggshells. [...]
>
> It is quite possible for particularly 'talented' narcissists to develop a whole arsenal of witty and sarcastic remarks in order to scare off potential aggressors – otherwise they fear they will themselves become the target of mockery. But witticism and sarcasm are nor synonymous with true humour; they can be used, rather, as defensive weapons in that they prevent feelings of hurt and embarrassment from 'coming too close'. They also keep people 'at a certain distance'.
>
> (Jacoby, 1999: 127).

The comedian's creativity relies on his relationship with the audience. The viewer aids the comedian in reflecting and re-integrating the lost, repressed and vulnerable parts of his or her psyche. The transference in the relationship with the audience brings together the different parts of the comedian's lost self while fulfilling his ego. In the words of another comedian, Steve Punt: 'I find it (...) upsetting when the audience ignores you. That's so depressing, because the whole illusion goes. Without that joke and response, there's nothing there at all' (Cook, 1999: 213).
American comedian Chris Rock agrees: 'It's weird. It's different every night because I change every day. Some nights I'm depressed, but as soon as they introduce me, it's all gone. I hear the music, and the people getting into it, and I know that as soon as I step out there, there will be a roar, so whatever down feelings I had are all gone' (Ajaye, 2002: 180). Chris Rock's words emphasise the importance of the collective energy affecting his engagement with a positive audience. Without the positive energy it would be difficult for individuation process to occur as the comedian would not continue to perform on stage.

Speaking generally and metaphorically, the comedic performance is the process of searching for the inner core. Ideally, the comedian unites the audience in such a way that it becomes the reflection of his unbroken inner core. Jung posed the statement that 'there is no light without shadow and no psychic wholeness without imperfection. To round itself out, life call not for perfection but for completeness; and for this the 'thorn in the flesh' is needed, the suffering of defects without which there is no progress and no ascent'. A comedian can recognise a glimpse of his Self, by uniting the disparate audience, who symbolically represent his psychic discord, by generating laughter thereby creating cohesion or wholeness, As Jung defined the Self in the psyche; 'natural man is not a 'self' – he is the mass and particle in the mass, collective to such a degree that his is not even sure of his own ego'.

Hence, the audience represents and externalises the unity the comedian lacks. It is the frisson activated by the inter and intra psychic unity of boundaries that the comedian feels ecstatic, oceanic, godlike and omnipotent. It is a heightened state similar to a religious revelation, which can prelude a numinous experience as a transcendent power. Edinger identifies in the alchemical process of 'solutio' that is summarised by the phrase 'dissolve and co-agulate' and that the greater solution is an encounter with the numinous as a profound symbol: 'what is worth saving by the ego is saved. What is not worth saving is dissolved and melted down in order to be recast in new life forms. Thus the on-going life process renews itself..........'(Edinger, 1994:81) The British comedian Bruce Morton describes his encounter with the numinous feeling of omnipotence that often occurs during a particularly powerful and successful performance:

> Some kind of chemistry happens in the first five seconds – something happens in the room. This'll look f*cking pompous in print but it's almost like a spiritual thing. I've felt like I'm actually half an inch off the stage. I'm not walking, I'm floating, and later I can't remember how I got from one end of the stage to the other. That's as good as it gets. You come off feeling not so much, "'God, I was such a star there!' but just, 'What f*cking fun I had there! No wonder I do this for a living!'"
>
> (Cook, 1994: 183)

The stand-up has a vital and critical voice, which allows the truth 'to slip out', as a slip of the tongue a parapraxis. (Freud, 1960: 126). This voice is 'free of pretence,' as he observes and exposes society and social change, resonating with members of the audience and drawing disparate members together through his humorous commentary.

Jung recognises the impact and value of the individual in relation to the group as audience; *'Although the dangers of the individual identifying with the collectivity are very great indeed, the relationship between the individual and society or a group*

*is essential, since no individual stands by himself but depends upon symbiosis with a group. The self, the very centre of an individual, is of a conglomerate nature. It is, as it were, a group. It is a collectivity in itself and therefore, always, when it works most positively, creates a group.*
(Adler, Jaffe, 1973: 508)

Chris Rock confirms the need for the connection with the audience: 'I am constantly looking for the ad-lib.... I am constantly feeling the audience' (Author, year: 179). It is within the 'connection' that the alchemical fusion takes place and transformation occurs which is similar to the process of transference and counter-transference within the therapeutic setting. As Jung states ' A person is a psychic system which, when it affect another person, enters into reciprocal reaction with another psychic system (C.W.16 par.1) and in particular ' the transference itself is a perfectly natural phenomenon which does not by any means happen only in the consulting room – it can be seen everywhere.... (C.W.16 par.420) It is through our projections that we find ourselves however the greater the identification with the object of our projections the greater the means of self-awareness.

The British-Jewish comedian David Baddiel draws a parallel between comedy and therapy although he does not believe that any creative process can solve one's personal problems permanently: 'It's so cathartic being onstage, when you're doing well, that you feel you should have come to some other point at the end of it, but your problems are still there at the end of the day' (Cook, 1994: 286). The American comedian Louie Anderson, however, has a different impression of therapeutic effects of self-comedy: '... I think a lot of my act is working out the problems I've had with my family, my father in particular. And I think that it really makes a difference. And I think it's healthy and helpful' (Ajaye, 2002: 54). Although both comedians are able to identify the root of their problem and they openly bring their complexes into the public domain they have different outcomes. This can depend upon the intensity of the primary relationship/s that is causing the anxiety. As with all therapies there is no guaranteed time for dealing with specific problems.

Individuation is both an internal and external process. The comedian's internal debate occurs as the audience response oscillates between the comedian and the audience. This means that the performance is always fluid and constantly changing; yet, at the same time, the comedian aims to remain in control of the whole process. Within this comedic process the comedian aims to appease if not heal the pain of the distortions in life. The comedian reveals his guilt, shame, taboos, desires both actual and delusional, which resonate with the core of personal and social psychic drives and anxieties. Individually they expose the collective complexes and give them a face, a Persona or even a Scapegoat. Within this process individuation potentially occurs.

## *7.2.2. Attachment and Seduction*

The key to the performer's success with the audience is 'seduction'. The audience is the symbolic mother who the performer has to attract and whose attention he has to capture and hold. On stage, comedians have to be self-deprecating and, at the same time, look powerful and in control.

The comedian's relationship with the audience may be theorised as pre-oedipal; based on the pure, intense, pleasurable and (ideally) unrestrained interaction between the person on stage and the people who are listening to him. One could say that the performer engages with a number of narcissistic processes and that his desire for the energy that he gets from the audience is also narcissistic, Freud's view is that he (the comedian) withdraws libido from the outside world and directs it to the ego.' (Jacobi. 31:1991) Freud postulates that mature adults never forget the affectionate fixations and the constant hunger for pleasure they had as children. He writes in the essay entitled 'On the Universal Tendency to Debasement in the Sphere of Love' (1912):

> These affectionate fixations of the child persist throughout childhood, and continually carry along with them eroticism, which is consequently diverted from its sexual aims. Then at the age of puberty they are joined by the powerful 'sensual' current, which no longer mistakes its aims. It never fails, apparently, to follow the earlier paths and to cathect objects of the primary infantile choice with quotas of libido that are now far stronger. […] These new object will be chosen by the model (imago) of the infantile ones, but in the course of time they will attract to themselves the affection that was tied to the earlier ones. […]
>
> (Freud, SE XI: 180-181)

In his close contact with the audience, the comedian may be said to be coming back to the early experiences of unity with the mother. His affectionate fixation on the mother is replayed on stage. There is an automatic anticipation that the audience should like the comedian. On his part, the comedian has to prove to the audience that he deserves to be liked. The performer has to go through the process of seducing the audience and proving to it that he is good enough to be loved and praised.

Ego problems and the problems of integration are a major aspect of the individuation process. They often congregate and vie for attention within the world. For instance, this is an excerpt from British comedian Eddie Izzard's show, which discusses his struggle to keep the balance between having a realistic view of his abilities and his ego:

It's ok to have an ego. […]
I went to see Jesus Chris Superstar in Wembley Arena
I got a taxi to Piccadilly
The driver said – 'Are you going back to Wembley?'
'Well I'm glad you asked'
My God my ego kicked in at this time. I'm getting through to the Asian Community!
'Yes I think I will be going back to Wembley'
I struggled so hard to get there.
Taxi Driver: 'Here is my card I'm working tonight. I can take you back'.
The demons they come in my mind.
The demons they come in my mind.

Izzard highlights the conflict of his narcissistic tendency towards his maturation, which results in what Kohut, defines as 'empathy, creativeness, humour and wisdom' thus embarking on the process of individuation.

The British comedian Steve Coogan talks about using creativity to get attention from parents in a large family as well as from random adults:

> I remember one weird thing I used to do, which was quite morbid. My sister brought me this wax skin and blood back from America, and I remember doing really detailed wounds on myself. I once went to get the family allowance from the post office with two really neat vampire bites in my neck, with blood down from them – just to see the reaction on the postmistress's face. She said: 'Excuse me. You've done something to your neck'. I said, 'Oh, that's OK'. […]

> It's definitely a case of having to get people's attention. I did do that in my family, because my sister tells me. She says I'd constantly be saying, 'Watch me! Look, watch me! Watch what I can do! Look, I can do this! Watch me do this!' When you're in a big family, you need to fight for attention.
>
> (Cook, 1994: 80)

It is interesting that Coogan speaks of 'fighting for attention' as a survival strategy in an environment in which attention is a resource, and it is sparse. Curiously, Woody Allen also talks about comedy as a way of getting attention and devising strategies to get it. He says in an interview to a fellow comedian Larry Wilde: '…it's some kind of privation or suffering not necessarily economic that turns someone into a comedian… that makes you squeeze humour from the world or twist the world out of shape' (Wilde, 2000: 27).

Steve Coogan's necessity to gain attention, triggered in the child a bout of creativity, which he structured and shaped in such a way as to entertain his audience in the most effective manner, and keep their attention for as long as possible. Using his creativity, he also found a way of expressing himself as well as allowing the audience to express himself. The strategy – as well as the attention he eventually received from family members – was not negative but positive.

A powerful combination of physical comedy and language is always bound to attract attention, either positive or negative, from an audience. Interestingly enough, John Bowlby links the acquisition of linguistic skills to attention-gaining strategies. He writes in *Attachment and Loss, Vol 1* (1969):

> Starting, we may suppose, towards the end of his first year, and probably especially active during his second and third when he acquires the powerful and extraordinary gift of language, a child is busy constructing working models of how the physical world might be expected to behave, how his mother and other significant persons might be expected to behave, how he himself might be expected to behave, and how each interacts with the other. Within the framework of these working models he evaluates his situation and makes his plans. And within the framework of these working models of his mother and himself he evaluates special aspects of his situation and makes his attachment plans.
>
> (Bowlby, 1969: 354)

Bowlby is right in discerning the issue of interaction here. As a child growing up in a large family, Steve Coogan had to plan his interaction in such a way as to provoke a particular response from his parents and siblings. He was already exploring different audiences and learning different reactions at a young age. He was learning how to establish a connection with a particular audience as well as gaining a better understanding of what makes people connect.

Similarly, when the comedian goes on stage, he has to ensure very early on during the performance that the audience likes him. This can be achieved with the help of a number of techniques and standard opening lines, announcing yourself and your identity; announcing and establishing your similarities and differences with the audience; being warm, welcoming and non-aggressive –most importantly self-deprecating. Occasionally comedians choose alternative ways of establishing contact with the audience, including being controversial and openly aggressive. However, before the comedian can start engaging with the audience fully, he or she must ensure that the initial contact has actually been made.

This is linked to another of Bowlby's ideas – the secure base. Bowlby devised this term in order to describe a whole range of behaviours going on between the child and the parental figure. He also links the secure base to human creativity and self-expression: 'Evidence is accumulating that human beings of all ages are happiest and able to deploy their talents when they are confident that, standing behind them, there are one or more trusted persons who will come to their aid should difficulties arise. The person trusted, also known as an attachment figure (…) can be considered as providing his (or her) companion with a secure base from which to operate' (Bowlby, 2005: 125). Bowlby also mentions that the need for the secure base is not limited to babies and children but continues into adult life, albeit in a modified form:

> The requirement of an attachment figure, a secure personal base, is by no means confined to children though, because of its urgency during those years, it is during those years that it is most evident and has been most studied. There are good reasons for believing, however, that the requirement applies also to adolescents and to mature adults as well. In the latter, admittedly, the requirement is commonly less evident, and it probably differs both between the sexes and at different phases of life.
>
> In the picture of personality functioning that emerges there are two main sets of influences. The first concerns the presence or absence, partial or total, of a trustworthy figure willing and able to provide the kind of secure base required at each phase of the life cycle. These constitute the external, or environmental, influences. The second set concerns the relative ability or inability of an individual, first, to recognise when another person is both trustworthy and willing to provide a base and, second, when recognised, to collaborate with that other person in such a way that a mutually rewarding relationship is initiated and maintained. These constitute the internal, or organismic, influences.
>
> (2005: 125)

Bowlby also mentions that his attachment concept discusses the same issues and phenomena that have been explored by other psychology schools in terms of 'dependency need' or of 'object relations' or of 'symbiosis and individuation' (Bowlby, 1980: 39).
The concept of secure base is useful for the analysis of live comedy. Comedians are dependent on the constant emotional feed generated by the audience. The comedian needs the audience to love him for his creativity to unfold. He needs to ensure that he will be accepted and loved *consistently* and *dependably* throughout the whole performance – otherwise he would not be able to function. Maternal mirroring – the audience's mirroring of the comedian – is very important for the psychological

wellbeing of the comedian during the performance. British comedian Jimmy Carr explains the comedian's need for the 'secure base' when he is on stage:

> In this precarious and unforgiving profession, the character trait that unites all successful performers is a kind of masochistic compulsion to make people laugh. It's pure, naked need: a need for love, for popularity, to be noticed, to show off. The great attraction of stand-up as a balm for the fragile ego – as opposed to, say, writing a book or appearing or a radio play – is the instantaneous nature of the audience feedback. Do they love me? Yes, they must do – they're laughing. Obviously, it's a double-edged sword: the medium's greatest attraction is also its cruellest disappointment, because when they don't laugh, it must follow that they don't love me. Actually, maybe they hate me. No, I know what it is – they don't get my jokes. I'm just *too funny* for them to deal with (… )
>
> (Carr and Greeves, 2006: 114)

Individuation can only occur when the secure base, a firm positive connection of acceptance between the comedian and the audience, is present. Absence of a secure base may provoke a strong emotional reaction in the comedian. Many comedians speak of nervousness in anticipation of being rejected or heckled. This is particularly true of female comedians whose 'masculine' profession often attracts envy and anger from the male portion of the audience. The American stand-up, television host and actress Ellen DeGeneres writes about her experience of not having a secure base during performances:

> Somehow you just learn to deal with it. You learn to handle your nervousness. You just kind of look at it, you know, you're not doing brain surgery. This is just a wonderful job you have(…….)
>
> If [hecklers] are really being mean, which I don't get anymore because my shows cost more money, so it's not like they won it or they already had passes or whatever, so people are not going to spend a lot of money to come to be mean. In the beginning when I had people like that (which I did) – being a woman on stage, you have these macho idiots who are drunk who want to get to you and upset you – they used to upset me all the time. I'd just walk off crying sometimes. I mean, they wouldn't see it, but I would be backstage crying.
>
> (Ajaye, 2002: 95-6)

Building a secure base during a live creative process is always two-way; both the comedian and the audience are involved. Only when this magical connection is present can the transformation of both the audience and the comedian occur. Bion's concept of *reverie* links with our analysis of the comedic creative process as an alchemical transformation, the success of which is founded on secure base. The term refers to a state of calm receptiveness that the infant requires of the mother. Her task is to take in the baby's feelings and to make them meaningful. The baby, through projective identification, would insert into the mother its feelings of anxiety and fear, and, through introjection of a receptive, calm mother image, the infant can develop his own ability to reflect on his states of mind, and deal with them successfully (Hinshelwood, 1991: 420).

The mother-audience has to be receptive – in a state of what Klein named as reverie, 'through introjection of a receptive, understanding mother the infant can begin to develop his own capacity for reflection on his own states of mind' (Hinshelwood, 1991:420) – in order to ensure that the comedian engages his capacity for self-reflection, his attachment needs have to be congruent with the audience.

In his essay 'Psychopathic Characters on the Stage' (1906), Freud writes that the audience is often seduced by the promise of heroic efforts from the performers on stage, as well as by the opportunity to live through powerful experiences, without having to actually suffer: 'For the spectator knows quite well that actual heroic conduct such as this would be impossible for him without pains and sufferings and acute fears, which would almost cancel out the enjoyment' (SE, Vol.7: 305-6). The necessity to introject heroic qualities comes from the feelings of inferiority and cowardice:

> The spectator is a person who experiences too little, who feels that he is a "poor wretch to whom nothing of importance can happen", who has long been obliged to damp down, or rather displace, his ambition to stand in his own person at the hub of world affairs; he longs to feel and to act and to arrange things according to his desires – in short, to be a hero. And the playwright and actor enable him to do this by allowing him to *identify himself* with a hero.
>
> (Freud, SE, Vol.7: 305)

Any creative process is an act of self-reflection, however mediated. Comedians are prepared to go through this ordeal, and they are prepared to endure the risk of failure if something goes wrong. Audience members, as a rule, are not prepared to take such risks but still wish to feel the adrenaline surge and the excitement that goes with identifying with the performer on stage.

## 7.3. After

After the performance two processes take place: reflection and repair. The comedians assess the creative process and the quality of their connection with the audience. This is when individuation – self-understanding and self-reflection – happens. Jung regarded the individuation process as a psychological phenomenon that can only happen when the individual interacts with his society. Similarly, the comedian's individuation only takes place when he manages to establish an emotional and intellectual connection with the audience. The connection with the audience is the magical, alchemical moment that assists the comedian's individuation process.

Many comedians do not reflect on their work *per se*, and do dwell on their self-improvement. However, all live comedy performers think and analyse the audience's reaction to their jokes. By assessing the success of the joke through laughter and emotional response, the comedian measures himself as a human being. By improving their material, they assess and improve themselves.

Like all creative people, including stand-up comedians, are often seen as narcissistic, self-obsessed, self-indulgent and unconcerned about society. As A Rothenberg informs us in Creativity and Madness (p38.1990) 'Among the mythical fallacies connecting mental illness with creativity is the idea of the creator's frenzy and transport in the experience of inspiration.' However, the comedian's connection with the audience disproves this view. Live creativity is a fair exchange of intellectual and emotional energies between the performer and the viewer. In Individuation and Narcissism (1999) Mario Jacoby draws the line between extreme individualistic comedic behaviour of railing against the inhibiting nature of social norms, accepted regulations and 'deadly seriousness of our activities' and true individuation.

'Humour may also be a help in attaining a somewhat workable relationship between the grandiose self and the realistic self'. Individuating on stage is not just about being visible, special and admired – it is also about giving something back to the people; being useful for your society. The comedian has to be in tune with the audience in order to please them. Being simply 'special' would not work. Jacoby writes: 'A sense of being special may mean: "I am especially beautiful, intelligent, good, clever, powerful, etc." It may also mean: "My sense of my own worth depends on whether this fact is seen and acknowledged by others; if that is not the case, then I am totally worthless, nothing. My very existence depends on whether my specialness is admiringly acknowledged or not". Meanwhile, Jung defines individuation as:

> … the process by which individual beings are being formed and differentiated; in particular, it is the development of the psychological *individual* as being distinct from the general, collective psychology. Individuation, therefore, is a process of differentiation, having for its goal the development of the individual personality… Since

individuality is a prior and physiological datum, it also expresses itself in psychological ways.

(CW6: paras. 757-758)

At the same time, human beings cannot survive physically or psychologically without the influence of the social. As Aniela Jaffe notes, consciousness always depends on external social conditions that should be taken into consideration when making individual decisions. The individual is never free from his family, his community, or his society. Whoever thinks that he is free from the social is seriously deceiving himself: '… one of the tasks of individuation for modern man is to recognise that his autonomous consciousness, which fancies itself so superior and yet so suggestible, is dependent on external social conditions as well as being determined by inner psychic factors and, in spite of this insight, to retain his sense of responsibility and freedom' (Jaffe, 1986: 93-4).

Thus, the comedian individuates by sharing his personal material, with his community, even if it is a group of strangers. He then gets feedback on this material, which feeds and furthers the processes of reflection and repair.

### 7.3.1. Reflection

In order to succeed the comedian reflects upon the audience's reaction to his often very personal material. Since some comedians make their material dangerously personal, it makes the self-reflective process therapeutic and cathartic. This catharsis, this sharing of emotions with an audience mostly consisting of strangers, is an important part of the comedian's individuation process. For instance, the very famous American comedian Joan Rivers was brave enough to joke about her husband's suicide, which happened a decade ago. The joke turned into a big scandal. Kate Lombardi writes about this incident in *The New York Times*:

> It was all done with Ms. River's brand of can-we-talk intimacy and wildly irreverent humor. And, yes, not surprising from a woman who played the role of herself in a television movie about her husband taking his own life, there were suicide jokes.
> 'After Edgar killed himself, I went out to dinner with Melissa," Ms. Rivers said. "I looked at the menu and said, 'If Daddy were here to see these prices, he'd kill himself all over again'.
>
> Or this: 'The first year after Edgar killed himself, I was so angry that if he had come home, I probably would have killed him'.

> Ms. Rivers is unapologetic about her attitude. Laughter, she says, is healing, and anger is natural. People have the right to grieve how they want and on their own schedule.
>
> (Lombardi, *The New York Times,* 29 January 1995)

## 7.3.2. *Repair*

Repair is a chthonic process primarily because of the chthonic nature of the joke as a phenomenon, but also because comedic creativity is particularly dark and bitter– often comes out of the depths of the traumatised psyche. It is the trauma that we can hear in the joke; and it is the trauma that speaks off stage during the performance. Trauma, which has for many years struggled to find an outlet, finally finds a voice in a joke.

The psychological phenomena in the form of myth and metaphor, traditionally describe revisiting of traumatic experiences as *catabasis* – the hero's visit to the underworld. The desire for repair essentially takes the individual back to the pre-sexual, pre-Oedipal stages of his existence. For instance, Jung writes in The Theory of Psychoanalysis (1912):

> The regressive libido apparently desexualises itself by retreating back step by step to the pre-sexual stage of earliest infancy. Even there it does not make a halt, but in a manner of speaking continues right back to the intrauterine, pre-natal condition and, leaving the sphere of personal psychology altogether, irrupts the collective psyche where Jonah saw the 'mysteries' ('representations collectives') in the whale's belly. The libido thus reaches a kind of inchoate condition in which, like Theseus and Peirithous on their journey to the underworld, it may easily stick fast. But it can also tear itself loose from the maternal embrace and return to the surface with new possibilities in life.
>
> (CW4: para. 171)

The *catabasis* mytheme is imperative to the joke-production process, the comedian descends into the depths of his psyche and revisits any dark places that still haunt him. He raids these places and takes all the treasure found in the process to the surface. These recovered personal and individual contents, become the foundation of the joke. For instance, the British comedian John Dowie openly says that therapy allows him to 'unearth' the contents of his psyche which could them be utilised for generating new material: 'A lot of the stuff in that [an act he used to perform in 1985] was improvised on stage – and also in therapy sessions, which were very useful for creating new material (…) it might start off having two laughs in five minutes; then the next night you might do three minutes and get four laughs; then if you're lucky you'll do six minutes and it'll all be funny' (Wilmut and Rosengard, 1989: 199).

The idea is reiterated by the famous actor, author, presenter and comedian Stephen Fry: 'I'm kind of actually kind of sobbing and kind of tearing at the walls inside my own brain while my mouth is, you know, wittering away in some amusing fashion' (Owen, *The Independent,* 16 September 2006). In the same interview he says: 'I always heard voices in my head saying what a useless bastard I am, but the voice is my own' (Owen, *The Independent*, 16 September 2006).

Fry has struggled with mental illness throughout his life, and at one point nearly gassed himself in a car: 'I had this image of my parents staring right in at me while I sat there for at least, I think, two hours in the car with my hands over the ignition key. [...] And so I decided not to do it. When you feel you can't go on - it's, it's not just a phrase, it is a ... it's, it's a reality. I could not go on, and I would have killed myself if I didn't have the option of disappearing because it was that absolute' (Owen, *The Independent,* 16 September 2006).

Repair thus happens upon the hero's return from the underworld of his psyche and re-joining his community. The comedian, like the mythological hero, gains the treasure and takes it to the audience – his community. Yes, he works for himself as he explores and recycles his personal problems – but he also works for the sake of the community; whether local or global; temporary or permanent. Jung writes about the role of the hero in myth: 'The hero who sets himself the task of renewing the world and conquering death personifies the world-creating power which, brooding on itself in introversion, coiled round its own egg like a snake, threatens life with its poisonous bite, so that the living may die and be born again from the darkness' (CW5: para. 592). The performer needs the audience because it allows him to see himself from the 'outside'. With the help of the audience, the comedian is able to see his jokes – as well as his personal narrative – in a different light. It is a question of meaning. The process of relating to the audience is also a meaning-making process, for only in relation to other human beings can we make sense of both our internal universe and the external world. To quote Jung again:

> We must interpret, we must find meanings in things, otherwise we would be quite unable to think about them. We have to break down life and events, which are self-contained processes, into meanings, images, concepts, well knowing that in doing so we are getting further away from the living mystery. As long as we ourselves are caught in the process of creation, we neither see nor understand; indeed we ought not to understand, for nothing is more injurious to immediate experience than cognition. But for the purpose of cognitive understanding we must detach ourselves from the creative process

> sand look at it from the outside; only then does it become an image that expresses what we are bound to call 'meaning'.
>
> (CW15: para. 121)

The comedian's discoveries and repair are not only personal but also social. The audience benefits from the jokes intellectually as well as psychologically. Not only do the spectators laugh at the joke, but they also absorb the issues and problems raised by the comedian during the performance. It also comes from announcing your vulnerabilities and your shame; announcing your problems, and from realising that you are not the only one who is suffering from these issues. It also comes from being accepted, in all your imperfection and with all your problems, by the audience who plays the role of the 'good enough mother'. To be in a situation when you realise that you are loved, despite being imperfect, is when the healing can take place.

Meanwhile, the audience finds the person they can identify with, and connect with the comedian – via mirroring. Jokes become reparative for the audience when a range of complex problems, otherwise hidden from view, is exposed, discussed and laughed at. The audience and the comedian regain control over their neuroses and vulnerabilities. Jokes, like creativity, mute the pain in a situation. Even though the pain is not gone entirely, the individual has regained the psychological control over it. It is within this fantasy situation, that replay and repair happens.

Jokes help the comedian and the viewer to reiterate, analyse and re-absorb the painful or problematic situation. The comedian is the hero who is brave enough to challenge the problems residing in the depths of his psyche, and members of the audience benefit from the hero's trip by gaining the picture of their own problems and by supporting the effort of the comedian become part of the heroic journey. Even if they do not recognise your problem, they like you enough to listen to you. The comedian Garry Shandling says: 'I think that acceptance is a springboard to go deeper, because once the audience accepts that you're funny, you no longer have to prove that. 'You're now free to explore' (Ajaye, 2002: 215).

Jokes work with the human ability to self-reflect as they defy the narcissistic desire to beat the world into submission without any self-reflection. Whereas a narcissist would simply act out the anger and pain, the comedian deals with the situation creatively and allows others to laugh at his misery and thereby laughs at it by proxy. Repressed aggression and anger are thus dissipated and the in time the pain is alleviated and consequently 'repaired' and resolved. Instead of being pushed to the limit until it becomes traumatic and potentially dangerous. Stand-up is thus a form of psychological self-sacrifice because, as a comedian, one has to expose one's personal life as he invites other people to laugh at his personal problems. He is more that societies scapegoat who would be used to carry the problems of society and made to run away, he is still present and standing in reality. As Donald Kalsched informs us, 'I believe that mythology has selected the birth of the divine child as its answer to the question, "Does God manifest himself in history... Yes, but the divine child (God/man) will have to be born again after a period of illusion, and this second birth will be equivalent to a sacrifice.' The audience learns from comedy by observing the *catabasis* and absorbing it via the processes of mirroring and self-reflection.

Thus, repair occurs through three factors: mirroring, empathy and recognition of the collective pain. The mirroring and empathy is mutual as the comedian and the audience enter a period of intense emotional transaction. This emotional link guarantees that the jokes and their author will be understood and accepted by the listener. For instance, the American television host and comedian Johnny Carson argues that the ability to establish an emotional bridge with the audience is the first skill the comedian should learn:

> ... first of all, the most important thing to me, in comedy – the greatest thing a performer can have if he is going to be successful, is an empathy with the audience. They *have* to like him. And if they like the performer, then you've got eighty per cent of it made. And if you don't have that, it's damned difficult to get the audience on your side. If they resent you or if they don't feel any empathy with you or they can't relate to you, as a human being, it gets awfully difficult to get laughs.
> (Wilde, 2000: 156)

Comedy also allows men to look at their feelings without becoming 'effeminate,' because humour allows them to remain masculine while discussing their emotions and vulnerabilities. It is a form of exposed and intense self-reflection, which is more 'masculine' than 'feminine'. It also invites a critical (but not judgemental) response from the audience in the form of laughter.

The collective nature of psychological problems is is demonstrated by Jung's concept of the collective unconscious and the archetype. The comedian often strives to embody 'the ordinary individual'. According to Jung, the archetypes reside in the collective, and the collective unconscious is shared by everyone: '(...) it is sheer objectivity, as wide as the world and open to all the world. There I am the object of every subject, in complete reversal of my ordinary consciousness, where I am always the subject that has an object. There I am utterly one with the world, so much a part of it that I forget all to easily who I really am' (CW9/I: para. 46).

Most importantly, the audience and the comedian must establish a link before the magic, the unquantifiable physics of comedy and subsequent repair can happen. The on-stage creative process is part of the individuation, which presupposes finding yourself in relation to your society. The supportive community of people is important for the comedian's individuation, as they guide him through the process.

## *7.4. Stand Up Comedy as a Maturation Process*

Jung displayed in his analysis of the Amfortas Wound that the male drive was towards a higher elevated spiritual and feeling instinct whereas, Freud believed that during the puberty stage both the male and female focus is sexual: 'This apparatus is to be set in motion by stimuli, and observation shows us that stimuli can impinge on it from three directions: from the external world by means of the excitation of the erotogenic zones ( ...) from the organic interior , and from mental life […] The mental indications consist in a peculiar feeling of tension of an extremely compelling character; and among the numerous somatic ones are first and foremost a number of changes in the genitals, which have the obvious sense of being preparations for the sexual act […]' (Freud, SE, Vol.7: 208).

It is this sexual excitement on stage, that is palpable and many members of the audience encourage comedians to have sex after the show. Freud also defined libido as 'invariably and necessarily of a masculine nature, whether it occurs in men or women, and irrespectively of whether its object is a man or a woman' (SE, Vol.7: 219). Libido is intrinsically linked with objects in the outside world. The ego-libido becomes visible when it cathexes sexual objects – that is when it becomes object-libido. The audience are the objects, which the libido aims to attract.

The comedian can use his stand-up performance as an explanation of the Oedipal stages that he did not experience through in his or her childhood. The performer gradually matures on stage and learns to be less obsessed with himself and more understanding towards the world. During the last stage of the Oedipus complex, when the child's ego turns away from its obsession with the parent of the opposite sex.

> (…)the object-cathexes are given up and replaced by identifications. The authority of the father or the parents is introjected into the ego, and there it forms the nucleus of the super-ego, which takes over the severity of the father and perpetuates his prohibition against incest, and so secures the ego from the return of the libidinal object-cathexis. The libidinal trends belonging to the Oedipus complex are in part desexualised and sublimated (a thing which probably happens with every transformation into an identification) and in part inhibited in their aim and changed into impulses of affection
> 
> (Freud, SE, Vol.7: 319)

As he grows up on stage, the comedian realises that the audience is a collection of individuals and as such real people not objects. His material often moves from the personal to the collective, and from personal issues to social problems. For instance, the British comedian Rudi Lickwood changed his material significantly in the past twenty years. In the early days of his career, his material used to be based on personal experiences and events. Later it became socially informed. As he mentioned to me in a recent private conversation on Facebook: 'My comedy is a reflection of the hidden racist barriers that create the glass ceiling for minorities that have given so much to the development of Britain today' (Personal communication on Facebook, 15 April 2015).

## 7.5. Conclusion

The stages are significantly different and yet overlap for the comedian and stages of reflection and development. They are a continuum and they do not exist independently. The preparative process creates an intent, which is reflected in the actual stand-up performance. However it is at this stage that the interaction and variable psychological interactions take place. These can be accommodated depending upon the quality of the material and the comics own performance skills. The love from the audience is then accepted or rejected as 'good enough" depending upon the comics own intra-psychic matrix. He has the potential to reflect and interiorise and potentially take a step towards repair and assimilation his experience during the post performance reflective period. If he is conscious of his 'purpose to serve' as opposed to 'ego fulfilment' alone and has learned to oscillate the conflict individuation has great potential.

# CHAPTER 8

## THE COMEDIAN AND DEPRESSION

The comedian's creative process is often related to a type of depression and a feeling of being empty. Performing is emotionally and intellectually intensive that the 'normality' off stage feels grey and boring. All comedians experience a sense of loss after the performance, and also between shows.

They feel the need to fill the psychological void, the so-called inner emptiness, which is similar to the mourning process after the loss of a loved one. Freud defined mourning as ' loss of a loved person'. (Vol X1V p243) The removal of the audience (as the mother) for the comedian into his reality can have a melancholic and in certain cases depressive affect on the comedian.

It could be argued that it is a narcissistic issue and has to be analysed as such. One could argue that the comedian who has lack a sense of self and seeks to replace the void with a temporary emotional energy such as the audience attention and reaction. It is also directly linked to the question of identity. A variety of approaches to this issue will be used in this chapter, including a number of Freudian and post-Freudian ideas (Freud, Klein),

*8.*
### *8.1. The Insecure Comedian*

Comedy as a profession is often linked to mental health problems including depression and even suicide. There is an observable link between mental health issues and stand-up comedy. In the article *'The Great Comedians: Personality and Other Factors'*, the psychotherapist Samuel S. Janus argues that the fathers of the fifty five comedians with whom he happened to work were 'described for the most part as either absent, uninterested, or overtly disapproving' (Janus, 1975: 171). Later in the article he remarks that as many as eighty per cent of comedians hope that therapy will relieve them of 'a power struggle with an overwhelming father' (1975: 172).

On the surface, it sounds impossible: how can someone whose profession implies making the audience laugh and making people happy (even if temporarily) can think about ending his life? Besides, does he not get his dose of attention from the grateful audience every time he performs? Surely, his dose of attention should be enough to keep him going for a while? Robin Williams is a comedian who committed suicide for whom the act of being funny did not assuage his own depression.

Apparently, not many performers are capable of retaining the 'memory' of 'being happy' while on stage. The adulation of the audience is not enough to alleviate the comedian's depression. There are many examples of comedy stars fighting with depression and other mental health issues. For instance, in his autobiography *Camp David* (2012) the famous British TV comedian David Walliams reveals details of his suicide attempts – the latest being in 2003 (Walliams, 2012: 14). In an interview given to *The Independent* in 2012 he also discusses his life-long battle with depression. His depressive roots he says lie in his experiencing bullying as a youth. (Dex, *The Independent,* 4 October 2012). During his appearance in the Radio Four programme *Desert Island Discs,* he said that he would take a gun as his luxury item to a desert island so that he could shoot himself if he got lonely. He also says:

> I can't stand being on my own. I hate it. I have a pathological fear of being on my own. When I am with my own thoughts I start to unravel myself and I start to think really dark thoughts, self-destructive thoughts.
>
> I am trying to deal with it. I have learnt I have to make plans. I have to see people and do things because I don't want to get myself in that state and I can keep it at bay by being creative.
> (Hastings, *The Mail on Sunday,* February 22, 2009)

Other comedians, including Richard Jeni, Charles Rocket and Ray Combs, lost the fight with depression and committed suicide.

Many more stage and television comedians have been depressed at some stage of their life, or are chronically depressed but manage the condition relatively well – for instance, Steven Fry, Spike Milligan, John Cleese, Michael Barrymore, Tony Hancock, Woody Allen, John Belushi, Peter Cook and Jimmy Carr. For instance, Tony Slattery has admitted having a series of severe breakdowns complicated by alcohol and cocaine. (Sawyer, *The Guardian,* 6 July 2003).

Jimmy Carr battled with depression beginning in his twenties when, having graduated from Cambridge with a degree in Political Sciences, and then getting a good marketing job, he nevertheless felt dejected: 'my job, my life, how I was, who I was, how I was living (...) I didn't like it'. He turned to therapy and chose to train as a psychotherapist (Jones, *The Independent,* 18 November 2008). However, it was the decision to become a comedian changed his life:

> Somewhere along the line came comedy. "It almost sounds retarded, but I was very unhappy and I thought, 'What would make me happy? Comedy would be a joyful thing to do.' I was sad for a good few years, then I got into doing this and got happy." His father, Jim formed J C Productions Ltd and made Jimmy a director to get his career going. His mother, who encouraged him to take the plunge, died from pancreatitis when he was 28. She had amicably separated from his father, Jim, an entrepreneur, seven years earlier. Her death convulsed the family. Carr has an older brother, Colin, a City banker, and a younger brother, Patrick (currently doing a Masters in film in California).
> 
> (Jones, *The Independent,* 18 November 2008)

After Robin Williams's suicide in August 2014, the producer and performer John Lloyd explained that it was very common for comedians to struggle with mental health issues:

> Robin Williams was a complete genius and did an enormous body of work. You can't do that if you're just depressed. You're more likely to do that if you're bipolar and you have terrific bursts of creative activity.
> 
> "And there's a price for everything. Often, and I know this as a television producer, if you've finished a series and you've been on a high with pumping adrenalin every day, when you come down from it you're really low. It's punishing.
> 
> (Youngs, *The BBC Website,* 12 August 2014)

The comedian Ruby Wax is also very open about her clinical depression – as well as about her treatment at the Priory, the acute mental health rehabilitation centre, where she 'sat catatonically in a chair, staring catatonically into space' (Grace, *The Guardian,* 12 December 2011). Wax is also open about the roots of her unhappiness – an overly strict father and a mother who was depressive and prone to fits of rage raised her. Her main complaint is the internalized authority, which she inherited from her inadequate parents. She calls it 'the voices in her head' which have been with her ever since and resulted in a 'roller coaster of depression' for most of her adult life. She says in an interview with *The Mirror:*

> I'm sure [my mother) was loving but she was also nuts. She had OCD and couldn't stop cleaning. And screaming. She was very critical. And

> usually when you have the critical voices in your head you pass them on to the next person.
>
> I didn't know it but I was even depressed in my teens. I used to go to sleep for a few days at a time. But nobody knew what it was back then.
> (Gask, *The Mirror,* June 2013)

Unlike with other comedians, Wax's depression is life-long and powerful. At times she felt completely out of control, and she had to take extra care to hide her condition from her two children. She says candidly: 'I never contemplated suicide, but when you're in that much agony, mental pain is so much more agonising than physical and all you want it to do is stop. So I didn't plan on jumping from a building but I thought something's got to give' (Gask, *The Mirror*, June 2013).

The comedian and television personality Michael Barrymore, suffered from depression also, following the disclosure that he was gay. After the disclosure, Barrymore lost some of his fans, and his marriage became complicated. At some point, in 1996, he was admitted to hospital. Barrymore openly discusses the feelings he had during the time of emotional instability: 'I fear I'm going out of my mind. My brain jumps all over the place, from one thought to another. Quite literally I don't know my own mind. I try to be all things to all people and then when I start feeling pressure I do a runner. I don't know how to be happy' (Laville, *Evening Standard,* May 6, 1996). Lenny Henry also admits suffering from depression which left him 'fighting for his life' at the Priory Clinic (Chalmers and Hewett, *Daily Mail,* June 11, 1999).

Gender does not seem to affect the propensity for comedians to become depressed. Female and male comedians, alike, struggle with low self-esteem and a lack of control over their lives. Below is a short biography of Giada Garofalo, an Italian comedian and photographer:

> Giada Garofalo has a penchant for pointlessly over-thinking things – an activity she calls 'mental wanking'. Her *Fringe* debut is the result of her taking a one-year-sabbatical from sex, in order to clear her mind and focus on herself, a show that explores grief, and courage. With her unbridled thought exercises, and by trawling through her troubled adolescence, Garofalo takes us through why, until recently, she was so prone to depression or, as her therapist put it, had a "tendency to be bipolar". Though she warns that it can get dark at some points, the more personal her material became, the more interesting it was. Laughter came naturally and frequently in this show, that displays a young woman's honest and courageous confrontation with herself.
> (Oh, Three Weeks Edinburgh, 22 August 2013)

Ruby Wax has also become an advocate of announcing her mental health issues:

> There is still a huge stigma attached to mental illness in this country. Being depressed has become the modern-day witch trials. People can't see it and they don't understand it: some are worried it might be catching. For those who do come clean about their illness, the consequences can be catastrophic. While some industries are now more relaxed about it, there are still many in which your career is effectively over. You can't run a company once you've declared you've been diagnosed as clinically depressed. So the pressure to keep it to yourself, to try and tough it out, can be overwhelming. And, almost invariably, the longer you wait to get help, the worse the problem gets.
> (It's Grace, *The Guardian,* and 12 December 2011)

She has even become 'the poster girl for depression', encouraging people to share their experiences of being unhappy. (Crace, *The Guardian,* 12 December 2011). This, of course, is a curious and paradoxical position for a comedian to assume – talking publicly about sadness and depression instead of promoting jokes and laughter.

## *8.2. The Audience as Psychological Filler: the Hunger for Love*

A media psychologist and consultant Andrew Evans remarks that comedians get most of their love and affection from the audience and therefore the smallest rejection can lead to depressive thoughts: 'Because of their keen sense of injustice, they will feel criticism much stronger than us. Some of my patients ignore ten good reviews and are then cut in half by one mediocre one' (Sheffield, *The Guardian*, January 27, 1998).
Chris Rock admits in an interview with Franklyn Ajaye that his depression immediately goes away once he gets the undivided attention of the audience: 'Some nights I'm depressed, but as soon as they introduce me, it's all gone. I hear the music, and the people getting into it, and I know that as soon as I step out there, there's going to be a roar, so whatever down feelings I had are all gone' (Ajaye, 2002: 180).

Chris Rock's description of his stepping out on stage becomes his psychic nourishment– the physical, palpable manifestation of being loved and accepted. For some comedians it brings about a state of inflation, a compensatory state for their lack of self-worth – a semi-delusional, temporary state of being unconditionally loved by a large group of people. To an extent, this state is also dangerous because it gives one the impression that one will be loved and accepted by the 'surrogate mother' forever whereas, in fact, this is only a temporary happening which, when it ends, might trigger a bout of depression and hunger for more attention. Often a depressive episode happens immediately or shortly after the performance. As the comedian leaves stage the intensity of psychic energy which has been expended and expanded into the audience is re-internalised. The awakening that the Zwang nature of his material compulsively re-experiencing the catabasis of the neurosis has not dissoluted but amplified the affect of the core incident. Betrayed by the audience's oceanic sole attention has moving on to the next performer creating a relapse of the depressive state due to the reminder of losing or sharing or not being able to retain his mother's attention. Combining of all these successively paradoxical experiences replaying and re-igniting the feeling of emptiness and rage forces the comedian's psychological state to plunge.

The state of inflation is thus very addictive in order to avoid the potentially dejected and isolated state, and can be analysed either from a Freudian or Jungian perspective. For instance, from the Freudian (or the post-Freudian) angle, audience addiction can be explained by the narcissistic hunger and the need for mirroring. The intensity of the performance can be compared to the omnipotent Kleinian paranoid-schizophrenic position of the early pre-Oedipal stage. It is so all-absorbing that one cannot separate oneself from the audience. There is an addiction to the challenge of being on stage – as well as addiction to the feeling of being the centre of attention.

Being on stage is part of a powerful experience, similar to the Jungian interpretation of *participation mystique,* when the performer merges with the audience. As Jung describes, 'the more we see personality disappearing beneath the wrappings of collectivity. And if we go right back to primitive psychology, we find absolutely no trace of the concept of an individual. Instead of individuality we find only collective relationship or what Lévy-Bruhl calls *participation mystique* (Jung, [1921] 1971: par. 12).

The affect of the *participation mystique* makes the comedians' soul feel connected, this corresponds to the term *abbaisement du niveau mental,* which borrowed from Janet by Jung as 'The tonus has given way, and this is felt subjectively as listlessness, moroseness, and depression. One no longer has any wish or courage to face the tasks of the day. One feels like lead, because no part of one's body seems willing to move, and this is due to the fact that one no longer has any disposable energy. . . . The listlessness and paralysis of will can go so far that the whole personality falls apart, so to speak, and consciousness loses its unity . . . . this listless depression is experienced as the 'loss of soul'. It is during the performance that the richness of soul connection is experienced and through all consuming experience the comedian become depleted both in terms of libido, as spiritual and sexual drive, but also in spiritual connection. Following the performance the performer feels like he doesn't need anybody else, but gradually he realise that he does. Depression slowly emerges through the haze of being hysterically loved and admired by a crowd of people, and the performer realises that, in the real world, he needs to make contact with other people; to make an effort to connect with others and he will never be loved in the same way. The love from an audience can make him feel omnipotent, where everything he does is right and is omniscient back in his uroboric state of a newly born infant truly adored, he becomes a demi-God, his mother's attention is total.

This state is so emotionally intensive that it can become addictive. The feeling is totally absorbing, it takes one over; and if there is a small sign of success, it gives one a feeling of completeness. Many comedians go back to this state over and over again to get their supply of the drug that is attention. During the live creative process and the resultant emotional exchange with the audience, the comedian's self-esteem inflates, and then it may deflate sharply or gradually after the performance. Depending on how broken the comedian's sense of Self is, his ego either holds to some of the self-esteem extracted from the audience, or fails to store it up and feels the need to go back for more.

Mario Jacoby mentions that Freud linked self-regard directly to narcisstic libido. Freud wrote in *Narcissism: an Introduction* (1914)*:* In the first place self-regard appears to be an expression of the size of the ego; what the various elements are which go to determine that size is irrelevant. Everything a person possesses or achieves, every remnant of the primitive feeling of omnipotence which his experience has confirmed, helps to increase this self-regard' (Freud, 1914: 98).

However, for Kohut, the broken or fragile self has difficulty joining its different parts together as the walls of the psychological container are too thin. Kohut writes that such a self is

> ... the self of the child that, in consequence of the severely disturbed empathic responses of the parents, has not been securely established, and it is the enfeebled and fragmentation-prone self that (in an attempt to reassure itself that it is still alive, even that it exists at all) turns defensively toward pleasure aims through the stimulation of erogenic zones, and then, *secondarily,* brings about the oral (and anal) drive orientation and the ego's enslavement to the drive aims correlated to the stimulated body zones.
>
> (Kohut, 1977: 97)

Klein links greed for attention which emerges during the depressive position during the ego's realisation that it is separate from the external world, similar to the narcissistic longing discussed by Kohut and Jacoby. The baby goes through a number of physical and psychological changes, which are evidence of the gradual development of the ego. She writes in the essay 'Some Theoretical Conclusions Regarding the Emotional Life of the Infant' (1952): 'Integration, consciousness, intellectual capacities, the relation to the external world and other functions of the ego are steadily developing' (Klein, 1988: 72). However, Klein continues, when the baby dreads, 'that the real, loving mother may be lost and that the girl *(or boy)* will be left solitary and foresaken'. (Klein, 1929 p 217) Klein argues that the baby cannot deal with the loss of a good object, the mother, who aids the formation of a strong ego. The baby is greedy for the mother's attention – which in adults turns into the greed for attention to alleviate the dominant 'bad objects and by hatred and destructive impulses' (Klein 1957 p181). During the depressive position the baby cannot also cope with the loss of an external good object as it amplifies the initial loss of the mother resulting in feelings of mourning guilt and need for reparation.

Besides, the baby starts to realise that, even when the objects are 'internalised', they still exist in an 'external' form and are therefore outside of the baby's influence. The baby has ambivalent feelings about the whole situation – it is a love-hate relationship. Klein writes:

> The various aspects – loved and hated, good and bad – of the objects become closer together, and these objects are now whole persons. The processes of synthesis operate over the whole field of internal and external object-relations. They comprise the contrasting aspects of the internalised objects (the early super-ego) on the one hand and of the external objects on the other; but the ego is also driven to diminish the discrepancy between the external and internal world, or rather, the discrepancy between the external and internal figures. Together with these synthetic processes go further steps in integration of the ego, which result in a greater coherence between the split-off parts of the ego. All these processes of integration and synthesis cause the conflict between love and hatred to come out in full force. The ensuring depressive anxiety and feeling of guilt alter not only in quantity but also in quality.
>
> (Klein, 1988: 72)

Meanwhile, the baby feels guilty about its 'bad' feelings towards the objects, now perceived as whole people, and its own desire to destroy or devour them: 'Greed and the defences against it play a significant part at this stage, for the anxiety of losing irretrievably the loved and indispensable object tends to increase greed. Greed, however, is felt to be uncontrollable and destructive and to endanger the loved external and internal objects' (1988: 72-3).

However, the attention received by the comedian on stage does not always fill the void – or sometimes fills the void, but only temporarily. Whereas the 'logical' thing would be to use the state of elation experienced during the performance to make the self feel more 'whole' and 'complete' in the long term, comedians often fail to use the attention generated by the audience for therapeutic purposes. They 'spend' the attention and 'love' granted by the audience in unproductive ways. Eventually, after the performance, the inflated sense of self disappears and the comedian is left emotionally worse off than he or she had been before the performance. This post performance state is similar to Depressive Anxiety, which as Klein suggests can be fulfilled by an external object but only as a compensatory act. The comedian must repair this state in order to reduce the anxiety.

This acknowledgement can facilitate the process of individuation for the comedian. However, for some comedians the depressive anxiety is so great that to repeat the stand-up performance which magnifies the anxiety as a 'wound' is constantly opened and re-engaging with the ambivalent nature of interacting with the 'internal and external (mother) object' can throw the comedian into a deeper depression and despair.

Jungian individuation, as discussed in previous chapters, presupposes that one can become 'oneself' only in relation to one's society. One looks for completeness in others, one can only find self-fulfilment in one's friends, partners and relatives. One is supposed to truly branch out into the world, to get outside one's limited area of subjective consciousness, to engage with other people – not as objects (which would still count as 'looking into the mirror') but as human beings. That's precisely what many comedians fail to achieve. They cannot afford to 'relate' to the audience because their performance is structured, and because they are insecure, and any attempts at aggressive engagement on part of the audience, such as heckling, is usually stopped abruptly by the comedian.

On the one hand, the performer has no intention or resources to get into a proper 'dialogue' with the audience outside the narrow framework of a pre-planned performance, in which there is no space for the public's 'true' reactions, and in which the public is only expected to provide positive reactions such as laughter or applause.

Effectively, they do not want a dialogue with the public, they do not want a 'genuine' engagement. What they want is to establish control over their audience in order to make it safe for themselves. The format of a stand-up comedy slot does not presuppose a 'proper' dialogue with the audience, which means that the comedian can control both the audience and the flow of the performance.

Often the audience challenges the comedian (which is a forced way of attempting to establish a dialogue in a format in which any verbal exchanges are strictly controlled), and it may even be that comedians subconsciously want to be challenged. There is an attraction in this kind of conflict, although it can be a potentially traumatising experience. Trauma, as Donald Kalsched reminds us, can be addictive because the traumatized psyche is self-traumatizing:

> Trauma doesn't end with the cessation of outer violation, but continues unabated in the inner world of the trauma victim, whose dreams are often haunted by persecutory inner figures. The second finding is the seemingly perverse fact that *the victim of psychological trauma continually finds himself or herself in life situations where he or she is retraumatized.* As much as he or she wants to change, as hard as he or she tries to improve life or relationships, something more powerful than the ego continually undermines progress or destroys hope. It is as though the persecutory inner world somehow finds its outer mirror in repeated self-defeating 're-enactments' – almost as if the individual were *possessed* by some diabolical power or pursued by a malignant fate.
>
> (Kalsched, 2010: 5).

Once the trauma is internalized, it lives through 'internal persecutors':

> Most contemporary analytic writers are inclined to see this attacking figure as an internalized version of the actual perpetrator of the trauma, who has 'possessed' the inner world of the trauma victim. But this popularized view is only half correct. The diabolical inner figure if often far more sadistic and brutal than any other perpetrator, indicating that we are dealing here with a *psychological* factor set loose in the inner world by trauma – an archetypal traumatogenic agency within the psyche itself.
>
> (2010: 4)

Sandor Ferenczi also wrote in his essay 'Narcissism *and the* Search for Interiority' (1980):

> A surprising but apparently generally valid feature of this process of self-splitting is the sudden change of the object relation that has become intolerable, into narcissism. The man abandoned by all gods escapes completely from reality and creates for himself another world in which he, unimpeded by earthly gravity, can achieve everything that he wants. He has been unloved, even tormented, he now splits off from himself a part which, in the form of a helpful, loving, often motherly minder, commiserates with the tormented remainder of the self, nurses him and decides for him, and all this is done with the deepest wisdom and most penetrating intelligence. He is intelligence and kindles itself, so to speak a guardian angel. This angel sees the suffering of a murdered child from the outside, he wanders through the whole

universe seeking help, invents fantasies for the child that cannot be saved in any other way, etc. But in the moment of a very strong, repeated trauma even the guardian angel must confess his own helplessness and well-meaning deceptive swindles to the tortured child and then nothing else remains but suicide, unless at the last moment some favourable change in the reality occurs. This favourable even to which we can point against suicidal impulse is the fact that in this new traumatic struggle the patient is no longer alone.

(Ferenci, Kalsched, 1980: 49).

To apply Kalscheds' theory it is possible that comedians deliberately look for trauma and find it in their relationship with the audience during the performance. They look for compliance and love, or, conversely, for a proof that 'the perfect connection' with the loving audience-mother is impossible. Since no equal interaction is possible within the tightly regulated format of stand-up performance, the comedian ends up having a controlling relationship with the audience which either results in 'love and acceptance' or 'conflict and 'rejection'. However, even the best-loved and accepted comedians get depressed. In this case, neither outcome seems to be favourable as far as depression is concerned, and any confidence gained by the comedian during the performance is spent very quickly and the comedian is left depleted, empty and wanting more attention and control.

## *8.3. Audience as an Abusive or Neglectful Parent*

Instead of the kind and accepting mother, the audience might start playing the role of the bad mother, a neglectful parent. In this case the comedian spends his emotional resources on pleasing the audience and 'forgets' about his needs. His personality remains 'unfed' and unsupported. This inability to nurture one's personality creatively might be one of the reasons comedians become depressed and dissatisfied with their lives and career.

In this case, the comedian's role as 'the leader' on stage is questioned. The audience is seen as attacking, and the performer may become aggressive and defensive in order to precipitate any attacks. These attacks can be a reminder and re-enactment of earlier childhood attack. In fact, there are two ways for the comedian to deal with this kind of audience – to try to please them or, by contrast, to go into the defensive mode and attack them (before or after their attack). It takes some comedians a lot of time to learn the correct emotional and behavioural ways of dealing with an aggressive audience – the metaphorical non-accepting mother.

For instance, the British comedian Stewart Lee explains that the ability to deal with the audience's destructiveness is a matter of time. Performers eventually learn to contain and manage both their own and the listener's feelings and behaviour:

> I suppose, I've done a thousand gigs, and I've only been heckled about ten times. It used to always absolutely destroy me, but when it happens now, I can usually go with it, because I can stay in character and deal with it in a way that seems appropriate to the act. I got heckled off two years ago in Southend, for being gay. I hadn't done any material about being gay – and that was reason enough to get someone offstage. There was nothing I could say about it. It wasn't even as if I've made a point about it – it came out of nowhere. The whole audience was chanting at me. It was a weird sort of hatred. I don't know where it came from. I was on for only about ten minutes. As soon as I went on, people started shouting at me. Somebody shouted out, 'Are you gay?' And I did not know what to say. And then they all started chanting, 'Crucify him!' Which was really strange. I don't know what I did – I've never had anything like it. Afterwards, the bloke who ran the gig said, 'I can't pay you – you didn't do the set'.
>
> (Cook, 1994: 224-5)

Another comedian, Eddie Izzard, outlines his own ways of deflating the hecklers – creatively. He would confer a whole new identity on the heckler, thus wrestling all control from him or her, and re-establishing mastery of the audience and the situation. His technique means that disruptive audience members did not divert his attention from the material he wanted to present. He learned to skilfully inoculate himself against the aggressive hecklers:

> I first dealt with hecklers on the street. I'd developed what I called the Imposing Scenario technique. Someone would say, 'Fuck off!' and I'd say, 'This is Steve. He is going to be saying "Fuck off" at regular intervals. He's a beginner heckler from Kent – he's driven up here for the day'. You'd impose a whole identity on to him and although the audience knew it was all bullshit, he became your assistant. Every time 'Steve' said, 'Fuck off – you're crap', I'd say, 'Good! Keeps me on my toes. Thank you, Steve!' And that deflected all the heckles.
>
> (Cook, 1994: 225).

Most importantly, Izzard points out that the performer should under no circumstances show their anger or annoyance at the heckler. This would mean that the comedian lost control over the audience, which was exactly what the heckler wanted:

> There are so many nutters on the street. They wander past and say, 'Hey! There's a show here!' And they actually come into the show. If

you ever get angry, you lost it. One time, seven guys started heckling – they do it in groups in the street. They attacked me really early, so the audience weren't with me. They were doing mindboggingly crap heckles and they ruined the show. I had to cancel, and at the end they came over and said, 'That was great, mate! Well done! We loved it! Great fun! Did we help you? We were trying to help you!' I wanted to kill them. It's some sort of spill over from the vaudeville of yesteryear.
(1994: 225-6)

The comedian expects the audience to create a safe environment, which would allow the performer to fully express himself as well as to rebuild his self-confidence and self-esteem. At the same time, heckling is a practice that is only allowed in a limited number of contexts, and stand-up comedy is one of them. Heckling is a form of expression of aggression, and therefore has to be controlled and managed in a 'civilized' context for the sake of all participants in a framed experience. According to Van Gennep (169:2004), 'especially during the transition periods, a special language is employed which in some cases include an entire vocabulary unknown or unusual in the society as a whole.' This can apply to the heckling process in stand-up. Stand-up comedy is one of the last remaining places where this kind of liminal experience is still allowed, almost in its primal form. A performance is still a framework, and any aggression – or any other liminal phenomena – still has to be captured and framed. This residual liminality is a leftover from traditional slapstick comedy, the pre-modern comedy which was 'in touch' with the masses, and which gave individual members of the audience the right to meddle with the performance. The audience was allowed to participate in 'the ritual'. It is plausible that 'heckling' can be seen as what Turner in The Ritual Process (p175/6) informs us is 'status reversal.' Rituals of status reversal (…) according to this principle, mask the weak in strength and demand of the strong that they be passive and patiently endure the symbolic and even real aggression shown against them by structural inferiors.'

With contemporary stand-up comedy it is more complicated. Such 'medieval' liminal 'status reversal' ritual as heckling can be psychologically or even physically dangerous. However, the comedian is already an individual performer, attempting to express his own self and establish himself as an individual on stage. Victor Turner would call this kind of performance 'liminoid' as opposed to the pre-individual expressions of creativity typical of small communities and pre-industrial societies. While liminality is matched with pre-modern consciousness and expresses itself in the rebellious, healthy, spontaneous creativity of the carnival, liminoidness renders the meaninglessness of contemporary mass entertainment. In social context, liminality describes transitional periods in pre-industrial societies. By contrast, liminoid phenomena, although they may also be collective (rock concerts, big sports events, mass spectacles), are rarely spontaneous and are carefully pre-planned, organised and produced. Unlike pre-modern liminal events, which denote change of personal, social or calendrical status within a given community and do not have a commercial purpose (or, at least, if it exists, it is not decisive), contemporary liminoid phenomena are becoming commercialised. In other words, a liminoid event or artefact is usually a one-off product of individual creativity or small constellation of creativities. Liminoid products are not cyclical but continuously generated; tend to be more idiosyncratic, quirky, radical and subversive than liminal phenomena (which are 'generalised and normative'); develop 'outside the central economic and political processes' and are 'plural, fragmentary, and experimental' (1992: 56-57). Liminoid phenomena 'flourish in societies of more complex structure. They are not cyclical but intermittent, generated often in times and places assigned to the leisure sphere' (1977b: 50-51, quoted in St. John, 2008: 133).

This situation accesses the early primal motivations the performer may feel like a child building his world with the help of the Winnicottian transitional object – the maternal audience. The audience is expected to support and buffer the performer against any aggression, shown in the form of heckling or even climbing on their stage, as well as to be accepting and friendly. Most importantly, the comedian does not want too much challenge from the audience, and many performers deal with hecklers (who, essentially, narcissistically injure them) in rough and ruthless ways. One such story involves Jimmy Carr who was annoyed by an audience member who was trying to show off:

> The last time I saw Jimmy Carr, he was having a decent gig, until some idiot interrupted him. Suddenly Carr was entirely in the room with us. He looked genuinely annoyed, but he never lost control. He chided the heckler for interrupting him while he was working. "How would you like it if I came to your workplace," he asked, "and knocked the sailors' cocks out of your mouth?" For all I know, Carr uses that line three times a week. But the speed, the aggression, the casual filth of it, felt entirely bespoke. It was the head rooster pecking out his challenger's eyes. Great Saturday night entertainment, in short.
> (Maxwell, *The Times,* October 13, 2011)

Other examples include rude jokes by Markus Birdman ('Sssh, madam. Pay attention and you'll realise we have a lot in common, not just the beard') and Arthur Smith ('Is that your real face or are you still celebrating Hallowe'en?' Female heckler: 'That is an ugly shirt'), Rufus Hound ('Sister, unless you're the mayoress or the world's shittest Mr T impersonator, I'd lose some of that cheap, gold jewellery before you criticise how people look') and Hal Cruttenden ('That's fine, you're very young and very pretty, but one day your looks will fade and you'll have to rely on your personality and you'll be screwed') (Maxwell, *The Times,* October 13, 2011).

Maxwell also outlines the psychology behind hecklers' behaviour:

> A heckler looks at the act on stage, sees how in control of the room they are, how everyone facing them seems to laugh on cue, how they have a microphone (so are therefore louder than anyone else in the room by far), how well lit and visible they are ...the heckler looks at all that and thinks: "I can take him/ her." This is because the heckler is a moron.
> (Maxwell, *The Times,* October 13, 2011)

Sometimes hecklers – and the audience with them – engage into a 'power reversal' and struggle with the audience. However, there are times the struggle for 'power reversal' becomes one of 'status reversal,' in which it is the aim of the heckler to become superior to the comedian. The superior comedian will permit this status superiority 'by making the low high and the high low, they reaffirm the hierarchical principle.' (Turner:1974) One famous anecdote involves Eric Douglas and his risky response to a witty heckler:

> Eighteen years ago, Eric Douglas, Kirk Douglas's son, was a bit upset at the audience reaction to his routine and shouted back: "You can't do this to me – I'm Kirk Douglas's son!" Some wag in the audience stood up and shouted out: "No, I'm Kirk Douglas's son," swiftly followed by the rest of the audience. He died on his arse.
> (Ward, *The Guardian,* May 16, 2009)

Hecklers can be even more problematic for a female comedian who might be regarded as vulnerable and as an easy target. For instance, the black female comedian Ava Vidal talks about her experiences of dealing with male hecklers who, she says, are 'evil' because they attempt to divert the attention away from the female comedian and claim power and control for themselves:

> The Heckler is evil. It is the person that you are warned about when you first start doing stand up. The person that you dread will be in your gig interrupting the show with slurred insults usually yelled out just at the precise moment that ruins the punchline you've been building up to. The Heckler is the person that is so powerful that they can ruin the whole night for every single comedian on the bill.
> Unlike Superman, David or Wonder Woman, we don't know our enemy's name and won't be able to instantly recognise their face in a crowd. He or she can be old or young, black or white. The only clue that you have to possibly identify this purveyor of all evilness is that

they will probably be drunk, (which to be honest, on most comedy nights doesn't really narrow it down).

(Vidal, *The Telegraph,* 5 Nov 2013)

Ava notes that there is a special dynamic between the female comedian and the male heckler – an almost Oedipal dynamic. The male heckler desperately wants to be noticed and attempts to prove and establish his superior status, encouraged by other the attitude of male comedians whose on stage material can be sexist, by challenging the dominant female:

> I have been performing stand up comedy for about 10 years now and have inevitably met several hecklers along the way. Hecklers don't really bother me. I was a prison officer at Pentonville, a male prison in North London, before becoming a comedian, so I have been heckled by people with time on their hands. However, there does seem to be a special dynamic between comedian and heckler when the comedian happens to be female.
>
> I have always stated that most comedy clubs are sexist places. Especially the big weekend ones that have lots of stag and hen parties in attendance. They are of course a reflection of society but everything is heightened. A comedian typically has 20 minutes on stage to perform their set and they are not going to be up there sharing their blandest, most middle-of-the-road views. They are often very extreme and things get exaggerated. Some of the sexism that I have heard come out of the mouths of male comedians is so shocking that if I were not paid to be there, I would just get up and walk out. It is this same machismo that often makes comedy clubs an unsafe space for lesbians and gay men

(Vidal, *The Telegraph,* 5 Nov 2013)

Vidal also emphasises that the comments from hecklers tend to combine sexuality and aggression in attempt to subdue the female who is currently getting the most attention from the sheer fact of being on stage and being given the opportunity to express herself. However, the good thing about it is the opportunity to answer back in a colourful language and to use her female power – the power to reject and to refuse to give attention to a male.

> One of the most standard heckles that female comedians receive is: 'Show us your tits love!'

> Jo Enright gave the most beautiful answer to this that I ever heard when she simply replied in a puzzled tone: 'Why should I be the first woman in the world to show you her tits?'
>
> When a man tries to exert his authority over me when I'm onstage, I normally put him down very quickly. 'I want you to treat me like every single woman that you've ever met and assume that I am not interested,' is one of my favourites.
>
> I was once told by male heckler that I was 'about as funny as a headache'. I replied: 'I am sure that you know a fair bit about headaches as I am guessing that your girlfriend has one every night.'
>
> The audience love it when you slam a heckler firmly back in their place, especially when you are female and they are male. Most men take it in the spirit in which it was intended and will offer to buy you a drink afterwards to show there are no hard feelings. But I have had a couple that have turned nasty. I had one guy who had come to the club with some colleagues and they told me they worked as bouncers. One decided to show off and started to heckle me. I responded and he carried on and he was losing badly. His friends really enjoyed it and they then started teasing him. Afterwards he came over to me and said: 'Are you that funny when you're at home in the kitchen washing up? Do yourself a favour and stay there.'
>
> (Vidal, *The Telegraph,* 5 Nov 2013)

Female hecklers, meanwhile, despite being harmless in terms of comments and language, are nevertheless 'the worst kind of heckler' when they get drunk in groups and attack the performer because they are difficult to control:

> The way that I deal with a female heckler is very different from the way that I would treat a male one. In the spirit of sisterhood I will always give a woman a couple of chances but I firmly let her know that if she continues I will go off on her. If you're a female comedian and you steam in and destroy another woman immediately then you can often lose the audience. You're seen as being bitchy, and unless that is part of your onstage persona, then you don't want that. You don't come out of the exchange looking good at all.
>
> (Vidal, *The Telegraph,* 5 Nov 2013)

Hecklers disrupt the basic trust expected of an 'ideal audience'. The comedians' responses can be seen as defensive as the psyche can interpret the heckle as an attack which replays their early trauma on stage. The rude responses are managed, triggered and guided by defence mechanisms. The defence mechanism activated can be seen as the 'protective "agent" of the self-care system.' Joseph Redfearn (1992) described a specific primitive defensive "complex" originating in trauma and acting between two inner sub-personalities, one a vulnerable child, the other "the omnipotent, apocalyptic God sub personality" who threatens to annihilate everything with " the bomb". The 'bomb' is the 'put-down' that comedians use to annihilate the heckler or to minimise their impact, so that the comedian's superior status is maintained.

The performer thus becomes defensive and aggressive on stage when the world he is trying to create for himself – an ideal world of love and acceptance – is threatened by some members of the audience. The audience is symbolised as that of the supporter, of the mother – and is not wanted in a 'paternal' role of Oedipal rival and challenger. What is therefore addictive is the positive and warm response, the elation that is shared both by the audience and the performer, but is initiated, produced and controlled by the performer.

There is a third view on the comedian-audience relationship and its relation to depression. The person on stage can be seen metaphorically as a child, fragile and exposed, who needs a lot of 'feeding' and understanding. The audience can be more accepting or less accepting, but the comedian's vision of it is always going to be biased and subjective. His view of the audience is similar to that of the baby's perception of his mother as an ambivalent object whose behaviour is directly linked to the baby's survival. As Fairbairn states;

> It is the experience of libidinal frustration that calls fourth the infant's aggression in relation to his libidinal object and thus gives rise to a state of ambivalence […] Since it proves intolerable to him to have a good object that is also bad, he seeks to alleviate the situation by splitting the figure of his mother into two objects. Then, in so far as she satisfies him libidinally, she is a 'good' object, and, in so far as she fails to satisfy him libidinally, she is a 'bad' object.
> 
> (Fairbairn, 2013: 110)

Meanwhile, the non-accepting audience, which may result in re-creation of an early trauma, can give rise to an ambiguous ambivalent internal response for the comedian who can show frustration that he is weak and defeated.

> If, on the one hand, [the child] expresses aggression, he is threatened with loss of his good object, [she rejects him all the more] and if, on the other hand, he expresses libidinal need, he is threatened with the singularly devastating experience of humiliation over the depreciation of his love, shame over the display of needs which are disregarded or

> belittled, [or] … still at a deeper level, an experience of disintegration and of imminent psychical death.
>
> (2013: 110)

The comedian does not trust the audience; he simply does not believe that he can be loved and accepted unconditionally. His depression, when it happens, is a profoundly existentialist feeling, and his dissatisfaction with the ungrateful and unfaithful, betraying audience is the frustration of an agent over the fact that the world cannot be entirely managed and controlled;and highlights that he is imperfect. . To an extent, the comedian fails to see the audience as having 'a mind of its own' and having its own needs and emotions, none of which are related to the comedian outside the framework of the performance. During the performance, the comedian sees the audience as either a 'bad' or a 'good' object depending on how well the satisfy his or her emotional needs and hunger for attention and acceptance. In sense, the value of the audience-object, from the point of view of the comedian, depends on its ability to be 'a good mother' and to look after the performer during the course of the set.

## *8.4.* *Early Childhood Experiences and Depression*

Many comedians link their depressive episodes to their childhood experiences. Stephen Fry, who, by his admission, has had two suicide attempts in a recent interview he talks about depression and suicidal tendencies being part of his family history.

> In 1987, when I was 31, I suffered a suicidal episode, which I fortunately lacked the courage to bring to its conclusion. I stood swaying on high buildings; I teetered on the edge of Tube platforms. I was only relieved of the symptoms by taking medication – a course that I had resisted for four years, because taking antidepressants was to admit that I was mentally ill.
>
> Shortly afterwards, my mother committed suicide, a story that I recounted in my "coming out of the depressive closet" memoir, The Scent of Dried Roses. These are facts, even now, that I find hard to recount, because part of me is blighted by shame.
>
> (Lott, *The Telegraph,* 7 June 2013)

Fry reportedly struggled with manic depression and his suicide attempts include trying to kill himself with exhaust fumes. He says:

> I went into my garage, sealed the door with a duvet I'd brought and got into my car. I sat there for at least, I think, two hours in the car, my hands on the ignition key. It was, you know, a suicide attempt, not a cry for help. In the end, he did not go through with it and instead fled to Belgium. [...]
>
> But after a week I secretly returned to England, to this hospital, and to a doctor telling me I'm bipolar.
>
> I'd never heard the word before, but for the first time at the age of 37 I had a diagnosis that explains the massive highs and miserable lows I've lived with all my life. There's no doubt that I do have extremes of moods that are greater than just about anybody else I know.
> (The Daily Mail, 21 July 2006)

It is notable that he links suicide to the feeling of being ashamed of being out of control. Fry describes the feeling of shame as being unstoppable, and the suicidal thoughts as being unmanageable. These thoughts cannot be cured by wishful thinking, or with the help of folk wisdom such as 'just do it' or 'you've got everything, what else do you want'. By his own admission, his desire to die was mostly unconscious ('teetering on the edge of platforms', 'standing swaying on high buildings'), which added to its basic and terrifying uncontrollability:

And yet nowadays a larger part of me is ashamed of being ashamed. I cannot say what the source of this shame is, other than the thought of being "a bit weird". I recognise this as absurd, even harmful, but it is hard to wish away, because the prejudice of society is still strong, even if it is, like racism, kept behind closed doors nowadays. His shame is exacerbated by his interaction with the audience who show love for his 'shameful' personality, the aspect of his personality has not been accepted by the mother and hence not contained. The 'shameful' aspect of his personality has no right to the love which he's shown by the audience as the mother, since it is paradoxical to self-reality. Should the audience reflect the 'real' mother, as opposed to the 'archetypal mother,' for whom the comedian has to be perfect, his shame can become overwhelming exacerbating the internal conflict of elation of self-expression versus the depression of super-ego admonishment, coinciding with deserving the adulation versus the shame of being ill -warranted over which he has no control and from which he wants to remove himself.

Suicide and depression are not seen as morally neutral, like a heart attack or any other kind of purely physical ailment is. They imply personal failure, madness, neuroticism, but the intensity of all events converging creating the desire for suicide can be overwhelming and move the individual to attack the very essence of his existence, his defensive protective ego mechanism has been weakened. "Ordinary" depression, from which I suffer, along with a huge number of other people in this country – including such famous victims as Ruby Wax and Alastair Campbell – is more complex and more liable to be mixed in with psychological factors. It is such sufferers whom idiots like to tell to "pull their socks up and stop whining". Yes, there is an element of personal responsibility in depression, which is why non-drug treatments such as Cognitive Behavioural Therapy and various forms of analysis and counselling can have a positive effect, and why sometimes antidepressants have no effect whatsoever.

But this is not the same as saying that depression is something that depressives "do to themselves", an idea that encourages stigma; one that retains traces in the media. It is true that we have come a long way since The Sun's infamous "Bonkers Bruno Locked Up" headline, when the boxer Frank Bruno was hospitalised after suffering depression in 2003. But the illness is still very much misunderstood by anyone who hasn't suffered from it.

> Naturally, onlookers are puzzled when they see apparently successful people wanting to die, even though they seem to have what the man in the street could only dream of. It is seen as self-indulgent by some – certainly I was aware that people called my mother "selfish" after she killed herself.
> (Lott, *The Telegraph*, 7 June 2013)

Another comedian, Freddie Starr, admits to suicidal thoughts and has to take antidepressants every day. He says in an interview to *Belfast Telegraph:* 'It's come into my mind once or twice. And I think, "what's it all about? Why am I going through this?' Why is this happening?" You think, "Maybe I'd be better off out of the way"' (*Belfast Telegraph*, May 18, 2000). Starr ended up taking handfuls of antidepressants, sometimes as many as thirty-six a day. At some point they stopped working: 'No matter what anti-depressant you take, you become immune to it after a while so they stop working' (*Belfast Telegraph*, May 18, 2000). His difficulties began in childhood when a speech impediment led to him temporarily losing the ability to speak, and he had to spend two years at home. Starr said that he covered his insecurities by being nonchalantly funny and relaxed: 'I play the person that doesn't care or with no feelings but little do people know how seriously I do take my job. I just like to make people laugh. We're not talking about brain surgery here or saving people's lives, we're talking about laughter, which is one of the greatest medicines in the world. I can give some of that to an audience and that's great' (*Belfast Telegraph*, May 18, 2000).

Audience reactions to comedians' 'behind the scenes' life is also interesting. As Roger Dobson argues in *The Independent,* spectators are often surprised or even shocked by the fact that comedians suffer from mood swings and melancholy. There is a discrepancy between 'the real person' with his or her deep problems and insecurities, and the mask of the clown, brave and defiant. After all, the comedians are the ones who are supposed to make us feel better about the human condition.

One could agree that from the audience's perspective as the symbolic mother, the comedian is the baby who is the new born and able to make her world better. However, if the internalised mother is unhappy, depressed or suicidal then the weight of responsibility internalised by the comedian, as baby, can be crushing. His role to 'rescue' the mother can be too great and the repetition of this problem by re-engaging with an audience that has such a great an expectation of him to be more than a 'hero' but the 'saviour' can further diminish the comedians' self worth. She can become, as Neumann states, the 'terrible mother' who is a 'goddess of death' ( 245:)

If the comedian cannot overcome the mother's needs and transform himself by integrating the overpowering feminine, from whom he had no protection, either via the father or another family trusted member, alongside his weaker under-developed masculine then the inevitable demise in some form of depression will take place.

Whenever, the male's ego-development is disturbed and he has not attained independence – e.g., where his ego has remained infantile due to a mother fixation and has not achieved the "combativity" necessary for the heroic ego- each demand for "transformation," every demand to develop towards something unknown and away from whatever provides security is answered with fear and defensiveness'. (254:1994)

He can either use the material he develops as a stand-up to determine his therapeutic process or aim to compensate by over-indulging the audiences expectations of himself or by finding a partner with whom he can externalise the 'anima' figure and play out and transform his internal patterns. If he cannot transform 'the mother' both internally as the actual experience of his mother, or externally as the audience or giver of love. This means he can stop performing in front of the audience as 'devouring mother' or chooses to perform in a more restricted and controlled environment as television or film. If the call of the creative and spontaneous is too great and he cannot consciously engage in the symbolic process then the outcome has a futility and the creative productive life-giving mother becomes invested with immense authority and numinous affects which leads to traumatic darkness and its affect.

## *8.5. Conclusion*

Some comedians are depressed, which sounds paradoxical and out of sync with their profession. Many famous stand-up comedians have even attempted to commit suicide. The roots of their continued depression often lie in their relationship with the audience, which replays its origins from their childhood. The performer wants to establish an ideal situation of acceptance and trust with their listeners; often feeling unfulfilled since the cause is not identified meaning that, he or she feels constantly unloved and rejected. Ultimately, however, being accepted by the audience is important in the short term but not in the long term because the 'trust' and 'connection' established with the audience is transient and can immerse the comedian in a recollection of painful unresolved experiences activating a psychic attack where the depression feels like a traumatic event. The temporary on stage relationship has to be counterbalanced with a lasting relationship and realisation of the cause of her depression or vulnerability can become exaggerated and potentially devastating.

# CHAPTER 9

## GENDER, CULTURE AND COMEDY

This chapter discusses the difference between male and female stand-up comedians, and the role of female comedians in the industry. It discusses a range of issues associated with women in live comedy: the female voice, sexist and patronising treatment by the male representatives of the industry, male envy, the compatibility of comedy and femininity, of the material of female jokes, and gender identity on stage. The best theoretical base for discussing these issues are a combination of Jungian psychology (particularly the concept of the animus), Freud's ideas (the link between jokes and aggression) and gender studies.

Western society largely ignores the proactive, creative, decision-making female, particularly in such male-dominated areas as politics, entertainment and corporate culture. Society's main socio-political structures are still predominantly masculine principles and male-dominated. There is no place in them for the woman who does not fill the what was until recently viewed as the traditional feminine role as the receptive vessel who listens, soothes and does not show much of her own personality. The woman, prototypically the mother, is the object who is always there to accept and to deliver love. The mother who 'does her own thing' is a bad mother, a selfish mother who neglects the children instead of spending all her energy on her family. This outmoded role is automatically transferred onto mature familial relationships as well as penetrating the entire social structure. A woman is the one who is expected to assume a passive role: the listener who does not have – or does not expresses her own views. Her creativity is linked to her 'biological destiny'. It would therefore be dangerous to grant a woman the full rights for self-expression; to allow her to have her own voice and to let it be heard.

Certain types of female creativity are 'suitable' for the patriarchal society because, by keeping the woman in the position of the object, they do not challenge the social masculine structure.

A female comedian does not have to look beautiful, or be slim, or wear perfect make-up and nice clothes because her creativity centres around her jokes and not her looks.

She cannot afford to be passive: has to be assertive in order to make her voice heard in an environment that has the potential to be hostile to her both as a woman and as a comedian. Any type of creativity, which involves 'speaking her mind.' for instance, writing or politics, which leads the woman to be seen as a person and not an object. An object is something without history, biography, desire, ideas or opinions; whereas a person is someone who is not scared to be herself regardless of the social consequences.

Stand-up comedy is a male-dominated industry. It is therefore difficult for a female comedian to break through because she is immediately seen as someone who is trying to be too visible for her sex. There are three main barriers to her success. The first is the audience, which is used to, and consequently expects, a certain type of comedy – a male style comedy, predominantly illuminating male issues. The second is the booker who looks mostly for male comedians because they mirror their own views, are not competition for the female booker and are overall a safer option. (The role of the booker is to engage the acts at the comedy clubs. It has become a ritualised corporate role accepted by venues and purveyors of comedy. The majority of whom are female.) Male comedians who often keep the woman at a distance simply create the third barrier because she is not 'one of the guys': she is different. Besides, there is a silent implication underlying all these barriers: that female comedy is different, that it touches upon the subjects that are either not too 'interesting' or are too sensitive for the general public.

It is much harder for a woman to engage in the process of individuation as a comedian on the circuit. There are many obstacles to her individuation: on average, women have fewer opportunities to perform, and, when they are given a chance, it does not mean that they would be heard (as opposed to be heckled or insulted). Female comedians also have to be more defensive or offensive than their male counterparts to get through to the audience. This also colours their psychological processes before, during and after the performance.

In this arena female individuation is a battle for acceptance, for transformation, and for the acceptance of this transformation. Neumann states that 'this secret inner world of to a woman's life, the result is a decisive enrichment of productivity'. Female comedians have to go through a very public and extreme type of individuation.
Neumann continues; 'due to the cultural symbiosis of the patriarchal marriage works out much less favourably for the Feminine and for women that it does for the Masculine and for men.[...] Due to the circumstances that women are compelled to embrace an unequivocal femininity, while the values of consciousness in patriarchal culture are masculine, women remain underdeveloped in this domain and are continually dependent on the aid of men'. (33:1994)

The audience will not necessarily try to 'mother' the female comedian the way they 'mother' the male performer, and respond with a higher degree of resistance both to her personality and material. She has to break through resistance and envy coming from the audience, and still be funny. She has to trust the process, and she has to allow the shadow to come to the fore before the communication process between her and the audience becomes stabilised.

## 9.
### 9.1. *Baubo – the Greek Goddess – the First Female Comedian*

Baubo (also Iambe) is an old woman who makes indecent jokes and exposes her genitalia for laughs. Her sexually liberated behaviour and her ability to laugh in the face of difficulties and loss enable her to transgress the barriers of depression and social norms. Various accounts depict Baubo as lifting her skirts and exposing her genitals in order to make the grieving Demeter, who lost her daughter Persephone, laugh. Even though Baubo is a minor character and mythological accounts about her are often incomplete or contradictory, she has great power over Demeter. 'That such a minor character should have such power over the great Demeter has led some to propose Baubo as a form of Hecate, who plays significant roles in Demeter's legend. Baubo's part in the Demetrian mysteries was re-enacted at a bridge between Athens and Eleusis, where participants engaged in ribald speech before more serene ceremonies' (Monaghan, 2014: 231). In the book *Goddesses and Monsters: Women, Myth, Power and Popular Culture* (2004) Jane Caputi writes that Baubo is associated with 'lewd jokes and the exposure of the vulva: Baubo's name is said to derive from a word meaning a body cavity, belly, womb, vulva. Images show her sometimes as a full-bodied old woman lifting her skirt, sometimes only as a vulva, and sometimes as the lower half of a female body with a face in place of the vulva' (Caputi, 2004: 382).

Baubo is associated with what we today see as 'stereotypical male' behaviour: indecent joking and lack of concern for one's appearance. Marguerite Rigoglioso also notes that figurines of Baubo often contain phallic references, which brings Baubo even closer to the image of the hermaphrodite:

> The image of the 'hermaphroditic/phallic' Baubo renders sensible something that has puzzled scholars for quite some time: the significance of her strange name in the larger schema of the Eleusinian complex. As Lincoln (1981, 80) notes, Baubo's name "literally means 'vagina', or a 'mock vagina', counterpart to a dildo (*baubon*)". Baubo was frequently represented iconographically as a naked headless torso with her face appearing in the abdomen as her vulva serving as her chin. Lincoln (81) also remarks on the 'markedly phallic shape' of the figurines, which renders them 'reminiscent of Baubo's implied male

counterpart, Baubon (dildo)'. What we see in this constellation of meanings and allusions is this: Baubo was the dildo, the dildo that was at once phallic and vulvar. A penis-within-a-vagina, a vagina-within-a-penis, she was, indeed, the ultimate symbol of parthenogenetic reproduction in a mother-centered universe.

(Rigoglioso, 2010: 180)

Baubo's exposure is very obviously non-sexual: the vulva is shown solely for entertainment purposes, and only when all other resources are depleted (Demeter insists on grieving and refuses to laugh until Baubo lifts the skirts). Baubo acts as a proto-comedian, by using references to pre-shame and pre-civilised phenomena (genitalia, scatology). In so doing, she rejects the constraining, male-centered framework of civilisation, which sees the woman as a well-behaved and passively sexual creature, always at the mercy of male aggression and male desire.

Also important is Baubo's part in the myth of Demeter and Persephone. In a way, with her humour, Baubo rectifies the crime committed by a man. Demeter is mourning her daughter having been abducted and raped by Hades. Baubo hauled Demeter out of her depression, caused by a man and brought nature back to life. In the myth Baubo is acting as both a healer and a comedian, reminding another woman of the power of the feminine; not the mysterious, fragile, passive and sexual feminine who can be desired, objectified, raped and abducted – but a powerful, ancient woman who is in charge of life and death, whose vagina is a symbol of the ability to create life; to 'make' human beings. Such a power places her above men, and is a reminder of the lost matriarchy. This power is true creativity, and its – albeit rude – symbol is the vulva.

Clarissa Pinkola Estes notes that Baubo – the Greek female proto-comedian, the goddess of obscenity, 'speaks from between her legs' (Estes, 1994: 336). Baubo, Estes writes, 'gives us the interesting idea that a little obscenity can help to break a depression. And it's true that certain kinds of laughter, which come from all those stories women tell each other, those women stories that are off-colour to the point of being completely tasteless … those stories stir libido. They rekindle the fire of a woman's interest in life again. The belly Goddess and the belly laugh are what we are after' (1994: 339).

Contemporary comedians can be said to be following in the footsteps of Baubo by discussing typically female – rather than male problems on stage. They may be even said to be metaphorically 'exposing' themselves on stage by discussing the issues that are simultaneously personal and social. The healing aspect of female humour is the catalyst and barometer for change because, on the one hand, it is rough and rowdy, and on the other, she is also caring. By making Demeter laugh, Baubo shows her motherly, soft, feminine side, which peacefully co-exists with the rude behaviour, which is sexual exposure.

The idea of 'sexual exposure' has always been associated with male indecent behaviour, and has not been applied to women except for Baubo. In ancient Greek comedy, actors were equipped with large leather phalluses, which were seen as a necessary part of the comedic routine. There are no records of 'leather vaginas' or female breasts being made part of comedic plays. The phallus is thus 'funny' whereas the vagina is not. Parts of female physiology (or female identity) were not thus in the spotlight because putting them in the spotlight would mean foregrounding the woman with her problems and thoughts, and this is what patriarchal cultures – including Classical Greece – have always been trying to avoid. In Classical Greece, women were completely excluded from the public sphere, and Baubo – the reminder of older fertility rituals – was thus regarded as a dubious and suspicious figure. The Mystery Cults revered the feminine but she would be hidden in a temple. The Vestal virgins were chosen at a young age and six were chosen to keep the flame alight in the temple in Rome. The Mysteries at Eleusis of Demeter and Persephone is recognised today as the myth concerning fertility, feast and famine.

She defied the power of the phallus – the symbol of order, civilisation and patriarchy.

Unlike the examples of Demeter or Penelope both of whom prefer the passive, masochistic, suffering stance, Baubo signifies a proactive and creative female:

> … complex and elusive persona who is sometimes a nurse, servant or priestess, sometimes a participant with goddesses in the *hieros gamos* (sacred marriage) ritual of certain ancient rites. She was also referred to as *Bona Dea*, goddess of women, while others saw her role simply as bawd, night demon, or the Evil Eye. […]
>
> Baubo was probably an extremely ancient aspect of certain agricultural rituals of fecundity, when specially appointed women squatted over the newly ploughed fields and gave their 'mood blood', their menstrual fluid, back to the earth; or of a time when priestesses may have officiated over archaic puberty rites.
>
> (Lubell, 1994: 5)

Lubell adds that 'in the fiercely misogynist climate of later patriarchal cultures, these old, female rituals that had been closely connected with the earth and its cycles faded away or were effectively obliterated. The concept of menstrual blood as part of the earth's sacred energy no longer fitted the ideology of the emerging aggressive civilisations that had seized power. Gradually, Baubo was transformed into an obscure creature of long-forgotten rituals. Her "moon blood", once understood as "wise blood" or "magic blood", became something to be feared and was rejected as an obscenity' (1994: 5).

Baubo is an expression of female creativity. She is both an artist and a creative person with the powers of making the crops grow. Classical Greece is, undoubtedly, the cultural and ideological base of the Western world. We have inherited the lamentable patriarchal attitude towards female creativity.

There is no consensus as to gender influencing comedian's material and performance manner. The American comedian Elaine Boosler explains that, for her, there are no 'male' subjects and 'female' subjects or 'male' and 'female' comedy styles:

> Once you ghettoize yourself, you're dead. I'm a comic. It's very important to me, and I fight hard. I don't let them write 'comedienne' when referring to me. People don't say doctorette, or dentistista, do they? I always did it funny, but I wanted to get the point across. I'm a human being trapped in a woman's body. Most people still think that a woman comedian is Totie Fields and nothing else. That's one of the reasons that I don't do television because the parts they write for women are so bad. They'll bring me something like ugly best friend who can't get laid. I said: 'I get laid in life. I see no reason to stop on television'. I think that I'm in an entirely different category and I will eventually carve that out. And that's what I hold out for.
> (Ajaye, 2002: 76).

The British comedian Sarah Millican also thinks that gender has no relevance as far as writing and performing jokes is concerned. It also does not affect the success of the joke: 'Gender doesn't come into it. And it's too easy to use it as an excuse. If I don't do well at a gig I could come off and go, well it's because they don't like women, but it's much more likely your jokes weren't good enough or you didn't have the confidence, or it's just a hard gig. There's a million reasons why an audience might not like you and it's almost never to do with gender.' (Viv Groskop, *The Daily Mail,* 6 July 2013).

Female comedy becomes the voice of the female condition and, as such, represents direct criticism of the patriarchal organisation of society. When women laugh at another woman's joke, they are experiencing a more direct (as opposed to a mediated) relationship with the content of the joke. They see the issue through another woman's eyes and criticise it using the female voice.

Typically, a female comedian going on stage feels isolated and pretty much outnumbered by her male colleagues. The American comedian Ellen Degeneres speaks about the difficulties females have to face *because of their gender* while on stage: female jealousy, male envy, sexism, hecklers and the macho attitude. For instance, proving to a group of men that you are capable of telling a joke may end up in a serious disaster because there is a level of prejudice that cannot be overcome. Degeneres says: 'I remember playing a boot camp for like four hundred Marines, and I thought, Gee, they're going to like seeing a woman. And that was a bad thing. They were screaming out the most obscene things. They didn't give me a chance to say anything. You're going to have times like that. It's just that everything builds character, everything makes you stronger, and it's just like life' (Ajaye, 2002: 100-101).

In the world of stand-up comedy, inter and intra-psychic processes surrounding the performance entail dealing with a high degree of aggression – and often female comedians deal with more emotional violence than their male colleagues. They are insulted both on their appearance and their abilities. For instance, Jo Brand recalls being called 'a fat cow,' who should 'fuck off' by one very persistent male audience member (Cook, 1994: 135). Her decision to remain calm did not help her in those circumstances: 'I wasn't scared – I was just fed up. I was angry because I was expected it to be better than that. I didn't get any laughs at all – he did. I slid off, humiliated, and packed it in for four months' (1994: 135).

Donna McPhail notes that men often insult female comedians because they suspect a powerful, talented woman who receives all the attention would reject them:

> Men feel threatened by a woman assuming authority over them. Some men have an emotional problem with you getting that attention and praise. They say 'I wouldn't fuck you' when you hadn't even asked them. You hadn't even noticed them. They want to be noticed, and put you in your place. You learn to use an outrageous heckle like that to your advantage, if it's, 'You're crap!' then the audience can agree or disagree. Also, women don't like it. If they're out with their boyfriend, and their boyfriend's laughing at you, which translates to them that they fancy you, that's when they heckle. Everyone is very attractive onstage, even if off stage in normal life they are quite ugly. It's something about the light shining in the eyes of someone onstage that makes them look more appealing.
>
> (1994: 206)

McPhail also recalls a man in the audience telling her to 'get her tits out' (1994: 207). Interestingly enough, McPhail also mentions her own envy and jealousy – this time related to the matters of social class and privileges. She prefers working class audiences to middle class ones because she feels intimidated by the latter.

The body and appearance is a particularly difficult area for female comedians to handle. When a women appears on stage in public, standing on an elevated surface and therefore pretty visible, the expectation is that she will look like a performer: entertaining, pretty, feminine, dressed up and made-up.

Jo Brand often talks about her appearance and her body. Many of her performances include jokes about being fat, unattractive, weird, and the now famous metaphor of the 'sea monster'. At first sight, this is deeply personal material. Yet, at the same time, she identifies an area of herself that is both intimate and vulnerable, and relevant and understandable for the audience. The audience can easily relate to the problem of excess weight or being unattractive in a society that places emphasis on model appearance, eternal youth and cosmetic surgery. She feeds on contemporary issues and is inspired. Moreover, these contemporary socio-cultural myths coincide with her internal psychological state. She aims to build the bridge between her identity and the ideal female image propagated by her social surroundings. In this respect, her attempts at reconciling the 'identities' – the personal, the real, and the ideal – is a good example of the inter-psychic process that takes place during the preparatory, pre-performance phase.

David Quantick argues in *The Daily Telegraph:*

> To be a female stand-up is a bit like volunteering to be water boarded while accompanying yourself on the banjo; it's hard enough just to keep going, never mind being entertaining as well. And there is – not with all women comedians, but a lot – a difference in comedic styles as well. Male comedians can be bullish testosterone-fuelled lads. A lot of male stand-up revolves around blokiness, and is rooted in the "real" world of observation comedy. Female comics are often either whimsical and surreal (Issie Suttee) or rooted in a gentler, dafter kind of comedy, which is notably female (Millican). There are exceptions – the American Sarah Silverman is terrifyingly obscene – but comics like Silverman rely on being outside the norm for part of their impact (a male comic such as Frankie Boyle has to be either really good or really vile to stand out in a more crowded field).
> (Quantick, *The Daily Telegraph,* 22 December 2011)

In a *Daily Telegraph* article Sarah Millican comments on the success of her DVD, *Chatterbox* and discusses the problem of sexism in the industry: 'I don't think there's an awful lot of sexism in this industry – I think if an audience is watching you and you're a bloke - it's the same as if you're a woman, they're expecting the same, to be entertained. But there were a handful of people who haven't seen any women comics on DVDs before and were suggesting it wouldn't happen' (Cavendish, *The Daily Telegraph,* 21 December 2011).

Male and female comedians include sensitive issues in radically different ways. Sexual violence towards women in male comedy sets is one of them. Rape jokes usually reflect a serious gap in confidence, but it does not make them less controversial or less acceptable. In this sense, nobody is interested in the psychological motifs of the comedian joking about violating a woman, but only about the effect that his words have on the audience.

For instance, the American comedian Patton Oswalt made headlines when he was trying to defend a fellow stand-up, Daniel Tosh, who, after being heckled by a female spectator about earlier rape jokes in his set, announced to the audience: 'Wouldn't it be funny if that girl got raped by, like, five guys right now?' To the moral outcry Patton responded with a long essay in which he explained his position as regards rape jokes, and assured his audience that he has no intention of raping anyone:

> A lot of times, a setup is deliberately meant to shock, to reverse your normal valences, to kick you a few points off your axis. If you heard the beginning of Lenny Bruce's joke where he blurts out, "How many niggers do we have here tonight?" and then stood up and mother fucked him into silence and stormed out? You'd be correct—based solely on what you saw and heard—that Lenny was a virulent racist. But if you rode the shockwave, and listened until the end of the bit, you'd see he was attacking something—racism—that he found abhorrent and was, in fact, so horrified by it that he was willing to risk alienating an audience to make his point.
>
> So that's how I saw the whole "rape joke" controversy. And, again, my view was based on my experience as a comedian. Twenty-five years' experience, you know? This was about censorship, and the limits of comedy, and the freedom to create and fuck up while you hone what you create.
>
> (Oswalt, *The Slate,* June 16, 2013)

Patton explains his defending of Tosh by naming this topic a taboo. In his view, no subject should be off-limits as far as stand-up is concerned. Joking about rape is not the same as raping women, Patton claims. This is only about making sure that no social or political taboos are left unexplored, and therefore left in the dark where they would fester:

> In fact, every viewpoint I've read on this, *especially* from feminists, is simply asking to kick upward, to think twice about who is the target of the punch line, and make sure it isn't the victim.
>
> Why, after all of my years of striving to write original material (and, at times, becoming annoyingly self-righteous about it) and struggling to find new viewpoints or untried approaches to any subject, did I suddenly balk and protest when an articulate, intelligent and, at times, angry contingent of people were asking me to apply the same principles to the subject of rape? Any edgy or taboo subject can become just as hackneyed as an acceptable or non-controversial one if the *exact same approach* is made every time. But I wasn't willing to hear that.
>
> And let's go back even *further*. I've never wanted to rape anyone. Never had the impulse. So why was I feeling like I was being lumped in with those who were, or who took a cavalier attitude about rape, or even made rape jokes to begin with? Why did I feel some massive, undeserved sense of injustice about my place in this whole controversy?
>
> The answer to that is in the first incorrect assumption. The one that says there's not a "rape culture" in this country. How can there be? *I've* never wanted to rape anyone.
>
> (Oswalt, *The Slate,* June 16, 2013)

Adrienne Truscott, the female comedian, treated the controversial subject differently by basing a whole show, '*Asking for It: A One-Lady Rape About Comedy*', around the subject of rape. Shockingly she performs naked from the waist down. She emphasises that her nudity is not intended to be sexual or attractive. In fact, it is quite aggressive, 'a subversion of how women are conditioned to perceive and use their own bodies' (Brockes, *The Guardian,* 1 January 2014). The show is a response to Daniel Tosh's joke about rape and Patton's subsequent failure to condemn it. During the show, Truscott jokes about women's right to make decisions about their bodies. She focuses on various aspects of rape. Emma Brockes writes:

> For anyone who has watched with dismay as rape jokes became standard fare in comedy – or just anyone who wants their stand up to mean something – this is an exhilarating tour. Truscott's got something major to get off her chest – and I'm not talking about the strip-tease

sight gag that punctuates a date-rape routine mid-show. That sounds like strong stuff? It is, and Truscott knows it: 'anybody need the [rape] whistle? - she'll ask. "Everybody fine?"
(Brockes, The Guardian, 1 January 2014)

Truscott's decision to partially undress, from the waist down, echoes Baubo's undressing and squatting for comedic purposes. Here Truscott denies two main assumptions about the female body that are prevalent in our patriarchal culture: that breasts symbolise the caring and nurturing aspect of the woman, and that the vagina should always be 'sexual'. The vagina without the breasts 'should not be seen'. Shown without the breasts, the vagina becomes the world of chaos, and the world of darkness. Another issue is that, unlike the phallus, the vagina has never been seen as funny; as something that can be 'displayed' in a non-sexual way. Whereas the phallus can be seen as a symbol of strength and a giver of life, and even laughed at as such, vagina as a symbol has an aura of danger to it.

Interestingly enough, Truscott's challenge to mainstream perception of female nudity is not funny probably because it is based on aggression. It is a forceful rejection, a form of pushing the boundary, a radical erosion of traditional roles and perceptions. The idea behind the image of the semi-naked woman (but naked 'on the wrong end') is to assert the power of the feminine, to go back to the ancient idea of the vagina as a source of creativity.

> 'The room, a bookstore in Edinburgh, was nerve-rackingly personal: no lights, no stage, no distance between Truscott and the front row. No one could leave without the entire room noticing – given the material, it amused Truscott to note that this acted as a powerful disincentive. "You can't get up because it's like," – sotto voce – 'is that the rapist?!' She laughs.
>
> Although it is more challenging, Truscott's preference is to perform before a mainstream audience, rather than a self-selected group of woman-friendly activists or supporters. (She is canny enough to know that being described as a "feminist performance artist" even though she is a feminist performer, "would be the death of it")'.
> (Brockes, *The Guardian*, 1 January 2014).

According to Freud, jokes are a form of passive aggression; they represent instincts diffused in 'civilised' ways. Jokes have traditionally been used to disguise both sexual and non-sexual aggression (Freud, 1960: 118-129). Obscene jokes, for instance, mask 'undisguised obscenity' which, in its crude form, cannot be enjoyed by a civilised person because of 'repression'. In a comedic form, however, sexuality is more palatable and acceptable:

> It is our belief that civilisation and higher education have a large influence in the development of repression, and we supposed that, under such conditions, the psychical organization undergoes an alteration … as a result of which what was formerly felt as agreeable now seems unacceptable and is rejected with all possible psychical force. The repressive activity of civilization brings it about that primary possibilities of enjoyment, which have now, however, been repudiated by the censorship in us, are lost to us. But to the human psyche all renunciation is exceedingly difficult, and so we find that tendentious jokes provide a means of undoing the renunciation and retrieving what was lost. When we laugh at a refined obscene joke, we are laughing at the same thing that makes a peasant laugh at a coarse piece of smut.
>
> (Freud, 1960: 120-121)

A woman who delivers jokes, expresses her primal aggressive instinct, and also accentuates her aggression – which is an intrinsically male milieu. If a woman diffuses her aggression, this means that she has aggression to diffuse. In addition, language and particularly speech can be perceived as crude and powerful tools of communication because they can be used to offend and humiliate people; they can be used as means of establishing hierarchies and explicitly demonstrating power. A female comedian is automatically regarded as a forceful woman, who, from a traditional perspective, is seen as aggressive and even dangerous because she seeks to challenge the patriarchal order. Truscott's aggression is both deliberate and explicit, and its aim is to reverse the 'victim psychology' often conferred onto women who have suffered rape. She wants to empower the victims with her show, and to prove that naked women do not necessarily look alluring or vulnerable – they can also be hostile:

> No one said, 'Dude, that was a bad joke'. The response to criticism was, 'Oh, you don't believe in free speech?' Oh, for fuck's sake, it's not that black and white'.

> She also wanted to make a point about emphasis. 'To show the flip side of the attention that's always on victims – the worst version of which is 'You asked for it', and the best version, 'That shouldn't have happened to her'. No no no. He shouldn't have done it. That was my whole thing: to bring that into the room'.
>
> (Brockes, *The Guardian,* 1 January 2014)

Some female comedians choose to perform in a deliberately 'non-feminine' way. For example, the British comedian Mandy Knight tends to be very rude on stage and tries to sound 'like a man'. Here are a few lines from her show in Oxford, which took place on the 6$^{th}$ of July 2001:

> No, look at you, you little couple, what's your name? Stephen. And your name? Emma. Emma, hello, Emma… that's quite posh, isn't, Emma? Excuse me, it's a little princess if I may say. A little bit posh – you've sort of got that middle class body language, haven't you, Emma?
>
> Hello? Yes, down the front, dress circle. 'I'm so posh I don't have periods, far too messy'. It's like, 'goodness me, I don't mess down there every month – I have a woman in from Bicester who does'.
>
> And look at you! Raaah! You're about twelve, aren't you? You're all ehhhh. Oh and you, take your glasses off – you'll find I'm a stunner. Look at you! What's your name, sweetheart? Mick. Um, foreplay over with… oh bless him, he's going, look, 'I'm with my friends, don't make me fuck the scary red lady'. I'm only teasing, Nick – take your hands out of your lap, though, I'm doing the entertainment. I'm only teasing, bless, I don't do anything dodgy, Nick, never taken it up the tradesman's. Alright once. But no, girls, you know what it's like – I jumped on his lap too quickly, it went up the wrong hole. No harm done, once the stitches were out.
>
> Oh, you're looking at me, going 'it's too much'. Relax, for fuck's sake. I'm in drag. Eh, luck, suckie suckie, five dollars.
> (*Jongleurs* show, Oxford, 6 July 2001, Recorded and transcribed by Maria Kempinska).

Knight is deliberately offensive to audience members of both genders, putting them down and inserting sexual allusions here and there. It is as if she is trying to break all possible boundaries, and to scandalise and disgust the audience with her comments. She is not scared of people's reactions, and is not shy of making her material and delivery sound aggressive and attacking. In this sense, her approach is no different from that of a male comedian, yet her allusions contain traditionally 'female' material and expose 'female' concerns – female biology, finding a partner, female sexual aggression, the issue of appropriate 'feminine' behaviour (invariably linked with the class issue), etc. She talks about 'posh' periods, deciding 'how 'approachable' a woman should appear to men, dealing with shy men, and openly sexualises men.

Gina Yashere, adds the race issue to the list of taboo subjects, which are not normally discussed openly in public. She brings up the problem of the cultural ghettoization of black people in Britain. For instance, she says in one of the shows she performed in 2001 at the *Jongleurs* club in London:

> None of you know me – that's cool, that's cool. In the black community, I'm a star! I had to say that 'cos there's only ten black people here. If black people recognise you on the street, they are like this… [gestures]
>
> Black people are not into all that talking and stuff. We're not into sleeping outside pop stars' houses and stuff. Black people like what? You mean sleep on the floor. I don't think so. Where am I going to plug my charger?
> (*Jongleurs* London, 20 July 2001, transcribed by me)

Like Knight, Yashere discusses the uncomfortable sexual and scatological issues. She breaks the same boundaries, but is less aggressive towards the audience and probably less annoying. Although her approach seems to be more 'feminine' than Knight's, Yashere still manages to produce some outrageous material. Interestingly enough, her take on sexual rejection echoes traditionally male complaints that it is difficult for both a man and woman to 'get laid'.

> It's all the male comics that get all the groupies… they get all the women queuing up outside their dressing rooms. Sex, sex, sex! I don't get shit.
>
> The other day, there was a man standing outside my dressing room. And I was like, "yes! Could be sex, could be sex, could be sex for me". And he was like – "No, I'm a minicab, mate".
>
> I shagged him anyway. £3.50 and a lift home … think I was worth a fiver, though, you know what I mean. Obviously not.
> (*Jongleurs* London, 20 July 2001, transcribed by Maria Kempinska)

Although Yashere's delivery of her material is 'softer', the material nevertheless shows no signs of 'femininity'. Moreover – she aims at the same degree of exposure of taboo subjects as Knight, Truscott and many other 'rude' female comedians. She still talks about the differences in attitudes between men and women; yet her language and subject matter are not at all 'feminine'. It is deliberately coarse, and aimed at breaking the 'civilized' social attitudes and challenging accepted behaviours. Being a comedian – going on stage and being physically 'seen' and 'heard' gives one a degree of power and authority.

## 9.2. *The Issue of Male Envy*

A woman making jokes on stage often evokes envy from both male comedians and the male audience. The comedian Lee Mack claims that women make worse comedians than men because they are not as 'boastful' and 'competitive':

> When men sit around and talk, they are very competitive. One person will tell an anecdote and the next person will try to top that. When you get six women together, they share a lot more.
>
> They will be far more interested in what the other person has to say. The conservation is more interactive and less about individually showing off.
> (Hastings, *The Daily Mail*, 28 September 2013)

The female comedian Josie Long wonders why out of the twenty highest-earning comedy performers there is only one woman:

> In fact, the numbers in the industry are even worse. Of the 20 highest-earning stand-up comedians in Britain at the moment, just one – Sarah Millican – is a woman. In the 31-year history of the Edinburgh comedy award, there have been only two solo female winners, Jenny Eclair and Laura Solon. A 2010 poll conducted by Channel 4 found that 94 out of the 100 greatest stand-ups were men, with Eclair, Victoria Wood, Jo Brand, Shappi Khorsandi, Joan Rivers and Roseanne Barr being the exceptions. Last month's shortlist for the Chortle awards named just two solo women comics in a list of 54 nominations (Dana Alexander and Susan Calman; on Tuesday night, Calman won the compere award). Never mind equality – these lists don't even give women 10%. Is any other art form so skewed?
> (Benedictus, *The Guardian*, 20 March 2012)

In the same article in The Guardian, Leo Benedictus tries to understand why the general socio-cultural view is that female comedians cannot be funny: 'There is an opinion at large out there, which Long estimates she hears three hundred times a year: that women aren't funny. Or, the deluxe version: that women are only funny rarely, and certainly less often than men. Some evolved genetic disadvantage (the details of which we'll gloss over) is apparently holding women back. A bold theory, is perhaps the politest thing to call that' (Benedictus, The Guardian, 20 March 2012). Benedictus attempts to find the answer to the problem. He thinks that this is the issue of social conditioning: 'So what is the problem? Lara A. King, recent winner of the Funny Women award, does not believe that men are funnier. 'Just because there are more men doing it, that doesn't necessarily mean they are better at it. I think they get given the breaks a bit more, and they get given a little bit more slack. I think women are less encouraged and less supported. People who book comedy nights do tend to think that one woman on the bill is really quite enough' (Benedictus, The Guardian, 20 March 2012).

Women on the circuit are still seen as a 'novelty', as something unusual and exotic. 'Bookers will spread you out ' explains Sarah Millican 'maybe because there's only about 10 or 12 [women] at [a particular] level. A bit like they might spread out the one-liner guys. You're kind of a bracket on your own – which is fine. I understand that people want variety on a bill. It's also positive discrimination in a way. They might like to have a woman on the bill' (Benedictus, The Guardian, 20 March 2012).

Another female comedian, Viv Groskop, shows that women in comedy often have to deal with male patronising behaviour:

> There are times when you just have to be grateful for sexist condescension. Without it I would not have got any laughs at all when I did a stand-up comedy set for the first time. As the compère handed over the microphone to me, he announced – not inaccurately, but totally cringeworthily – that we were moving 'from one lovely lady to another'. The comic on before me was a woman. There were four of us on a bill of 25. (Yes, 25 comics. Welcome to the open-mic circuit.) But the MC then sealed the deal in the worst way possible by patting me on the arm, looking at me pityingly and mouthing, "Well done, love." I thought out loud into the microphone: "Hmm, that wasn't very patronising or anything…" Big laugh. Sadly I then proceeded to die for most of the next five minutes. But that was not because I was a woman. It was because I was rubbish. And a beginner. But mostly rubbish. There's a stereotype that stand-up comedy is more difficult for women. But it is rapidly being overturned.
> (Groskop, *The Daily Mail,* 6 July 2013).

Interestingly enough, Groskop chooses financial success to show the measure of female comedians' popularity. Criticising, author and journalist Christopher Hitchens's statement that 'women cannot be funny', she gives examples of DVD sales of a fellow woman comedian:

> The infamous Christopher Hitchens accusation 'women aren't funny,' has been buried under the weight of Millican's DVD sales (more than 175,000, a record for a female stand-up), Miranda's best-selling book (over £1 million in sales in the run-up to Christmas) and the film *Bridesmaids*' box office takings ($228 million).

If anyone still thinks women aren't funny, they would be well advised not to bet any money on it.
(Groskop, *The Daily Mail,* 6 July 2013).

Overall, it seems that female comedians' material contains both gender-specific and non gender-specific elements. At the same time, women in the live comedy business still feel insecure enough to talk about their success in terms of the number of DVDs sold and money earned. They are still unsure as to their place and role in this thriving and complex business.

## *9.3. Gay Women on the Circuit*

Female comedians who are gay do not like the idea of the audience being too obsessed with the performer's sexuality. James Rampton writes in *The Independent* about Donna McPhail's 'coming out' on stage:

> Like it or not, Donna McPhail is known as the comic who 'came out' on stage. With some justification, she feels the seven minutes of her hour-long show devoted to her sexuality at Edinburgh last summer have been blown out of all proportion. 'All that lesbian stuff annoyed me,' she asserts. 'I hid it in the middle of the show, but all the reviews still read, 'Donna McPhail . . . LESBIAN' . . . But I'm a stand-up who's a woman who's a lesbian – in that order. I want to be a funny person, not a funny lesbian - which is a contradiction in terms anyway.
> (James Rampton, *The Independent,* 2 March 1994)

What McPhail implies here is that the content and quality of her work is not in any way influenced by her sexuality; she is a primarily a comedian who has to be judged on her professional qualities; and only then a gendered person. At the same time, McPhail observes, her sexuality affects the way the audience reacts to her – and particularly its male members. She admits that she has to develop an aggressive persona in order to protect herself from the men who feel offended by the fact that she is gay:

> Part of her appeal lies in her aggressive stage persona, developed as a way of counteracting nerves. Crunching on a croque monsieur in a Regent St cafe, McPhail explains: 'The adrenalin you get before a show is equivalent to a car crash – that's why your bowels open so regularly. Your body is in shock. If you show that on stage, you're dead. So I give the feeling that you don't mess with me'.

> Some beer-swilling, rugby-club types have certainly learnt not to mess with her. 'They heckle on a very personal basis. They shout, 'You've

> got no tits, I wouldn't shag you. You haven't got a boyfriend'. If they're trying to humiliate you sexually, all you have to do is turn around and do the same to them: 'What do you use for contraception - your personality? Where's your girlfriend - outside grazing?' Although it's not my bag politically, you have to do that to shut them up.
>
> (James Rampton, *The Independent,* 2 March 1994)

She also admits that lesbian audiences also present problems – albeit of a different kind. Gay audiences tend to be defensive, and their defensiveness results in an impaired ability to enjoy jokes. They need to make sure that the jokes are not too flighty, too feminine or not in any way diminishing the achievements of the LGBT movement:

> Sometimes lesbians forget to have a laugh, because we have to be so defensive all the time. That attitude can be very frustrating when you're doing a comedy show. They all mentally flick through their Politically Correct Dictionary before they laugh. You get women coming up and saying, "It's not right to say you're a bird', and I have to reply, 'It's a joke. Shall I give notes out before you come in?'. I love having dykes in, but they take a long time to relax".
>
> (James Rampton, *The Independent,* 2 March 1994)

Often the degree of power, aggression and masculinity that the female comic possesses is mistaken for being a matter of sexuality, rather than as an exercise in the female right to express aggression more openly.

Another British gay comedian, Zoe Lyons, called one of her shows '*Miss Machismo*'. The title itself implies a masculine approach – but should not be seen as specifically gay. In an interview to *Time Out London,* Lyons talks about her argument with the philosopher and feminist Germaine Greer. Greer was scandalised by Lyons's jokes about female self-harm, and pointed out to her that subjects like this were not funny – particularly because the target of the joke was Amy Winehouse (who was still alive at the time).

Lyons calls 'lazy journalism' the attempts of some representatives of mass media to stick labels to gay comedians' jokes. For her, there is no such thing as 'lesbian comedy.

She says in the interview with Tim Arthur:

**Was this the inspiration for your show, 'Miss Machismo'?**

'Partly, yes. Also in the same year I got voted the eighty-first most influential gay in Britain. And that was another moment where I went: "You're joking!" I literally spat my coffee out. The two things came together so I thought I'd write a show about having a bit of a swagger. And then, like most shows, you start off with a kernel of an idea and you end up talking about gay penguins and the Pope.'
(Tim Arthur, Lyons was Quoted in Time Out London, 23 March 2010)

She also points out that the way the public still sees female comedians is shaped by traditional attitudes:

**Why do you think that the out dated misconception still exists?**

'I haven't focused on it that much, because it doesn't really bother me. But I think it probably goes back to the old tradition of blokes sitting in pubs telling each other jokes. Men told jokes and ladies gossiped. But that's all nonsense. Like I said, it's not something I really focus on. I'm not a flag waver of any kind. I just enjoy going out there and making people laugh. I think if you can't hack it don't do it.
(Tim Arthur, *Time Out London,* 23 March 2010)

The problem is that the genre itself originated as a male one, and has been dominated by male performers for a long time. The first comedians were male, and female comedians have had no choice but to copy their format and style. Besides, the format and style of stand-up performance presuppose a fair amount of aggression, both on the part of the comedian and the part of the audience. This format, which implies aggressive, untamed exchanges between the performer and the audience, is only suitable for certain personality types. It is very different from contemporary theatre performances which are geared up for polite audiences and which would not test the actor's confidence.

Female comedians adopt of the male street entertainment tradition by including psychological, political and particularly social issues. The female comedians work in the best popular entertainment traditions, and incorporate into their performances and engineer crude jokes that often go beyond the 'norms' of the middle class. They do this on purpose, knowing that crudity is going to embarrass and test the limits of tolerance of any 'decent' people (particularly women), present in the audience.

There is a psychological aspect to the masculinisation of stand up comedy as well. The adoption of the 'male' style also may be the result of the generally accepted view that masculine means of dealing with the outside world are more advantageous and, in the long run, more productive. They bring financial and social security. It was Freud's assumption that both sexes assign a higher value and universally masculine behaviour, and 'that one's image of masculinity should provide the baseline in reference to which femaleness is considered' (Mitchell, 1995: 220).

Freud himself was puzzled by femininity and wondered about how it came into being. He paid attention to both its biological and social aspects. Ultimately, he admits that disentangling the one from the other, and creating a single psychological picture of human sexuality is the kind of task of which psychoanalysis is incapable:

> The distinction is not a psychological one; when you say "feminine", you usually mean "passive" Now it is true that a relation of the kind exists. The male sex-cell is actively mobile and searches out the female one, and the latter, the ovum, is immobile and waits passively. This behaviour of the elementary sexual organisms is indeed a model for the conduct of sexual individuals during intercourse[......]
>
> One might consider characterizing femininity psychologically as giving preference to passive aims. This is not, of course, the same thing as passivity; to achieve a passive aim may call for a large amount of activity. It is perhaps the case that in a woman, on the basis of her share in the sexual function, a preference for passive behaviour and passive aims is carried over into her life to a greater or lesser extent, in proportion to the limits, restricted or far-reaching, within which her sexual life thus serves as a model. But we must beware in this of underestimating 'the influence of social customs, which similarly force women into passive situations. All this is still far from being cleared up. There is one particularly constant relation between femininity and instinctual life, which we do not want to overlook. Suppression of women's aggressiveness which is prescribed for them constitutionally and imposed on them socially favours the development of powerful masochistic impulses, which succeed, as we know, in binding erotically the destructive trends which have been divested inwards.
> (Freud, XXII: 114-11)

Freud's analysis of 'mislaid aggression' is far from displaying self-destructive masochistic trends for women on stage who find healthy, creative and socially useful ways of channelling their aggressive impulses. Moreover, they are not afraid to admit that they have these impulses, and openly display them in rude jokes and arguments with hecklers. Their impulses are expressed both verbally and visually.

Gay female comedians do not emphasise their sexuality deliberately, and do not make their performances look or sound explicitly gay. In this way, self-expression is equated with aggressive impulses. Writing and performing jokes is an act that is both linguistic and political. It threatens the patriarchal structure of society and questions male control over language and discourse.

## 9.4. *The Comedic Animus*

Female desire to write and perform comedy can also be explained using the Jungian concept of the animus. The animus is one of the archetypes and represents the male counterpart of the female psyche. Marie-Louise von Franz defines the animus as 'the male personification of the unconscious in woman' which 'exhibits both good and bad aspects, as does the anima in man' (Jung, 1964: 198). Von Franz describes the animus as a kind of voice that can be dangerous if not controlled:

> [...] the animus does not so often appear in the form of an erotic fantasy or mood; it is more apt to take the form of a hidden 'sacred' conviction. When such a conviction is preached with a loud, insistent masculine voice or imposed on others by means of brutal emotional scenes, the underlying masculinity in a woman is easily recognized. However, even in a woman who is outwardly very feminine the animus can be an equally hard, inexorable power. One may suddenly find oneself up against something in a woman that is obstinate, cold, and completely inaccessible.
>
> (1964: 198)

The animus, adds Jolande Jacobi, seldom appears as a single figure. Moreover, Jacobi writes, it often takes the form of 'uncritically accepted opinions, prejudices, principles, which make women argue and bicker. This happens most often to those whose main function is that of feeling and whose thinking function is undifferentiated. They seem to make up a fairly high percentage of their sex, though there may have been some change since the turn of the century, perhaps as a result of the emancipation of woman' (Jacobi, 1973: 121).

Jung's own view of the animus had negative connotations, and, at times, was openly hostile. Thus, the animus expresses itself in 'opinionated views, interpretations, insinuations and misconstructions, which all have the purpose (sometimes attained) of severing the relationship between two human beings' (Jung, CW 9/II: para. 32). This particular definition is also profoundly insulting to women:

> No matter how friendly and obliging a woman's Eros may be, no logic on earth can shake her if she is ridden by the animus. Often the man has the feeling – and he is not altogether wrong – that only seduction

or a beating or rape would have the necessary power of persuasion. He is unaware that this highly dramatic situation would instantly come to a banal and unexciting end if he were to quit the field and let a second woman carry on the battle (his wife, for instance, if she herself is not the fiery war horse). This sound idea seldom or never occurs to him, because no man can converse with an animus for five minutes without becoming the victim of his own anima.

(CW 9/II: para. 29)

This sexist outburst is, to an extent, compensated by his remark that the animus also has a useful side to it. A woman's animus originates from her father's conduct, and 'expresses not only conventional opinion but – equally – when we call "spirit", philosophical or religious ideas in particular, or, rather the attitude resulting from them. Thus the animus is a psychopomp, a mediator between the conscious and the unconscious, and a personification of the latter' (CW 9/II para. 33). Meanwhile, 'the animus gives to a woman's consciousness the capacity for reflection, deliberation, and self-knowledge' (CW 9/II: para. 33). Jung in general did not have a favourable attitude toward the female expression of the animus and often demeaned it as overbearing, and loud. In his own life's work he harnessed a number of female disciples work and either integrated their ideas or collaborated with them, including, M. L Von Franz, Speilrein, Wolff, and his own wife Emma. This act of identification of the animus and yet distain has remained within the social patriarchal culture.

The female on the circuit is often seen as having an overwhelming presence and 'loud mouth'; she is a creature who expresses her views openly and has the pluck to discuss a range of 'sacred' things which had traditionally been taboo subjects for 'decent' women: being sexually promiscuous, refusing to please men emotionally, being physically aggressive, being morally strong, being emotionally or financially independent, often consciously and proactively choosing the man for procreation, criticising their own children (showing no love towards their children), weight and appearance, and single motherhood.

Erich Neumann expresses a similar sexist view of the animus, which is experienced as an intrusion: 'the animus world expresses itself in opinions and assertions that, on closer inspection, prove to be the property of the archetypally masculine, patriarchal spirit. They arise from the world of male consciousness and of the masculine spirit that is extrinsic and foreign to woman and the Feminine. They express the patriarchate's inner rule over woman. This is why this level of animus actually belongs not to woman's nature but to male culture' (Neumann, 1994: 80).

The idea that a female comedian should be brave in the way she express herself, is echoed by another American comedian, Elaine Boosler who remarks that comedians should not shy away from difficult subjects: 'The paper doesn't change every day.

The abortion fight's going on, the economy's been going on. This is all four to eight years old already. So it just festers. Someone once said to me, "I've figured you out. You either want to be outrageous or outraged." I can live with that. I don't enjoy the jokes that are just jokes for me as much as the jokes that have a little political punch on the end (Ajaye, 2002: 73).

'The loud animus' can be explained by the fact that self-expression is still an uncommon development for women in Western societies. In order to be heard, one has to shout loud and be proactive and in a culture where women are not listened to the volume has to match the masculine. As Viv Groskop explains, 'this leads to many female comedians becoming 'bullish' on stage because they are still unsure about their position in society as well as about their position within the hierarchy of the circuit'. Kit Hollerback an American comedian in England echoes the sentiment, 'they didn't life the idea of girls telling jokes' (p207 Didn't They Kill My Mother in Law) Therefore, women on the circuit are often treated as 'fragile' – particularly because they are 'prone to failure'. Comedians like Millican and Groskop argue that women are no more prone to failure on stage than men; and when they fail, it happens for reasons other than their gender:

> While no one would argue more funny women is a bad thing, many successful women in comedy are bullish, saying they don't want special treatment and they wish everyone would just forget the whole thing. Miranda Hart has said that women love her show because it's like "having a friend who does things you fear you might do or have done". But she's also known as "the female Eric Morecambe" and has pointed out that her comedy is far more about being a fool and a clown than being a woman.
> (Viv Groskop, *The Daily Mail,* 6 July 2013)

As Tessa Adams writes, Jung saw the animus as a form of possession, and contrasted the 'active' nature of the male psyche with the innate female 'passivity' (Adams and Duncan, 2003: 97). Although Jung's idea of the animus may be intuitively correct and has a degree of psychological truth to it, the forms and language in which it is expressed are clearly conservative and even sexist. This sexism is the result of his conservative background:

> …it is hardly surprising that Jung psychologizes women's passivity in a society that needed women to subdue intellectual enquiry in the service of domestic concerns. The simplification of a woman as a nurturer and a man as thinker needed to be perpetuated and Jung's amalgam of gendered attribution and biological difference – masculine/male; feminine/female (albeit mitigated by the contra-sexual archetypes) does little to ensure change. Since Jung was

renowned for encouraging many women to enter the analytic profession, this raises the question as to why Jung was not more radical.

(Adams and Duncan, 2003: 97)

Polly Young-Eisendrath also notes that Jungian psychology has a blatant misogynist and patronising bias, and that many women interested in Jung often feel confused and torn between Jung's vision of the female voice and their own perception of their voice as it should be – expressed openly and clearly (Young-Eisendrath, 2004: 90). Young-Eisendrath eventually realises that she had no other choice but to become a Jungian feminist (which, in itself, is an oxymoron):

> My own definition of feminism shares its principal themes with many others' definitions. Feminism is a discipline of thought and action that aims to enhance mutuality and trust; to reveal the meanings of gender differences; especially as these might interfere with mutuality or trust; and to oppose all models of methods of dominance-submission for relationships among people. Feminism is not a "power-over" movement. It is not women wanting power over men. What feminism has revealed, in its many forms from theology to literary criticism to psychology and philosophy, is that silencing and trivializing of women and their ideas affect all of us all of the time in the way that we expect the world and ourselves to be.
> 
> (Young-Eisendrath, 2004: 90)

Is the decision to go on stage, make oneself visible, make oneself heard, understood and accepted, a sign that one has become a feminist ideologically and politically? This profession is based on the ability to manipulate language in a certain way; it is all about the mastery over language. Thus, female comedians reclaim power by having access to live language – the bedrock of the society and the keeper of the rules. Female comedians can choose their own subjects, and manipulate these subjects in their own way. Feminist psychologists Rachel Hare-Mustin and Jeanne Marecek explain: 'Language highlights certain features of the objects it represents, certain meanings of the situations it describes. Once designations in language become accepted, one is constrained by them […]. Throughout history, men have had greater influence over language than women' (Hare-Mustin and Marecek, 1988: 455). Young-Eisendrath also highlights the fact that women themselves are often guilty of using patriarchal language to describe and criticize 'the weaker sex' because creating and popularizing a female-friendly (let alone feminist) language is a task that is difficult socially, culturally and linguistically:

> Currently, we are still in the position of being dominated by gender stereotypes that function to limit our experiences, expressions, and

expectations of the lives we live. We all necessarily participate in everyday conversations in which the given worldview includes assumptions of female inferiority, inadequacy and weakness. Inevitably, all female people arrive at adulthood with feelings and significant beliefs about their own inferiority. […] Attributions about women's weaknesses and narcissism, about their lack of competence and objectivity, are sustained on an on-going conversations in which both verbal and non-verbal communications are structured by the hard-core belief that female persons lack something. Inevitably all female people develop individual theories about themselves, their families of origin, their bodies, their intelligence, their competence, their nurturance, or the like, that indicate to themselves and others: "Something is wrong with me personally".

(Young-Eisendrath, 2004: 91).

Young-Eisendrath emphasises the fact that women tend to be less 'adventurous' (intellectually as well as in any other way) than men because being proactive sends all sorts of signals to society (2004: 91-92). However, female comedians are adventurous and in this context they take emotional risks in order to activate her animus voice a partial or even a full freedom.

They also take narcissistic risks – including the ones associated with their appearance. For instance, they are not afraid of looking silly or even 'ugly'. The very idea of being funny (and comedy has a physical aspect alongside the intellectual aspect) contradicts society's expectation that women look good and look after their appearance. Robert Lynch, a cultural anthropologist from Rutgers University, attempts to explain this phenomenon: 'Maybe women have to go overboard with the self-deprecation because comedy can be an alpha thing, the alpha being the class clown, the attention-grabber, the presence dominating the room. Women alphas in general tend to be disliked. They can sometimes be distrusted, I think. And they're not sought after. The female stand-ups I know, they don't get a lot of dates out of it' (Fetters, *The Atlantic,* 23 August 2012).

Lynch also points out that this can evolutionarily be explained, and that both men and women look for a sense of humour in their partners, but tend to see it differently: "What men mean by 'a sense of humour" is that they want someone who laughs at their jokes, Lynch explains, "and what women want is [someone who's] funny" (Fetters, *The Atlantic,* 23 August 2012).

It might as well be that men regard women, who are allowed free self-expression on stage, as some kind of archetypal ambivalent mothers, devouring, seductive and poisonous. They are mothers who demand all attention for themselves, and therefore deprive men of care and warmth. Like the Freudian's, the Jungians traditionally objectify and poeticise the mother figure. However, there are significant differences in the way in which the maternal is objectified. The mother in the Jungian thought, albeit still not a 'real' woman, is nevertheless seen as the seat of power and action. She has the right to create and destroy; she is potentially dangerous. Far from being the castrated, downtrodden creature residing in the imaginary, her power is all too real. Jung writes that the 'negative' mother."

> …may connote anything secret, hidden, dark; the abyss, the world of the dead, anything that devours, seduces and poisons, that is terrifying and inescapable like fate. […] Perhaps the historical example of the dual nature of the mother most familiar to us is the Virgin Mary, who is not only the Lord's mother, but also, according to the medieval allegories, his cross. In India, the 'loving and terrible mother,' is the paradoxical Kali. Sankhya philosophy has elaborated the mother archetype into the concept of *prakrti* (matter) and assigned to it the three *gunas* or fundamental attributes: *sattva, rajas, tamas*: goodness, passion and darkness. These are the three essential aspects of the mother: her cherishing and nourishing goodness, her orgiastic emotionality, and her Stygian depths.
>
> (CW 9/I: para. 158).

A female comedian is not an object because she is not beautiful, passive or voiceless, which means that male members of the audience cannot project onto her. Men in the audience may even feel psychologically 'starved' because all the attention goes to the female on stage who is automatically elevated to the status of the leader. The female performer is not 'feeding' the man; instead, she is taking something for herself. In fact, female comedy is a matriarchal situation. Erich

Neumann writes that in the realm of 'the Great Mother' the role of the masculine is limited:

> In the matriarchy – that is, under the hegemony of the Great Mother – the Masculine can be experienced only in diminished form. The matriarchy regards the masculine side of the uroboros, which of course is bisexual, as part of the Great Mother, as her tool, helper and satellite. The male is loved as child and as youth, and used as her tool of fertility, but he continues to be integrated in and subordinated to the Feminine, and his authentic masculine being and uniqueness is never acknowledged.
>
> (Neumann, 1994: 15).

The 'masochistic' and passive tendencies are only brought about by 'the invasion of the patriarchal uroboros,' which seeks to oppress and control the dark and overwhelming power of the Feminine (1994: 14). At the same time, Neumann distinguishes between masculine tendencies in women and truly feminine power. He writes:

> Often a woman's neurotic animus-possession is the expression of her inability to differentiate her Self from the Masculine. The woman becomes the victim of her tendency to identification and alienates herself from her own nature by over-developing the masculine, animus side. This identification with the spiritual and the Masculine can find expression in truly tragic conflicts. By identifying with the transpersonal Masculine that takes the place of authentic surrender and devotion, the woman relinquishes her own earth nature and thus becomes a helpless victim of masculine powers.
>
> (1994: 23)

Female creativity, particularly of the proactive, comedic kind, can be regarded by society as a claim to have 'too much creative power'; as a claim to give birth in several ways instead of just one. This can even take a form of double 'womb envy' – male envy of the woman's ability to produce both biological and metaphorical children. Every time a female comedian makes a joke, it is like a child. The female comedian is the matriarch who has the most power in the room, and who expects male members of the audience to give her attention and praise.

Neumann expects a woman to be both 'powerful' and 'non-masculine'. He implies that there exists some specific female power, grounded in biological reproduction: 'Nature has granted the mystery of the Feminine its fulfilment both in the primal relationship and in pregnancy, a fulfilment that ever and again comes to pass even without consciousness and even if it is not expressed in ritual; the male mystery is the deed and something to be earned' (1994: 23-24).

Neumann apportions ambiguity within the female herself. He believes that her intrinsic power is diminished and distorted because she is over identifying with the masculine. Hence the female who enters into the masculine world of stand-up comedy has to entertain the rules of performance and consequently becomes overtly antagonistic. It so happens that the moment the woman starts expressing her ideas, making jokes or appropriating language in other ways, she is immediately seen as 'aggressive', rough and unfeminine. She is seen as someone who has lost 'a vital, soft maternal aspect of herself. Moreover, the female performers themselves seem to be struggling with self-definition, self-image and the persona acceptable for success. Female comedy is still at the crossroads, whilst society is transforming its patriarchal and inherently masculine expectations, she has to accommodate her own and society's transition. Hence her route to individuation is fraught with many obstacles.

## 9.5. *My Own Experience as a Comedian*

In my own performance on the 26<sup>th</sup> of April 2013 at the Covent Garden branch of *Jongleurs* I encountered all the issues that professional female comedians have to deal with on a regular basis. First of all, I felt like my performance had to contain some taboo material; to be shocking in some way. Shocking in this context means 'not feminine', challenging, rude. I opened the performance with a joke about multiculturalism in London, and concluded it with jokes about sex and promiscuity.

The opening line was: 'I am fascinated by languages. Did you know that, in London, Polish is officially the second language. First of course is Jamaican patois. English is fifth, after Rumanian and Arabic!'. The closing paragraph sounded like this: 'Sexual politics has to change in this country. For years men have said to women: "Lie back and think of England". I think in this day and age there should be something women can say to men in the bedroom, like "Thrust forward and think of football... and let's see if you can last 90 minutes and score a goal, but I prefer a hat trick! But really its better with rugby players as they always have a few tries?'
I needed help so I asked a friend and master comedian Sean Meo to help me. As I have already stated this is a male-dominated industry and I chose a male for several reasons, firstly because I respected Sean's style and his ability to create sharp new political, cultural and personal insights into on-stage material. He also delivers his material in a sharp, fast and efficient manner. Secondly, and most importantly, is that he avoided macho statements about women and relationships, which meant that he was confident enough to be friendly about women. I wanted to impress and deliver in a short, fast style and hopefully successfully.

The initial meeting with Sean was to discuss what sort of help I needed. He comically translated the areas of my life that I was prepared to divulge, and showed me how to engage the audience and to make the audience laugh. I talked about my upbringing at a council estate, being the daughter of Polish political refugees, being mistaken for a famous singer, my divorce and new relationships. Importantly, I suggested that underlying all this should be a feminist statement: the recent changes to the gender/control axis in relationships. I wanted to show that in this day and age, women were moving closer to having more control in relationships. I also realised that I particularly liked Sean as a stand-up with his style of one-liners, of short pithy stories or attitude statements. I had one shot at this, and had to make it work for me.

I was nervous prior to the performance. My world of comedy was watching me and one of the fears beginning to emerge was that other comedians would be derogatory of me. I was scared of being a bad performer, of other people thinking of me as hopeless, as someone doing 'not her own job'. My biggest fear was being criticised by other comedians. Thankfully, they were also supportive and helpful. It is only in a performance that a comedian can see if the material is funny.

I saw Sean a couple more times, and in between he sent me new one-liners or some of his old one lines that he no longer used and that could fit with my template. My whole being became enveloped by an emotional and energetic charge of potential failure, criticism, annihilation, and subsequent shame.

However, the sense of isolation for me was unnerving. Imagine: it would be me and only me on the stage doing the job for which I usually pay other comedians a substantial amount of money. Of course I wasn't being paid, but I wanted to be good.

On the day of the performance my fear made me myopic and my memory vanished. I couldn't remember my lines. Finally, the set began, and I engaged with the audience: 'Is anyone here Polish?' There was silence. The next question was: 'Not even behind the bar?' Laughter. Phew, I had a response! I divulged certain areas of my partying days, and these were viewed with interest and minimal laughter. I talked about my mobile phone and about people who talk in cinemas. A stag party to my right was looking at me intently. There was laughter, the audience was responding. The second half of my set was received better than my first. Overall, the response was generous, and I could breathe a sigh of relief. At the same time, I felt that I didn't get control of the audience fully. Audience control is an art in itself, and it comes with experience. I felt as if I was on a high speed train clinging on tightly, afraid to let go until the end of the set when the train stopped. The oceanic feeling of being in contact with so many people at once was enthralling and all consuming, so much so that I sat on my own for a while to understand my feelings. It was like moving to a different dimension. It was the amalgamation of my creativity with the audience reaction that consumed me. This alchemy made the experience totally enveloping. I hadn't failed, I was good enough.

The most exciting part of the performance was the feeling of having my own voice back; of discovering it anew. This was the 'loud', uncontrollable animus emerging from the depths of my psyche. For instance, half way through my set I changed my material from the perspective of the victim to being in control and fierce. This got the biggest laugh. I joked about not being married anymore because 'I don't want to be told off – I have predictive text for that'. I also joked about the sensitive issue of communicating with ex-husbands: 'The best way to contact them is at eighty mph in a three-litre Range Rover in the middle of the night on a quiet road with no witnesses or speed cameras'.

The louder my animus became, my jokes became sexually orientated. I realised that the soft mellow nurturing female aspect of myself, which I use mostly in my work, would have to be put aside, and the dark shadow of the careless, self-absorbed, proactive, offensive (as opposed to defensive) aspect of my nature would have to be accentuated. Now, for the first time, I was exposing an inner rarely expressed dynamic. There was a frisson between myself and the world of stand-up comedy, and I wanted to engage with this world. Secretly I was hoping that I might unveil an aspect of a creative life that I had never had the chance to explore. Never in the thirty years of watching stand-up had I hoped that one day I would be one of the people on stage.

Conversely, I was afraid that that dark side would get out of control, that I might enjoy it. For the sake of getting laughs I may expose the darker aspect of myself, and it may take over, and subsequently I may regret it. Conversely, it may work well in my favour. I was reclaiming my voice, and trying to discern the different shades within it.

My voice was unwittingly silenced throughout my entire childhood partially through language and that my interests differed from my family. Finally – and ironically – I re-discovered it in a format that was predominantly male! The analysis of what had actually happened here took a few days to understand, but the full realisation of what happened took a few months. It was as if my internal psychological mechanism changed. The performance encouraged me to do more, to be better, to be brilliant. It gave me confidence and realisation that I could create, to produce something new, and affect people in a positive way. Importantly, I don't have to behave 'like a woman' to be accepted: I can be rude and rough and challenging. I could even be unpleasant. I could show off my bete noir. It was now my choice. I was not projecting my shadow. There was no sharing of glory or pain. I had to take responsibility for the good and the bad. Thankfully, both the performer and the audience were good enough!

# CHAPTER 10

## CONCLUSION

The stand-up comedian is a modern artistic phenomenon who has an impact on society culture, politics and the global psyche. The comedian can be viewed as the embodiment of the creative process along with the therapeutic aim of confession, education, elucidation and transformation as a process to achieve individuation on both the personal and psycho-social level. The entire process is psychologically and socially unique as it can give the comedian regular employment while, at the same time, it is also transformative.

The comedian enters into the role of stand-up comedy much like Parzifal enters into the Klingsors' valley naively, yet with a serious mission: to make people laugh. He engages in the ritual of comedy, finding his persona, his comedic voice, his style of delivery, the composition of the joke, opening lines, timing, engaging with the audience and, ultimately, finding his comedic power. What becomes apparent is the intra-psychic changes of the comedian.

Comedy is a unique genre in terms of the intensity of emotional interaction between an individual performer and the audience. The comedian receives an immediate response from the spectators in the form of laughter. The audience's reaction is instantly visible and therefore feeds the comedian's ego and contributes to his sense of self-satisfaction. On the other hand, the audience is also basking in a variety of positive emotions and is intellectually stimulated. The exchange between them is mutually satisfying and can be therapeutic. With their routine, which is based on personal experiences, comedians also offer self-reflective experiences for the audience. This self-reflection is simultaneously personal and social, and can be seen as mini-steps on the path that is the Jungian individuation process.

In order for this personal and social individuation to occur, the Comedy Club transforms into an alchemical container, the Vas, and the audience becomes the symbolic mother who reinforces Bowlby's 'secure base' which, once found, helps the comedian discover his voice and sends him on a journey of self-discovery.

During the performance the comedian can uncover his shadow and disintegrate and re-integrate various components in a public manner.

It is the individual's search for individuation that promotes the self-reflection and actualization of society, which can be termed 'Supra-individuation'. Little by little, area-by-area, the comedian has an illuminating effect on society. His or her search for individuality and distinction, his Creatura, the creative instinct being revealed and recognised can give rise to society's disintegration and re-integration from the threat of Plerorma. There is a healing component to comedic individuation and Supra Comedy. The Supra-comedian consistently creates the Supra-jokes, which become the spark to make the fire in which the alchemy of change from the lead to gold takes place.

The question arises of the lack of Supra-comedian's amongst female performers. Whereas there are quite a few female comedians on the circuit (and several big stars such as Sarah Millican), there are still few female Supra-comedians such as Andi Osho and Ellen DeGeneres. This may be because it is difficult to tackle social issues and to be successful. Women are still yet to find their feet in the realms of stand-up comedy, and they have fewer chances to become Supra-comedians simply because there are many more obstacles on their way to success and acceptance.

In as much as a client cannot go into the ritual of therapy knowing how his individuation process will unfurl, all he knows is his need to be healed or for changes to be recognised and made. It could be suggested it is a similar process for a comedian, he knows he wants to make people laugh and for some individuation comes through the alchemy of the stand-up ritual.

The comedian's individuation is constantly on view to the audience, and the changes to his psyche are being encouraged by the verbal transaction much like the therapist and his client. The comedians' psychic development is being watched by a great number of people, and although the individuals in the audience are not personally selected, they potentially affect his development, and they monitor his or her progress by loving them and thereby following them or, conversely, disowning them.

The audience needs the comedian for guidance and illumination. It could be inferred that mankind is in need of the modern type of gods, not as celebrities who have an idealistic glow to them, but people who express their inadequacies, vulnerabilities and neuroses in a palatable and more immediate form that that of the stand-up comedian. The audience can watch and influence the comedian who performs for them but he also represents the ordinary man as he translates the struggles of his fellow human beings with humour. Humour, therefore, becomes a vehicle for change and personal transformation as it expresses the paradox of conflict in recognisable and relatable dramatic forms. It is arguable that the stand-up is representation of man's psycho-evolutionary drive.

The comedian is similar to a mini earthquake as he pulls apart the strata's of stability and potentially destroys the social scaffolding. It is his connection between the individual and society that can create the destruction and re-construction of previously held view, emotions and beliefs. As Jung wrote, 'in the last analysis, the essential thing is the life of the individual. This alone makes history, here alone do the great transformations take place, and the whole future, the whole history of the world, ultimately springs as a gigantic summation from these hidden source in individuals. In our most private and most subjective lives we are not only the passive witnesses of our age, and its sufferers, but also its makers. We make their own epoch' (Jung, CW10: para. 315).

As an individual and social agent, the comedian initiates change in society by looking at the political issues through the prism of his or her psyche. This is a heroic act, and by doing so, individual performers do make 'their own epoch'.

## *10.*
### *10.1. Developing Stand up Comedy Therapy:*

My parents were Polish Political prisoners of war and subsequently refugees. My early years were a struggle between existence, survival and enjoyment of life, echoed with mourning, depression and conflict. My father suffered from undiagnosed PTSD. These intense family emotions were accommodated and alleviated by play and humour. My mother made Christmas crackers and my father loved comedy shows. As a teenager I worked voluntarily in a large Victorian building housing a Mental Asylum and at the age of twenty I was a volunteer for the Samaritans. I trained as a teacher of English and Drama and through the process of teaching improvisation I understood that more people were prepared to discuss and involve themselves in personal reflection if it had a playful element to it. Taking all my learning on board I intend to create a series of Stand-up Comedy Therapy workshops in combination with psychotherapists. This will act as both a medium for behavioural change and personal change with immediate feedback. It can also give an opportunity for a creative outlet and potentially a new occupation.

# BIBLIOGRAPHY

## A

Adams, Tessa and Duncan, Andrea (2003) The Feminine Case: Jung, Aesthetics and the Creative Process, Karnac Books.
Ajaye, F (2002) Comic Insights, Los Angeles, CA: Silman-James Press
Arieti, Silvano (1967) The Intrapsychic Self: Feeling, Cognition and Creativity in Health and Mental Illness, New York and London: Basic Books.
Arthur, Tim (2010) 'Zoe Lyons: Interview', Time Out London, 23 March 2010.
Attardo, Salvatore (2001) Humorous Texts: A Semantic and Pragmatic Analysis, Berlin: Walter de Greyter.
Attardo, S and Ruskin, B (1985) Semantic Mechanisms of Humour, Dordrecht: D.Reidel

## B

Babad, E.Y (1974) 'A Multi-Method Approach to the Assessment of Humour: A Critical Look at Humour Tests', in Journal of Personality, 42(4), pp. 618-631.
Bacharach, Samuel (2013) 'Creativity Tips from Five Very Funny People', (http://www.inc.com/samuel-bacharach/leadership-tips-from-5-stand-up-comics.html).
Barron, J.W (1999) Humour and Psyche: Psychoanalytic Perspectives, New Jersey: Analytic Press Incorporated.
Bassil-Morozow, Helena (2012) The Trickster in Contemporary Film, London: Routledge.
Benedictus, Leo (2012) 'Where Are All the Female Standups?', The Guardian, 20 March 2012.
Berger, Arthur (1999) An Anatomy of Humour, New Jersey: Transaction Publishers.
Bergman, M.S (1999) 'Psychoanalysis of Humour and Humour in Psychoanalysis', in J.W. Barron (ed.), Humour and Psyche: Psychoanalytic Perspectives, Hillsdale, N.J: The Analytic Press, pp. 11-30.
Bollas, Christopher (1995) Cracking Up: The World of Unconscious Experience, London: Routledge.
Bowlby (2005) A Secure Base, London: Routledge.
—— (2012) The Making and Breaking of Affectional Bonds, London: Routledge.
—— (1969) Attachment and Loss, Vol 1, London: Pimlico.

Boyle, Frankie (2011) My Shit Life So Far, London: Harper

Brockes, Emma (2014) 'Adrienne Truscott: the Naked Comic', The Guardian, 1 January 2014

Brodzinsky, D.M and Rubien, J (1976) 'Humour Production as a Function of Sex of Subject, Creativity, and Cartoon Content', in Journal of Consulting and Clinical Psychology, 44 (4), pp. 597-600.

## C

Caputi, Jane (2004) Goddesses and Monsters: Women, Myth, Power, and Popular Culture, London: Popular Press.

Carr, J and Greeves, L (2006) The Naked Jape, London and New York: Penguin

Cattell, R.B and Luborsky, L.B (1947) 'Personality Factors in Response to Humour', in Journal of Abnormal and Social Psychology, 42, pp. 402-421.

Cavalli, Thom F (2002) Alchemical Psychology: Old Recipes for Living in a New World, New York: Jermy P. Tarcher

Cavendish, Dominic (2011) 'Sarah Millican Reflects on the Remarkable DVD Sales Success', The Telegraph, 21 December 2011

Clabby, J.F (1980) 'The Witt: A Personality Analysis', The Journal of Personality Assessment, 44 (3), pp. 307-310.

Cook, William (2001) The Comedy Store, Boston, MA: Little, Brown and Company

Critchley, Simon (2007) On Humour, London: Routledge.

## D

Dex, Robert (2012) 'David Walliams Reveals Suicide Attempts', The Independent, 4 October.

Doris, J and Fierman, E (1956) 'Humour and Anxiety', in Journal of Abnormal and Social Psychology, 63, pp.59-62.

Edinger, Edward. (1994 ) Anatomy of the Psyche,
Open Court Publishing; a Division of Carus
Publishing.

## E

Eliade, M (1987) The Sacred and the Profane, San Diego, CA: Harcourt

Estes, Clarissa Pinkola (1994) Women Who Run With the Wolves, London and Sydney: Rider.

Evans, Dylan (1996; 2001) Dictionary of Lacanian Psychoanalysis, Hove and New York: Routledge

The Sacred and the Profane, San Diego, CA: Harcourt

Eysenck, Hans (1942) 'The Appreciation of Humour: an Experimental and Theoretical Study', in The British Journal of Psychology, 32, pp.295-309.

—— (1943) 'An Experimental Analysis of Five Tests of "Appreciation of Humour"', in Educational and Psychological Measurement, 3, pp. 191-214.

# F

Fairbairn, W.R.D (2013) Psychoanalytic Studies of the Personality, London: Routledge.

Fetters, Ashley (2012) 'Why Do So Many Pretty Female Comedians Pretend They're Ugly?', The Atlantic, 23 August 2012.

Fisher, S., and Fisher, R.L (1981) Pretend the World is Funny and Forever: a Psychological Analysis of Comedians, Clowns and Actors, Hillsdale, NJ: Erlbaum.

Freud, S (1905; 1960) Jokes and their Relation to the Unconscious, London: W.W Norton and Co.

Freud, S (1905; 1975) Complete Psychological Works Of Sigmund Freud, London: Vintage

Fry, William (1963; 2010) Sweet Madness: A Study of Humour, New Jersey: Transaction Publishers.

Fyfe, Andy (2010) 'Bill Hicks: the Man who Said the Unsayable', in The Daily Telegraph, 12 May.

# G

Gask, Marina (2013) 'Ruby Wax: How I Learnt to Tame the Voices in My Head', in The Mirror, 6 June.

Goldberg, S et al (2013) (eds.) Attachment Theory: Social, Developmental, and Clinical Perspectives, London: Routledge.

Grace, John (2011) 'Ruby Wax: Depression, Me and You', in The Guardian, 12 December.

Groskop, Viv (2013) 'Miranda Hart, Sarah Millican, Jo Brand... So, women aren't funny... are you having a laugh?', The Daily Mail, 6 July

Grossman, Klaus (2013) 'The Evolution and History of Attachment Research', in S. Goldberg et al (eds.) Attachment Theory: Social, Developmental, and Clinical Perspectives, London: Routledge.

# H

Hannah, Barbara (1981) Active Imagination, Boston: Sigo Press
Hastings, Chris (2009) 'Comic Walliams Speaks of Depression Battle', The Mail on Sunday, 22 February
Harding, Esther (1948; 1973) Psychic Energy: Its Source and Its Transformation, New Jersey: Princeton University Press.
Hare-Mustin, Rachel T and Marecek, Jeanne (1992) Making a Difference: Psychology and the Construction of Gender, Yale University Press.
Hastings, Max (2013) 'Women can't do Stand-Up Because They are not Show-Offs', The Daily Mail, 28 September
Hauke, Christopher (2000) Jung and the Postmodern. The Interpretation of Realities, London and Philadelphia: Routledge.
────── (2005) Human Being Human: Culture and the Soul, London: Routledge.
Hillman, James (1975; 1992) Re-Visioning Psychology, New York: Harper Perennial.
────── (1987) Puer Papers, Dallas: Spring.
Hinselwood, Robert (1989/1991) A Dictionary of Kleinian Thought, London: Free Association Books
Huizinga, J (2009) Homo Ludens, London: Routledge
Hyers, Conrad (1996) The Spirituality of Comedy: Comic Heroism in a Tragic World, New Brunswick and London: Transaction Publishers.
Hynes, W.J and Doty, W. (eds.) (1993) Mythical Trickster Figures: Contours, Contexts, Tuscaloosa and London: University of Alabama Press.
Hynes, William (1993) 'Mapping the Characteristics of Mythic Tricksters: A Heuristic Guide, in W. J. Hynes and W. Doty Mythical Trickster Figures: Contours, Contexts, Tuscaloosa and London: University of Alabama Press.

# J

Jacobi, Jolande (1973; 1942) The Psychology of C.G.Jung (Eighth Edition), trans. Ralph Manheim, New Haven and London: Yale University Press.
────── (ed.) (1953) Psychological Reflections. An Anthology of the Writings of C.G. Jung, London: Routledge and Kegan Paul.
Jacoby, Mario (1996) Shame and the Origins of Self-Esteem, London: Routledge
────── (2010) Individuation and Narcissism, London: Routledge
Jaffe, Aniela (1986) The Myth of Meaning in the Work of C.G. Jung, Einsiedeln: Daimon Publishers.
Janus, Samuel S. (1975) 'The Great Comedians: Personality and Other Factors', in American Journal of Psychoanalysis (35), pp. 169-174
Jones, Alice (2008) ;Taboo-Buster: the Dark Side of Jimmy Carr', in The Independent, 18 November

Jung C.G. Except where a different publication was used, all references are to the hardback edition of C.G. Jung, The Collected Works (CW), edited by Sir Herbert Read, Dr. Michael Fordham and Dr. Gerhardt Adler, and translated by R.F.C. Hull, London: Routledge.

Jung, Carl Gustav (2009) The Red Book, New York and London: W.W Norton and Company.

Jung, Carl Gustav and von Franz, M.-L. (eds.) (1978; 1964) Man and His Symbols, London: Picador.

# K

Kalsched, D (2010) The Inner World of Trauma, London: Routledge

Klein, M (1975; 1997a) Envy and Gratitude, London: Vintage

—— (1975; 1997b) The Psycho-Analysis of Children, London: Vintage

—— (1975; 1988) Love, Guilt and Reparation, London: Vintage.

Kohut, Heinz (1978; 2011) The Search for the Self, London: Karnac.

—— (1971: 2001) The Analysis of the Self, Chicago and London: the University of Chicago Press.

Kulhman T. L (1994) Humour and Psychotherapy, New Jersey: Jason Aronson Inc.

# L

Lacan, Jaques (1998) Ecrits: a Selection, London: Routledge.

Laplanche, Jean and Pontalis, Laplanche (1976; 1973) The Language of Psychoanalysis, London: Karnac

Lasch, Christopher (1979; 1991) The Culture of Narcissism: American Life in an Age of Diminishing Expectations, New York: W. W. Norton & Co.

Leigh, Rob (2013) 'Jimmy Carr: Comedian's Forty Best Jokes', http://www.mirror.co.uk/tv/tv-news/jimmy-carr-jokes-comedians-40-1323055

Lemma, Alessandra (2000) Humour on the Couch: Exploring Humour in Psychotherapy and Everyday Life, Hoboken, New Jersey: Wiley.

Levine, J. and Abelson, R.P (1959) 'Humour as a Disturbing Stimulus', in Journal of General Psychology, 60, pp. 191-200

Lombardi, Kate (1995) 'Joan Rivers Offers Some Stand-Up Therapy', The New York Times, 29 January.

Lott, Tim (2013) 'Stephen Fry is the Brave Face of Suicidal Depression', The Telegraph, 7 June.

Lubell, Winifred MIlius (1994) The Metamorphosis of Baubo: Myth of Women's Sexual Energy, Nashville and London: Vanderbilt University Press.

# M

Martin, A. Rod (2007) The Psychology of Humour: an Integrative Approach, San Diego, CA: Elsevier Academic Press

Martin, Rod (2007) The Psychology of Humour: An Integrative Approach, Boston and London: Elsevier.

Maxwell, Dominic (2013) 'The Best Comedy Put Downs', in The Times, 13 October

Mitchell, A (1995) Freud and Beyond: A History of Modern Psychoanalytic Thought, Basic Books.

Monaghan, Patricia (2014) Encyclopedia of Goddesses and Heroines, Novato, CA: New World Library.

Morreall, J (1991) 'Humour and Work', in Humour: International Journal of Humour Research, 4 (3-4), 359-373.

Moss, Stephen (2009) 'Jimmy Carr: "I Thought My Paralympics Joke Was Totally Acceptable"', in The Guardian, 5 November.

# N

Neumann, Erich (1973; 2002) The Child: Structure and Dynamics of the Nascent Personality, London: Karnac.

—— (1994) The Fear of the Feminine and Other Essays on Feminine Psychology, Princeton University Press.

# O

Oh, Kyung (2013) 'Comedy Review: Flipper Committed Suicide', in Three Weeks Edinburgh, 22 August.

Oswalt, Patton (2013) 'Thievery, Heckling and Rape Jokes', in The Slate, June 16 2013.

Otto Beatrice K. (2007) Fools Are Everywhere, University of Chicago Press.

Owen, Jonathan (2006) 'Stephen Fry: My battle with Mental Illness', in The Independent, 16 September.

# P

Partington, Alan (2006) The Linguistics of Laughter: A Corpus-Assisted Study of Laughter-Talk, London: Routledge.

Provine, R.R and Fischer, K.R (1989) 'Laughing, Smiling and Talking: Relation to Sleeping and Social Context in Humans', in Ethology, 83 (4), pp. 295-305.

## Q

Quantick, David (2011) 'Female Comics Will Have the Last Laugh', in The Telegraph, 22 December.

## R

Radin, Paul (1972; 1956) The Trickster: A Study in American Indian Mythology, New York: Schocken Books.

Rampton, James (1994) 'Comedy: Prima Donna: She's a stand-up who's a Woman who's a Lesbian - in that order. James Rampton Talks to the Outgoing Donna McPhail', The Independent, 2 March 1994
Rank, Otto (1932l 1989) Art and Artist: Creative Urge and Personality Development, New York: W.W. Norton and Company.
Ricketts, Mac Linscott (1966) 'The North American Trickster', in History of Religion 5(2), 327-350.
Rigoglioso, Marguerite (2010) Virgin Mother Goddesses of Antiquity, London: Palgrave Macmillan.
Rodman, F.R (1987) The Spontaneous Gesture: Selected Letters of D.W Winnicott, Cambridge, MA: Harvard University Press.
Ruch, W (2007) The Sense of Humor: Explorations of a Personality Characteristic, Berlin: Walter de Gruyter
—— (1992) 'Assessment of Appreciation of Humour: Studies with the three WD Capitals Humour Tests', in C.D Spielberger and J.N. Butcher (eds), Advances in Personality Assessment, Volume 9, Hillsdale, N.J: Lorenz Erlbeum Associates pp. 27-75

## S

Samuels, Andrew (1985) Jung and the Post-Jungians, London: Routledge.
—— (1993) The Political Psyche, London: Routledge.
Samuel, Martin (2012) 'Why Did No One Listen to Jerry's Howl of Rage?', in Mailonline 12 October.
Samuels, Andrew, Shorter, Bani and Plaut, Fred (1992) 'Trickster', in Richard P. Sugg (ed.), Jungian Literary Criticism, Evanston, Illinois: Northwestern University Press, pp. 273-274.
Sawyer, Miranda (2003) 'Comic Relief', The Guardian, 6 July.
Segal, Julia (1995) Phantasy in Everyday Life, London: Karnac.
Stein, Murray (1993) In MidLife: A Jungian Perspective, Dallas, TX: Spring Publications.

St. John, Graham (ed.) (2008) Victor Turner and Cultural Performance, New York: Berghahn Books.
Strachey, J. (Ed. & Trans.). (2001; 1960) The Standard Edition of the Complete Psychological Works of Sigmund Freud, London: Vintage.
Storr, Anthony (1997; 1988) Solitude, London: HarperCollins
—— (1994) Churchill's Black Dog, London: HarperCollins
Strean, H. (1993) Jokes, Their Purpose and Meaning, New Jersey: Jason Aronson Press.
Sugg, Richard P. (ed.) (1992) Jungian Literary Criticism, Evanston, Illinois: Northwestern University Press.

# T

Tannen, Ricki Staphanie (2007) The Female Trickster: the Mask that Reveals, London: Routledge.

Turner, Victor (1974) Dramas, Fields, and Metaphors: Symbolic Action in Human Society, Ithaca, New York: Cornell University Press.
----(1975) Revelation and Divination in Ndemby Ritual, Ithaca, NY: Cornell University Press.
------- (1977; 2011) The Ritual Process, Aldine Transaction, A Division of Transaction Publishers, New Brunswick (U.S.A) and London (U.K)
—— (1979) Process, Performance and Pilgrimage, New Delhi: Naurang Rai
—— (1992) Blazing the Trail: Way Marks in the Exploration of Symbols, Tucson and London:

# V

Vaillant, George (1995) Adaptation to Life, Harvard University Press. The University of Arizona Press.
Vidal, Ava (2013) 'Shooting down evil male hecklers: A female comedian's guide', in The Telegraph, 5 November.
Van Gennep, Arnold (1960;2004) The Rites of
Passage. Routledge Library Editions – Anthropology and Ethnography
Von Franz, Marie Louise (1979) Psychotherapy, Colorado: Shambhala Publications.
Von Franz, Marie-Louise and Hillman, James (1979) Jung's Typology, Irving, Texas: Spring Publications.

# W

Waddell, Terry (2006) Mis/takes: Archetype, Myth and Identity in Screen Fiction, London and New-York: Routledge.

—— (2009) Wild/Lives: Trickster, Place and Liminality on Screen, London: Routledge.

Walliams, David (2012) Camp David, London: Penguin.

Ward, Don (2009) 'The guidelines: Don Ward's 10 greatest heckles', The Guardian, 16 May.

Wilmut, Roger and Rosengard, Peter (1989) Didn't You Kill My Mother-in-law?: Story of Alternative Comedy in Britain from the Comedy Store to Saturday Live, London: Methuen Drama

—— (2009) Wild/Lives: Trickster, Place and Liminality on Screen, London: Routledge.

Wilde, Larry (2000) Great Comedians Talk About Comedy, Executive Books.

Wilmut, Roger and Rosengard, Peter (1989) Didn't You Kill My Mother-In-Law?, London: Methuen.

Winnicott, Donald (1971; 2001) Playing and Reality, London: Routledge.

—— (1990) Maturational Process and the Facilitating Environment, London: Karnac.

Wright, Kenneth (2009) Mirroring and Attunement, London and New York: Routledge

# Y

Yarrow, P (2007) Sacred Theatre, London: Intellect Books

Young-Eisendrath, Polly and Dawson, Terence (eds.) (1997) The Cambridge Companion to Jung, Cambridge: Cambridge University Press.

—— (2004) Subject to Change: Jung, Gender and Subjectivity in Psychoanalysis, London: Routledge.

Youngs, Ian (2014) 'Robin Williams and the Link Between Comedy and Depression', The BBC Website, 12 August.

## Dictionaries and Encyclopaedias:

'Humour' (2010) in Encyclopaedia Britannica Online. Retrieved from http://www.britannica.com.

## Jongleurs Shows:

Jongleurs Club, Oxford, 6 July 2001
Jongleurs Club, London, 20 July 2001
Jongleurs Club, London, 26 April 2013

## Programmes and Performances:

Comedy Nights Russell Howard

## Unauthored Articles:

'Stephen Fry talks for first time about suicide bid' (http://www.dailymail.co.uk/tvshowbiz/article-396723/Stephen-Fry-talks-time-suicide-bid.html#ixzz3xRVhz0xQ)
'The Words of Sam Kinison', (http://www.comedyontap.com/jokes/kinison/skjokes.html).

www.ingramcontent.com/pod-product-compliance
Lightning Source LLC
Chambersburg PA
CBHW081107080526
44587CB00021B/3491